The Lord Will Give Grace *and* Glory

Other volumes in the

BYU WOMEN'S CONFERENCE Series

Continue Your Journey and Let Your Hearts Rejoice
Armed with Righteousness
By Small and Simple Things
Choose Ye This Day to Serve the Lord
In the Strength of the Lord
For Such a Time as This
Rise to the Divinity within You
A Light Shall Break Forth
The Joy of Our Salvation
The Power of His Redemption
The Rock of Our Redeemer
Ye Shall Bear Record of Me
Arise and Shine Forth
The Arms of His Love
May Christ Lift Thee Up
Every Good Thing
Clothed with Charity
Hearts Knit Together
To Rejoice as Women
Women in the Covenant of Grace
Women and Christ
Women Steadfast in Christ
Women and the Power Within
Women of Wisdom and Knowledge
As Women of Faith
A Heritage of Faith
Woman to Woman

The Lord Will Give Grace *and* Glory

Talks *from the* 2014 BYU Women's Conference

Salt Lake City, Utah

Visit us at DeseretBook.com

Library of Congress Cataloging-in-Publication Data

Women's Conference (2014 : Brigham Young University), compiler.
The Lord will give grace and glory : talks from the 2014 BYU Women's Conference.
pages cm
Includes bibliographical references and index.
Summary: A selection of talks given at the 2014 BYU Women's Conference in Provo, Utah.
ISBN 978-1-60907-995-6 (hardbound : alk. paper)
1. Mormon women—Conduct of life—Congresses. 2. The Church of Jesus Christ of Latter-day Saints—Doctrines—Congresses. 3. Mormon Church—Doctrines—Congresses. I. Title.
BX8656.W6 2014
289.3'32082—dc23 2014034331

Printed in the United States of America
R. R. Donnelley, Crawfordsville, IN

10 9 8 7 6 5 4 3 2 1

Contents

Sweet above All That Is Sweet

Sheri Dew

Our theme is filled with hope and power: "For the Lord God is a sun and shield: the Lord will give grace and glory: no good thing will he withhold from them that walk uprightly" (Psalm 84:11).

A dear friend, who knew I felt drawn to focus on the grace of Jesus Christ but was wrestling with this message, sent me an e-mail that I'm sure she meant to be helpful. Here is what she wrote: "Here is what I hope you cover in your talk. What is grace? How do I gain access to it? What difference does grace make in my life? Can it help me with loneliness, with overeating, with bad relationships, with weaknesses and temptations, with insecurity, with heartache and stress? Can it help me with my husband? Is grace always present, or do I have to do something to get it? Is it a feeling? How can I tell when grace is helping me? Okay, those are the questions I want you to answer."[1]

I responded with one line: "Are you sure that's *all* you want to know?"

Her e-mail led me to ask another friend what she wanted to understand about grace. "To tell you the truth," she said, "TV evangelists have wrecked that word for me. I almost feel disloyal to the restored gospel even talking about grace. I mean, do *we* believe in grace?"

I then asked a dear friend who is serving as a stake Relief Society

---

Sheri Dew is the CEO of Deseret Book Company, an executive vice-president at Deseret Management Corporation, and a former member of the Relief Society General Presidency.

president to ask her presidency what they wished the women in their stake understood about grace. This presidency is a spectacular quartet of women who have logged decades of service. And yet, after a long discussion, they said, "We don't think we know enough about grace to even know what to ask."

The disturbing irony in all of these comments is that *the central*, most compelling, most life-changing message of all time is that Jesus Christ already triumphed over sin, death, hell, and every kind of misery. Surely there is *nothing* our Father is more eager for us to understand than the breathtaking scope of the Atonement of His Son and the power the Atonement makes available to us. *Because the key to unlocking the power of His covenant daughters is covenant daughters learning to unlock the power of Jesus Christ.*

With this truth in mind, let's consider four of my friend's questions. First, what is grace? Second, what difference can grace make in our lives? Third, how *does* the Savior make His power available to us? And fourth, what must *we* do to gain access to that power?

Question Number One: What Is Grace?

My father had many virtues. He served faithfully in the Church his entire life. I doubt he ever missed home teaching in sixty years, though he had to drive a hundred miles every month to do it. My earliest testimony of priesthood power came from him. After his death, we heard story after story about his quiet generosity. And my father's word was gold. But my dad had an Achilles' heel—a temper he never conquered. We knew he loved us, but we often bore the brunt of his anger. Sustaining a loving relationship with him was a struggle for me.

One afternoon a few days before he died, I was sitting at his bedside as he slept. Suddenly I found myself asking the Lord to forgive him for years of angry outbursts. As I prayed, something unexplainable happened to me. In an instant, I felt decades of hurt simply fall away. The feeling was spiritual but it was also tangible. I could *remember* his anger, but I couldn't *feel* any of the pain. It was gone. It was beauty for ashes (see Isaiah 61:3). It was sweet.

That is grace. The amazing power of grace. No earthly remedy could have done for me what the Savior did in that moment. It was the redeeming power of Jesus Christ that prompted me to pray for my father—and even gave me the words to say—and it was His healing power that healed a lifetime of wounds.

The scriptures explain what I experienced. In Lehi's vision of the tree of life, most of those he saw either never entered the "covenant path" our leaders described in the April 2014 general women's meeting,[2] or they got lost somewhere along the way (see 1 Nephi 8:18, 23, 28). But one group *held fast* to the iron rod, pressed forward to the tree, partook of the fruit, and *heeded not* those who mocked them (see 1 Nephi 8:33). The fruit made them happy and filled their souls with "exceedingly great joy" (1 Nephi 8:12). It was "sweet above all that is sweet" (Alma 32:42).

What is this fruit that Nephi said was "*most* desirable above all things"? (1 Nephi 11:22). The fruit is the Atonement, which is *the most tangible evidence* of the Lord's incomprehensible love for us. Grace is the power that flows from the Atonement and is what the Savior uses to continue to manifest His love for us. The *Bible Dictionary* says that grace is "divine means of help or strength, given through the bounteous . . . love of Jesus Christ. . . . Grace is an *enabling power*."[3] The Savior empowers us with His grace, not because we've earned it, but because He loves us perfectly. That is why grace is sweet. It was grace that I experienced at my father's bedside.

I've never really liked the word *sweet*. I love things that *taste* sweet, let's be clear about that. But the word *sweet* has always seemed weak and insipid. When I was a student at Brigham Young University, being called a "sweet spirit" was *not* necessarily a compliment. But I have come to understand that when we feel unexplainable peace or hope, love or strength, when we want to linger somewhere because the feeling is sweet, the Lord is manifesting His grace.

Years ago, I heard a speaker at the BYU Women's Conference say that when she saw the word *grace* in the scriptures, she substituted the word *power*.[4] Her counsel helped me begin to make sense of many scriptures for the first time. *When we talk about the grace of Jesus Christ, we are talking about His power*—power that *enables* us to do things we simply could not do on our own.

The Savior has "all power" in heaven and on earth.[5] He has power to cleanse, forgive, and redeem us; power to heal us of weakness, illness, and heartache; power to inspire us; power to conquer Satan and overcome the flesh; power to work miracles; power to deliver us from circumstances we can't escape ourselves; power over death; and power to strengthen us. When the Apostle Paul said, "I can do all things through Christ which strengtheneth me" (Philippians 4:13), he was describing grace.

Grace is divine power that enables us to handle things we can't figure out, can't do, can't overcome, or can't manage on our own. We have access to this power because Jesus Christ, who was already a God, condescended to endure the bitterness of a fallen world and experience *all* physical and spiritual pain.[6]

In the April 2014 general conference, Elder David A. Bednar taught that "the Savior has suffered not just for our sins and iniquities—but also for our physical pains and anguish, our weaknesses and shortcomings, our fears and frustrations, our disappointments and discouragement, our regrets and remorse, our despair and desperation, the injustices and the inequities we experience, and the emotional distresses that beset us.

"There is no physical pain, no spiritual wound, no anguish of soul or heartache, no infirmity or weakness you or I ever confront in mortality that the Savior did not experience first."[7]

Because Jesus Christ atoned, His grace is available to us *every* minute of *every* hour of *every* day. It is this power that ultimately enables us to do what we came to earth to do. Grace is divine enabling power.

Question Number Two: What Difference Can Grace Make in Our Lives?

The last few months have been a little intense for me, and somehow I managed to make more commitments than I could possibly handle. Have you ever done that? One Saturday, I worked all day trying to make a dent in looming deadlines before joining my family at the temple for a niece's endowment. As I walked into the chapel and sat down, the tears started and they would not stop. Exhaustion and the sheer fear of letting people down had me totally undone. I opened the scriptures and through tears read, "The Lord God showeth us our weakness [and was He ever showing me mine] that we may know that it is by *his* grace . . . that we have power to do these things" (Jacob 4:7; emphasis added).

What the Nephites in this verse had power to do was work miracles, and I needed a miracle. Because of the Nephites' faith, they could command in the name of Jesus and the trees and mountains and waves of the sea would obey them (see Jacob 4:6). As I pondered these verses, my mind raced over countless times the Lord had helped me. I felt a surge of faith and knew He would help me again. Faith unlocks divine power. For the first time in weeks, I felt peace. Peace from the Prince of Peace. It was sweet.

We all know what "overwhelmed" feels like. Mortality gives us a visceral experience with the reality that without the Lord, we are nothing (see Alma 26:12). If there are times when you think, *I can't handle my children, or my checkbook, or my illness, or the urge to eat brownies at midnight, or the lack of a husband, or the lack of a good husband, or a family who doesn't appreciate me one more day*, you're not alone. The Savior's divine empathy is perfect, so He knows how to help us. He rarely moves the mountains in front of us, but He always helps us climb them.

Because of Him, you don't have to confront grief or insecurity or an addiction alone. With His help, you can resist temptation. With His help, you can change, forgive those who've hurt you, and start over. With His help, you can become your true self. With His help, your capacity and energy can increase. With His help, you can be happy again. The Savior promised, "My grace is sufficient for all men that humble themselves before me; for if they humble themselves before me, and have faith in me, then will I make weak things become strong unto them" (Ether 12:27).

We are among the "weak things" the Savior is talking about. His grace can change our very nature and, over time, transform us from who we are into who we can become.

What difference can grace make in our lives? It can make *all* the difference!

Question Number Three: How Does the Savior Make His Power Available to Us?

Elder Bruce R. McConkie said that "if it were not for the grace of God, there would be nothing—no creation, no fall, no mortal probation, no atonement, no redemption, no immortality, no eternal life. It is God's grace that underlies all things, [and] . . . that makes all things possible. Without it there would be nothing; with it there is everything."[8]

Elder Jeffrey R. Holland added this clarity: "Much of the miraculous help we find in the gospel is just that—a miracle from heaven, the power of divine priesthood, the attendance of angels administering to us through a very thin veil. These are gifts from God, manifestations of His grace."[9]

Every divine gift and *every spiritual privilege* that gives us access to the power of heaven comes from Christ or through Christ or because of Christ. We owe *everything* to Him and our Father in Heaven, including the privileges of receiving the gift and power of the Holy Ghost; of receiving personal revelation and gifts of the Spirit; of being endowed in the temple with knowledge and priesthood power; of learning the "mysteries of the kingdom, even the key of the knowledge of God" (D&C 84:19); of having angels on our right and on our left (see D&C 84:88); of receiving all the blessings of the Atonement; and of receiving eternal life, the "greatest of all the gifts of God" (D&C 14:7). We owe every divine gift and all access to divine power to the grace of Jesus Christ.

Eliza R. Snow said that we, as Latter-day Saint women, "have greater and higher privileges than any other females upon the face of the earth."[10] I stand with Eliza on this. If there were time, we could talk about how grace is involved in giving us access to the Holy Ghost, to angels, and to countless gifts of the Spirit.[11]

But briefly, let's consider the one privilege we are the most likely to overlook—the privilege of having access to priesthood power.[12] Too many of our sisters think we don't have this privilege. *But that is not true.* Women who have been endowed in the temple have *as much access* to priesthood power *for their own lives* as ordained men do.

Four key points underscore this truth: First, priesthood keys are the manner through which the Lord authorizes the use of His power, *for both women and men.* Second, there are distinctions between priesthood keys, priesthood authority, and priesthood power. Priesthood keys are required to authorize ordinances, priesthood authority is required to perform ordinances, and priesthood power is available to all who worthily receive ordinances and keep the associated covenants. Third, both men and women who serve under the direction of priesthood keys serve with divine authority.[13] In the April 2014 general conference, Elder Dallin H. Oaks said: "We are not accustomed to speaking of women having the authority of the priesthood in their Church callings, but what other authority can it be? . . . Whoever functions in an office or calling from one who holds priesthood keys exercises priesthood authority in performing her or his assigned duties."[14] And finally, fourth, men and women have equal access to the Lord's highest spiritual privileges.

Nowhere is this more apparent than in the house of the Lord. Elder M. Russell Ballard declared that "when men and women go to the temple, they are both endowed with the same power, which is priesthood power. . . . Access to the power and the blessings of the priesthood is available to all of God's children."[15] Though women are not ordained to an office in the priesthood, in the temple we are endowed with priesthood power and with knowledge to know how to use that power.[16]

We have other privileges as well. We aren't required to be ordained to enter the House of the Lord and officiate in priesthood ordinances there, though men are. Further, as already mentioned, when we serve *in any capacity* under the direction of those who hold priesthood keys, we have full access to the power that flows through those keys, just as men do. We as women *never* lack for divine authority. Further still, God's highest ordinances are available only to a man and woman together. In this single doctrinal provision, God indicates His respect for the distinctive but vitally interconnected roles of both men and women. And finally, women have claim to *all blessings* that emanate from the priesthood. Again, from Elder McConkie: "Where spiritual things are concerned, as pertaining to all of the gifts of the Spirit, with reference to the receipt of revelation, the gaining of testimonies, and the seeing of visions, in all matters that pertain to godliness and holiness . . . —in all these things men and women stand in a position of absolute equality before the Lord."[17]

Sisters, we may not presently have the answers to all questions. But we do know, as Lehi told his son Jacob, that "all things have been done in the wisdom of him who knoweth all things" (2 Nephi 2:24).

Most importantly, we live in the dispensation of the fulness of times, when no spiritual blessings are being withheld from the earth (see D&C 121:27–29). This means that no women living *anytime, anywhere* have had greater access to divine power than we do. If we seek for a lifetime, we won't plumb the depth of power and breadth of spiritual privileges the Lord has given us. Through His grace, He has made His highest, holiest spiritual privileges available to us. *That* is our doctrine. *That* is the truth.

Question Number Four: What Must We Do to Gain Access to the Savior's Power?

I recently visited Harvard and honestly felt a little smarter just walking across campus. But later that day, I went to the Boston Massachusetts Temple, and the contrast between that elite university and the Lord's house, which is *the* institution of highest learning, was striking. Everything felt different! The world's finest education simply pales when compared with the tutelage of God (see D&C 76:7–10).

Elder Dallin H. Oaks said that "in contrast to the institutions of the world, which teach us to *know* something, the gospel of Jesus Christ challenges us to *become* something."[18] Sisters, *our* access to divine power *hinges upon who we are becoming.*

I doubt we quote any scripture on grace more often than Nephi's: that "it is by grace that we are saved, after all we can do" (2 Nephi 25:23). As covenant women, we have a tendency to zoom in on the "*after* all *we* can do" part of the grace-and-works equation, but then wonder how we can possibly do more than we already are—though we're pretty sure whatever we're doing isn't enough.

This scripture is not about sequence, and it is not about feverishly working our way through an exhaustive list of good works. Jesus Christ is the only one to walk this earth and do all that could be done.

Instead, doing "all we can do" is about the direction we're headed and what kind of women we are becoming. There is nothing simple about this, because it isn't natural for the natural woman to want to do good *or* to be good. But the Lord's Atonement and His gospel are all about change, and particularly a change of heart. If we are willing to yield to "the enticings of the Holy Spirit," to stay on the covenant path, to hold tightly to the iron rod, and to partake of the fruit again and again, it is possible to "[put] off the natural [woman] . . . through the atonement of Christ" (Mosiah 3:19) and be transformed from fallen women riddled with faults into true disciples. *Doing "all we can do" is all about discipleship.*

Discipleship requires at least three things of us: first, coming to love the Lord more than we love anything in the world; second, experiencing a change of heart so that we have no "disposition to do evil, but to do good continually" (Mosiah 5:2)—which doesn't mean we no longer make mistakes, it just means we don't want to—and third, behaving like true followers. The road to discipleship leads away from all forms of ungodliness (see Moroni 10:32). That means resisting the gravitational pull of the world and shedding the attitudes, appetites, and behaviors of the natural woman. As Elder Neal A. Maxwell put it, "Personal sacrifice never was placing an animal on the altar. Instead, it is a willingness to put the animal in us upon the altar."[19]

At the heart of becoming disciples is *doing* what we promise to do every time we partake of the sacrament—which is to "always remember" the Lord (Moroni 4:3; 5:2). This means remembering Him when we choose what media we're willing to expose our spirits to. It means remembering Him in how we spend our time and when choosing between a steady diet of pop culture or the word of God. It means remembering Him in the middle of conflict or when temptation looms. It means remembering Him when critics attack His Church and mock truth. It means remembering that we have taken His name upon us (see Mosiah 5:7).

None of us have mastered this, but it is our quest, because conversion to the Lord requires immersion in His gospel. We baptize by immersion, not by sprinkling. A "sprinkling" of the gospel will never lead to conversion.

If we constantly immerse ourselves in a fallen world, how far can we really expect to progress in this life? I am not suggesting that there aren't fun and even inspiring opportunities all around us. I love ball games and four-wheelers and travel and snowshoeing and Broadway plays with the best of them. But mortality is a short-term proposition.[20] None of us will stay here long. Doesn't it make sense to devote as much energy as possible to things we can actually take with us into the eternities? To covenants, eternal relationships, our knowledge of truth, and to the blessings that come from devotion to the Lord? Those blessings are remarkable.

Elder D. Todd Christofferson related an experience of two sister missionaries serving in Croatia who were headed home late one evening after an appointment. He told the story this way: "Several men on the trolley made crude comments and became rather menacing. Feeling threatened, the sisters got off the trolley at the next stop just as the doors closed so no one could follow them. Having avoided that problem, they realized they were in a place unknown to either of them. As they turned to look for help, they saw a woman. . . . She knew where they could find another trolley to take them home and invited them to follow her. On the way they had to pass a bar with patrons sitting along the sidewalk. . . . These men also appeared threatening. Nevertheless, the two young women had the distinct impression that the men could not see them. They walked by, apparently invisible to [the men]. When the sisters and their guide reached the stop, the trolley they needed was just arriving. They turned to thank the woman, but she was nowhere to be seen."[21] How are we to explain this sequence of events? The discipleship of two sister missionaries gave them access to the Lord's protecting grace.

Discipleship is not easy, but it's easier than *not* becoming a disciple. Paraphrasing President Howard W. Hunter, if our lives are centered on Christ, nothing can ever go permanently wrong. But if they're not centered on Christ, nothing can ever go permanently right.[22]

As disciples, we can ask for more energy, more revelation, more patience, more self-discipline, more hope, more love, more healing, more happiness. We can ask for miracles, for freedom from pain, and for the desire to forgive. We can ask for more faith and for help in becoming better disciples.[23] We can ask for angels to walk with us, because if we live up to our privileges, angels can't be restrained from being our associates.[24]

The Lord is not saving up His grace, His power, for one dramatic display at the Final Judgment, nor is grace something that kicks in at the end of an ordeal. *It is there from the moment we exercise even a "particle of faith" and ask for His help.*[25] Jesus Christ is Alpha and Omega, literally the beginning and the end (see Revelation 1:8, 11; 21:6; 22:13; 3 Nephi 9:18; D&C 35:1; 45:7), which means He'll stick with us from start to finish.

Not long ago, I was assigned to make a sensitive presentation to a group of senior General Authorities—which is always a little nerve-wracking. I prepared the best I could and sought the Lord's help, and even asked if angels could accompany me to the meeting. Things went better that day than I expected—which should have tipped me off. As I walked back to my office thinking, *That went pretty well*, I had a very immediate and clear impression: *You don't think* you're *the one who did that, do you?* That's when I realized that the Lord had indeed sent help.

I can't think of a single thing I've ever been asked to do that I've been equal to. But therein lies the beautiful intersection of grace and works. When we as disciples do our best, whatever that is at a given moment, the Lord magnifies us.

Doing "all we can do" is about becoming and behaving like true disciples of the Lord Jesus Christ. That is our part. That being said, make no mistake about it: *notwithstanding* all we can do and *despite* the little we actually do, it is the Savior's grace that will ultimately save us (see 2 Nephi 10:24). We can never earn exaltation. But we can indicate by the way we live our lives that we want to be part of the kingdom of God more than we want anything else. *And that is discipleship.*

In the 2013 new mission presidents' seminar, Elder Jeffrey R. Holland encouraged new mission presidents to "have an eternal love affair with the life of the Son of God. I pray that you will . . . love everything He did, everywhere He went, everything He said, and everything He is. I would walk on hot lava, I would drink broken glass to find one more word, one more phrase, one more doctrine, *any* parable that *anyone* could give me of the life of Christ the living Son of the living God. The doctrine of Christ means everything to me as a result of [my feelings] for the author of the doctrine of Christ."

My dear sisters, what one thing would you be willing to give up, starting today, to put the Savior even more at the center of your life? What one thing would you be willing to do, starting today, to unlock more of His power? His grace is what will enable us to do what the Savior is counting on us to do in the twilight of this great, culminating gospel dispensation.

Elder Holland put the task before us in perspective: "'Something is going to be asked of this dispensation that's never been asked before.' [We] must be ready to 'present the Church of the Lamb, to the Lamb,' and when that happens, 'we must be looking and acting like His Church.'"[26]

The Lord is hastening His work, and we are right in the middle of the hastening. I loved it when a sister opened a recent Relief Society meeting in Houston by praying, "We are grateful to live in this day when we are preparing the world for the return of Jesus Christ."

Think of it! The eyes and hopes of every previous dispensation are upon us. We've been chosen to help prepare the world for the Savior. We are living in a day unlike any other, which means it is time *for us to do things we have never done before.* Because we are disciples of Christ, how will we make sure that we and our loved ones are converted? Because we're disciples of Christ, what will we never do or even tolerate again? Because we're disciples of Christ, what truths are we willing to stand for, even if they aren't popular? Because we're disciples of Christ, how will we treat those who see the world, and even the Church, differently? Because we're disciples of Christ, what are *we* willing to do to *build up* the kingdom of God? (see JST, Matthew 6:38). Because we're disciples of Christ, how hard will we work to unlock the Savior's power?

The more we unlock the power available to us as covenant-making women, the more vibrant our impact will be in the work of salvation. We will receive more revelation more often; we will learn to unlock the power we've been endowed with; we will perform more temple work and worship; our families will be more centered around Christ and more eager to share the gospel; and we will have more righteous influence. Period.

The key to unlocking the power of covenant women is covenant women learning to unlock the power of Jesus Christ.

I know how tangible the Lord's power is. I was in my early thirties when an opportunity to marry evaporated overnight and the heartache plunged me into depression. One day a friend called to say she'd had an impression that a verse in Mosiah was just for me, and then she read the verse over the phone: "I will also ease the burdens which are put upon your shoulders, that even you cannot feel them upon your backs . . . ; and this will I do that ye may stand as witnesses for me hereafter, and that ye may know of a surety that I, the Lord God, do visit my people in their afflictions" (Mosiah 24:14).

I'm sorry to say that I hung up even more discouraged. As foolish as it sounds now, I wasn't looking for the Lord to ease my burdens—I just wanted Him to send me my husband! I felt I couldn't face the burden of singleness *one more day.* I was sure that if I prayed and fasted and went to the temple enough, I could convince Him to bless me with this righteous desire. I wasn't thinking about standing as a witness. I was far too preoccupied with myself—which is what happens when we try to lift our burdens alone.

Weeks stretched into a year, and with all of my praying and fasting and temple-going, I was still single and still miserable. But then one day I noticed a verse in Luke where the Savior declares that He has come to heal the brokenhearted. The word *brokenhearted* jumped out at me, because my heart had been broken. I was still thinking about that verse a few days later when I found myself meeting with Elder Bruce C. Hafen about a manuscript he'd written on the enabling power of the Atonement. I took that manuscript home and devoured every word. It opened my eyes to scriptures and divine promises I had never seen before: that the Lord would heal our wounded souls, that He had already taken our pains upon Him, and that He would succor us (see Luke 4:18; Jacob 2:8; Alma 7:11–12). I realized then that I didn't know very much about the Savior, and *it simply isn't possible to be a disciple of someone you don't know.*

Fast-forward thirty years. In some respects, my life hasn't changed much. But in other ways, *everything* is different. That painful episode was a vital turning point, because it launched me on a continuing quest to understand the Atonement and the power that flows from it. Life would have crushed me long ago if I hadn't learned how to access the Savior's power. He has carried me and healed my heart again and again.

Sisters, just the last few days I have had yet another experience with the power and the grace of Jesus Christ. On Saturday I became quite ill, and by the time I could see my doctor on Monday, I was in a world of hurt. He took one look at me, took my temperature, ran some other tests, and told me how seriously ill I was and even threatened to send me to the hospital. He then told me it would take at least ten days to get me back on my feet. That was Monday at about 5:00 P.M. I said, "Well, that's great. But I have just one tiny problem with that. Regardless of what else you need to do, on Thursday morning I need to be able to stand at a pulpit for thirty-five minutes and talk to about fifteen thousand of my best friends." He looked at me as though every marble had just drained out of my head and then went to work to do everything he could medically to help me. And I am grateful for his help. But that is not why I'm here today.

I'm here because my family and many friends have been praying for me and fasting. I'm here because general auxiliary presidencies have been praying for me along with Sandra Rogers and her committee. I'm here because priesthood power is real. I'm here because angels are real and they really do minister through a very thin veil. All of these blessings that give us access to the power of God are manifestations of the grace of Jesus Christ.

Sometimes we think that the world around us is what is real. But this world is so fake, so much of it. What's real is our Father and His Son, the Atonement of the Lord Jesus Christ, and all of the power available to us to help us do what we came to this earth to do.

This recent experience is one of many that allows me today to say that I do stand as a witness that the Lord visits His people in their afflictions. I testify to you that He is filled with healing, enabling power, and that He can ease our burdens and strengthen us when we feel weaker than weak. I testify that the covenant path, the path of discipleship, is actually the easiest path. And I testify that His love for us has no end, which is why the fruit of the tree is sweet above all that is sweet.

This really is The Church of Jesus Christ of Latter-day Saints. Jesus Christ really *is* going to come again. Every knee really is going to bow and every tongue confess that He is the Christ. I know these things are true. As His covenant daughters, may we be determined to unlock His power to help us be the disciples we want to be.

NOTES

1. Personal correspondence in author's possession.
2. See Linda K. Burton, "Wanted: Hands and Hearts to Hasten the Work," *Ensign*, May 2014, 122–24; Bonnie L. Oscarson, "Sisterhood: Oh, How We Need Each Other," *Ensign*, May 2014, 119–21; and Rosemary M. Wixom, "Keeping Covenants Protects Us, Prepares Us, and Empowers Us," *Ensign*, May 2014, 116–18.
3. *Bible Dictionary*, s.v. "Grace," 697; emphasis added.
4. More recently, Elder David A. Bednar has suggested the same approach. See David A. Bednar, "In the Strength of the Lord," Brigham Young University devotional address, 23 October 2001; available at http://speeches.byu.edu/?act=viewitem&id=251; accessed 23 June 2014.
5. After His Resurrection, He declared to His remaining eleven Apostles, "*All power* is given unto me in heaven and in earth" (Matthew 28.18;

emphasis added). John later bore record that the Savior "received a fulness of the glory of the Father" (D&C 93:16). See also Mosiah 4:9.

6. Paul taught the Hebrews, "We have not an high priest which cannot be touched with the feeling of our infirmities; but was in all points tempted like as we are, yet without sin. Let us therefore come boldly unto the throne of grace, that we may obtain mercy, and find grace to help in time of need (Hebrews 4:15–16).
7. Bednar, "Bear Up Their Burdens with Ease," *Ensign*, May 2014, 89–90.
8. Bruce R. McConkie, *A New Witness for the Articles of Faith* (Salt Lake City: Deseret Book, 1985), 149.
9. Jeffrey R. Holland, *For Times of Trouble* (Salt Lake City: Deseret Book, 2013), 45. See also Psalms 18:36; 94:18–23.
10. Eliza R. Snow, "Great Indignation Meeting," *Deseret Evening News*, 15 January 1870, 2.
11. The Holy Ghost is one such avenue. Elder Parley P. Pratt described the breadth of the Holy Ghost's influence upon us: "The gift of the Holy Ghost . . . quickens all the intellectual faculties, increases, enlarges, expands, and purifies all the natural passions and affections. . . . It inspires, develops, cultivates and matures all the fine-toned sympathies, joys, tastes, kindred feelings, and affections of our nature. It inspires virtue, kindness, goodness, tenderness, gentleness and charity. It develops beauty of person, form and features. . . . It strengthens . . . and gives tone to the nerves. In short, it is, as it were, marrow to the bone, joy to the heart, light to the eyes, music to the ears, and life to the whole being" (Parley P. Pratt, *Key to the Science of Theology* [Salt Lake City: Deseret Book, 1855], 101).
12. Elder Bruce R. McConkie said that the "doctrine of the priesthood—unknown in the world and but little known even in the Church—cannot be learned out of the scriptures alone. . . . The doctrine of the priesthood is known only by personal revelation" (McConkie, "The Doctrine of the Priesthood," *Ensign*, May 1982, 32).
13. See Sheri Dew, *Women and the Priesthood* (Salt Lake City: Deseret Book, 2013), especially chapter 6.
14. Dallin H. Oaks, "The Keys and Authority of the Priesthood," *Ensign*, May 2014, 51.
15. M. Russell Ballard, "'Let Us Think Straight,'" BYU Campus Education Week devotional address, 20 August 2013; available at http://speeches.byu.edu/?act=viewitem&id=2133; accessed 23 June 2014; see also Ballard, "Men and Women in the Work of the Lord," *New Era*, April 2014, 2–5; see also D&C 109:15, 22. Elder D. Todd Christofferson taught that "in

all the ordinances, especially those of the temple, we are endowed with power from on high" ("The Power of Covenants," *Ensign*, May 2009, 22).

16. In the temple, we may "grow up" in the Lord, receive a "fulness of the Holy Ghost," and be armed with God's power (D&C 109:15, 22).
17. McConkie, "Our Sisters from the Beginning," *Ensign*, January 1979, 61.
18. Oaks, "The Challenge to Become," *Ensign*, November 2000, 32.
19. Neal A. Maxwell, "'Deny Yourselves of All Ungodliness,'" *Ensign*, May 1995, 68.
20. Cicero purportedly said, "I am more interested in the long hereafter than in the brief present" (quoted by LeGrand Richards in "I Am More Interested in the Long Hereafter Than in the Brief Present," BYU devotional address, 25 February 1975; available at http://speeches.byu.edu/?act=viewitem&id=500; accessed 23 June 2014).
21. See Christofferson, "When Thou Art Converted," *Ensign*, May 2004, 12–13.
22. See Howard W. Hunter, "Fear Not, Little Flock," BYU devotional address, 14 March 1989, available at http://speeches.byu.edu/?act=viewitem&id=828; accessed 23 June 2014.
23. Elder Marvin J. Ashton taught that there are "less-conspicuous gifts," such as the gift of being a disciple, the gift to calm, the gift of being agreeable, and so on (see "'There Are Many Gifts,'" *Ensign*, November 1987, 20–23).
24. See Joseph Smith, in Relief Society Minute Book, Nauvoo, Illinois, 28 April 1842, 38; available at http://josephsmithpapers.org/paperSummary/nauvoo-relief-society-minute-book#!/paperSummary/nauvoo-relief-society-minute-book&p=35; accessed 16 July 2014.
25. See Alma 32:27. Elder Bruce C. Hafen wrote that "the Savior's gift of grace to us is not necessarily limited in time to 'after' all we can do. We may receive his grace before, during, and after the time when we expend our own efforts" (*The Broken Heart* [Salt Lake City: Deseret Book, 1989], 155).
26. Holland, quoted in Elizabeth Taylor Frandsen, "Place of truth: Wilford Woodruff Building on Yale campus rededicated," *Church News*, 17 February 2007; available at http://199.104.95.22/articles/50143/Place-of-truth.html; accessed 24 June 2014.

A Personal Witness of the Atonement of Jesus Christ

Bonnie L. Oscarson

One of the great blessings of my current assignment is to serve side by side with these two remarkable women [Linda K. Burton and Rosemary M. Wixom] as we work together to serve the women of The Church of Jesus Christ of Latter-day Saints of all ages. We are unified in vision and in purpose. We do not see ourselves as being responsible for just one specific age group; rather, we feel deeply an urgency to work closely together in one single cause—to help children, youth, and adults to make sacred covenants and come unto Jesus Christ. I learn and am inspired daily through my association with Sister Rosemary Wixom and Sister Linda Burton. I truly love these women as well as all of our counselors.

I testify that the greatest event in all the history of mankind is the Atonement of our Savior, Jesus Christ. The Atonement is what gives our lives meaning, and without it, we have no hope or joy in this life.

If you will indulge me today, I want to share the personal journey which led me to this testimony. I was born into a Latter-day Saint home.

Bonnie L. Oscarson was sustained as the Young Women general president in April 2013. She has a bachelor's degree from Brigham Young University with an emphasis in British and American literature. She served with her husband, Paul, when he presided over the Sweden Göteborg Mission and returned to Sweden thirty years later when she and her husband served as matron and president of the Stockholm Sweden Temple. They are the parents of seven children and proud grandparents of twenty-seven amazing grandchildren.

I was taught about the Atonement in my home and in my Church classes growing up. I thought I had a good, basic understanding of what the Atonement was and of the role of Jesus Christ in our Heavenly Father's plan for us. I felt I had faith in Jesus Christ as our Savior. It is almost embarrassing to admit that it was not until I was married and was the mother of several small children that I came to realize that it is not enough to simply *know about* the Atonement. The Atonement must become personal and individualized, and we must all recognize the absolute necessity of the Atonement in each of our lives before we can fully draw upon the Savior's enabling power. I believe the Savior taught this principle when He invited the 2,500 individuals at the temple in the land Bountiful to come and see and feel for themselves the prints of the nails in His hands and in His feet: "And this they did do, going forth one by one until they had *all* gone forth, and did see with their eyes and did feel with their hands, and did know of a surety and did bear record, that it was he, of whom it was written by the prophets, that should come" (3 Nephi 11:15; emphasis added). When He invited the people to come to Him one by one, He taught that it is essential that our testimonies be individual and personal.

I was twenty-five years old when my husband and I were called to serve as mission president and wife in Göteborg, Sweden. We took four small children with us, including a one-month-old baby. It was an exciting but challenging time for us—and especially for me. I was struggling to care for a newborn and three other young children while traveling around our mission to meet our missionaries and members. I was running into restrooms as often as I could manage to nurse a newborn while trying to cover the meetings and assignments I felt were necessary. I was dealing with a foreign language and was expected to be a hostess in arranging and preparing dinners for missionaries and leaders. I wasn't familiar with the grocery store and didn't understand the language well enough to know what was in a can of food when I picked it up. Thank heavens for the pictures on cans and packages! In the midst of all these changes and challenges, I began to feel not only inadequate, but unworthy.

In retrospect, I may have been suffering in one degree or another from depression following the birth of my baby. What I was feeling was very intense and very real. I knew that, generally speaking, I was a good person and hadn't committed any major sins, but I felt as if every weakness, fault, and sin I had ever committed was being brought to my remembrance. I was struggling to meet the demands of my calling, and I wondered if I was acceptable in the eyes of the Lord, especially in my current situation.

I turned to the scriptures, to personal prayer, and to my husband for a priesthood blessing and counsel during this period. Slowly, I began to understand an important truth and to find relief. I realized that I could not do what I needed to do on my own. I needed help. I needed to apply the Atonement to my challenges, shortcomings, and deficiencies. Jesus Christ had already suffered for my sins, my trials, and my problems, and yet I was trying to carry them all on my own. I needed to accept His infinitely generous offer and let Him help carry my burdens. At some point, the Atonement of Christ was no longer an abstract principle of the gospel but a certainty and a sure reality. It became the lifeline which I reached out to hold onto in order to survive spiritually. I needed the Atonement to work for me. I was totally and completely dependent on what Christ had done for me personally to have any hope at all for help in this life and exaltation in the next.

Practically speaking, I went through the following steps:

- I asked for forgiveness of my shortcomings and tried to become a more patient and giving person.
- I realized that repentance is a daily necessity and that it simply means we are trying to be better each day.
- I prayed to understand how to prioritize the various things commanding my time. I tried to put the needs of my children first and to turn the things I just couldn't manage over to others—and to the Lord. I had to work at letting the Lord take over the many things I worried about.
- I prayed and I studied my scriptures. I learned to listen to the promptings of the Spirit more than ever and trust that the Lord understood me and stood ready to prompt and help. The busyness of my life didn't change, but my ability to handle things increased. I have never viewed the Atonement in the same way since.

I think that each individual in this life needs to come to the same realization. Everyone, without exception, needs the power of the Atonement of Jesus Christ. In the words of the prophet Helaman, who was quoting King Benjamin: "There is no other way nor means whereby man can be saved, only through the atoning blood of Jesus Christ, who shall come; yea, remember that he cometh to redeem the world" (Helaman 5:9).

A few years ago, my husband and I had the opportunity to visit the Holy Land. It was something I had dreamed of for many years. We traveled with my sister, one of my brothers, and their spouses, and we shared some wonderful experiences together. Our small group was given the opportunity to spend time alone in a private portion of the Garden of Gethsemane. The olive trees there are ancient and twisted. We were given the chance to read quietly and wander around freely. It was a quiet, reflective time as we pondered the events which had occurred there. Later, my sister and I stood together in the Garden Tomb, where it is believed the Savior's body lay after His Crucifixion. We looked at one another in wonder.

As I reflect on our experiences in the Holy Land, one memory stands out above all the rest. We had the opportunity to partake of the sacrament while we were there, and we drank the water from small cups carved from olive wood. As I was drinking, I noticed that something in the wood gave the water a very bitter taste. Immediately a scripture came into my mind: "I have drunk out of that bitter cup which the Father hath given me, and have glorified the Father in taking upon me the sins of the world, in the which I have suffered the will of the Father in all things from the beginning" (3 Nephi 11:11).

The taste of that bitter water in my mouth, combined with the experiences and sights of the previous few days, caused a swelling of gratitude to fill my heart for what Jesus Christ had done for me. I felt a confirmation of the reality of the Savior's sacrifice and felt amazement at the love He has for each of us.

We do not have to travel to the Holy Land to appreciate the Atonement of Jesus Christ. We understand it as we study the scriptures, listen to the words of our living prophets and apostles, and accept Jesus Christ as our personal Savior.

It has been said that the Bible describes what happened in the Atonement and that the Book of Mormon and the Doctrine and Covenants explain the doctrine. The Atonement is an event of monumental significance, and yet there are amazingly few verses in the New Testament which describe it. No wonder most of the world lacks a true understanding of it. It is through the dozen or so sermons in the Book of Mormon, the modern revelations of the Doctrine and Covenants, and the words of our latter-day prophets that we truly come to understand the significance of what Jesus experienced. One of the "aha moments" in the Book of Mormon is the teaching that not only did Christ suffer for all mankind's sins, he also experienced every kind of pain and misery known to mankind in a way that would have killed any mortal person. King Benjamin teaches us:

"And lo, he shall suffer temptations, and pain of body, hunger, thirst, and fatigue, even more than man can suffer, except it be unto death; for behold, blood cometh from every pore, so great shall be his anguish for the wickedness and the abominations of his people" (Mosiah 3:7).

In a memorable talk, Elder Jeffrey R. Holland described that, during the Savior's final moments on the cross, "the Father briefly withdrew from Jesus the comfort of His Spirit, the support of His personal presence. It was required, indeed it was central to the significance of the Atonement, that this perfect Son who had never spoken ill nor done wrong nor touched an unclean thing had to know how the rest of humankind—us, all of us—would feel when we did commit such sins. For His Atonement to be infinite and eternal, He had to feel what it was like to die not only physically but spiritually, to sense what it was like to have the divine Spirit withdraw, leaving one feeling totally, abjectly, hopelessly alone."[1]

Think of this! The only perfect man who has ever lived on the earth, the Creator of the universe, the literal Son of God, a member of the Godhead, was willing to do all of this for us—we who are imperfect, weak, and unworthy. He loved us enough to suffer all of that—for you and for me. To me it is beyond comprehension.

The Atonement of Jesus Christ is real and it is personal. Just as the Savior invited the people in the Book of Mormon to come "one by one" and witness His reality for themselves, He continues to invite us to believe and accept what He did for us—one by one. We must each, in our own way, examine the wounds Jesus received on our behalf and decide whether or not to accept Him as our personal Savior and Redeemer. I testify that as we accept His great sacrifice and allow Him to change our lives, we will never be the same.

NOTES

1. Jeffrey R. Holland, "None Were with Him," *Ensign*, May 2009, 88.

"Let Us Therefore Come Boldly to the Throne of Grace"

Gaye Strathearn

Hebrews 4:16 reads, "Let us therefore come boldly unto the throne of grace, that we may obtain mercy, and find grace to help in time of need." For many years this has been one of my favorite scriptures in all of holy writ. I love the emphasis that it has on the mercy and grace of our Savior Jesus Christ, and I love the invitation that it extends to me personally, and all of us collectively, to come boldly to the throne of Christ's grace. Of course, this is only one verse from the epistle to the Hebrews. In isolation and out of context I believe that it has power, but I believe that the richness of this verse is enhanced when we place it in its context. The epistle to the Hebrews is a fascinating and rich book of scripture. Although we know very little about its dating and provenance, Hebrews seems to be written to Jewish Christians who were struggling to remain firm in their profession (Greek *homologia*) that Jesus is the Christ (Hebrews 3:1; 9:11; 10:10; 13:21), the Son of God (Hebrews 4:14; 6:6; 10:29). The author of Hebrews tells us that the people had begun to "cast away [their] confidence [or boldness—Greek *parrēsia*]" (Hebrews 10:35) which had led them to "draw back" [or "retreat"—Greek *hypostellō*] (Hebrews 10:38–39).[1] To paraphrase President Dieter F. Uchtdorf, they

---

Gaye Strathearn is an associate professor of ancient scripture at Brigham Young University. Born and raised in Australia, she participated in the BYU Jerusalem Study Abroad program in the fall of 1987. She came to BYU as a student in 1989 and earned a BA and an MA in Near Eastern studies. She earned a PhD in New Testament at the Claremont Graduate University.

were beginning to doubt their faith, rather than doubt their doubts,[2] or, as Elder Jeffrey R. Holland taught, they were beginning to "pitch their tents out on the periphery of [their] religious faith."[3]

The author of Hebrews uses Old Testament people, stories, and images to help encourage his audience to appreciate Christ and his mission and to renew the fire of testimony in their souls. Today I would like to consider just two ways that the greater context of Hebrews can help us better understand and appreciate the nuances and power of Hebrews 4:16. The first, in Hebrews 3, is an appeal to learn from the mistakes of the Israelites in the wilderness as they rejected the invitation to enter the presence of God. The second, in the two verses that immediately precede Hebrews 4:16, is a description of Jesus as the great high priest. These verses, in particular, give us the *reason* that we can have boldness to come to the throne of his grace.

First, Hebrews 3:8–11 exhorts: "Harden not your hearts, as in the provocation, in the day of temptation in the wilderness: When your fathers tempted me, proved me, and saw my works forty years. Wherefore I was grieved with that generation, and said, They do alway err in their heart; and they have not known my ways. So I sware in my wrath, They shall not enter into my rest." Here the word *rest* is a metaphor for the Promised Land. The Old Testament provides many examples of times when Israel provoked the Lord with their murmurings. Even after the spectacular displays of God's power in helping them to escape from Egypt, they frequently complained about not having any water (Exodus 15:23; 17:1–7), or food (Exodus 16:2–3), or that the promised land was too full of giants (Numbers 14:2–23). Sometimes they even complained that it would have been better if they had stayed in Egypt! (See Numbers 11:5.) All of these incidents emphasized the physical challenges that Israel faced and their immature understanding of God and his plan for them.

But there was another event where they provoked the Lord that had more spiritual ramifications. When the children of Israel were camped at Mount Sinai, Moses went up into the mountain to commune with God. As he prepared to return from the mountain, "the Lord said unto Moses, Go unto the people, and sanctify them to day and to morrow, and let them wash their clothes, and be ready against the third day: for the third day the Lord will come down in the sight of all the people upon mount Sinai"

(Exodus 19:10–11). Unfortunately, as the time drew near, "all the people saw the thunderings, and the lightnings, and the noise of the trumpet and the mountain smoking: and when the people saw it, they removed, and stood afar off. And they said unto Moses, Speak thou with us, and we will hear: but let not God speak with us, lest we die" (Exodus 20:18–19). The Israelites, like the brother of Jared (see Ether 3:8) and many of the ancients, feared that if they saw God they would be consumed. To be sure, the thunderings and lightnings that were associated with God's presence on Mount Sinai probably didn't do much to alleviate their fear!

Doctrine and Covenants 84 gives us some additional information about this event. First, it puts the event in context of the importance of the Melchizedek priesthood and its ordinances to enable people "to see the face of God, even the Father, and live" (D&C 84:22). In other words, through the power of the Melchizedek priesthood, humans, even in their mortal condition, can enter the presence of God without being consumed by his glory. Then we read, "Now *this* Moses plainly taught to the children of Israel in the wilderness, and sought diligently to sanctify his people *that they might behold the face of God;* but they hardened their hearts and could not endure his presence; therefore, the Lord in his wrath, for his anger was kindled against them, swore that they should not enter into his rest while in the wilderness, which *rest is the fulness of his glory*" (D&C 84:23–24; emphasis added).

Notice how this revelation defines "rest." It is not the physical rest of the Promised Land, but the spiritual rest of the fulness of God's glory. The Israelites refused the opportunity to enter into the presence of God because they allowed their fear of the thunderings and lightnings to cast out their faith.[4]

Sisters, we live in a world where fear is a part of our mortal experience. Fear *can* be a positive thing that helps us to avoid dangerous situations. It is not *always* the antithesis of faith, but, if we're not careful in spiritual matters, it can be. In Shakespeare's *Measure for Measure,* Lucio declares,

> Our doubts are traitors,
> And make us lose the good we oft might win
> By fearing the attempt.[5]

For the Israelites at Sinai, their doubts made them fear to attempt to participate in a supernal spiritual opportunity. Their doubt was not about the normal fears of mortality: it was a fear to believe the Lord's prophet when he taught them that they could see God and live; it was a fear to move to a higher spiritual level; it was a fear to have God come and dwell with them.

Hebrews 3:12–15 then gives this exhortation to avoid the pitfalls of the ancient Israelites: "Take heed . . . lest there be in any of *you* an evil heart of unbelief, in departing from the living God. . . . For we are made partakers of Christ if we hold the beginning of our confidence [or boldness—Greek *parrēsia*] stedfast unto the end; While it is said, To day if ye will hear his voice, harden not your hearts, as in the provocation." At the end of the discussion on rest, 4:11 exhorts: "Let us labour therefore to enter into that rest." The word "labour" suggests that we have work to do, but the Greek word, *spoudasōmen,* also has the sense of "hasten," suggesting that there is an urgency to participate in the journey that will lead us into "that rest."

It is in response to the fears that keep us spiritually stagnant that Hebrews 4:16 issues the call for Israel to "come boldly to the throne of grace." In other words, Hebrews is a clarion call for Israel, both ancient and modern, to learn from the mistakes of Israel and not to lose spiritual opportunities, by "fearing the attempt." During the Savior's mortal ministry he repeatedly invited people to not only "come, follow me" but, perhaps more significantly, to "come unto me." He invited "all those who labour and are heavy laden" to "come unto me" so that he could also give them rest (Matthew 11:28). He invited the children to "come unto me" (Mark 10:14) and he invited anyone who was spiritually thirsty to "come unto me" (John 7:37). Sometimes, like the rich young man, the people went away sorrowful because of the cost of such a call (see Matthew 19:22). Others, like the woman with the issue of blood, came to the Savior tentatively, in a crowd, seeking to remain anonymous, but coming all the same, just hoping to have some kind of contact with her Lord (see Luke 8:43–48).

Sisters, are there ways that we sometimes allow our fear to replace our faith when it comes to our spiritual progression? For example, do we allow fear to surface when we are called to serve the Lord? President

Thomas S. Monson reminds us, "Now, some of you may be shy by nature or consider yourselves inadequate to respond affirmatively to a calling. Remember that this work is not yours and mine alone. It is the Lord's work, and when we are on the Lord's errand, we are entitled to the Lord's help. Remember that whom the Lord calls, the Lord qualifies."[6] Or, do we sometimes allow fear to prevent us from hastening the work of our personal salvation by fearing to move to a higher level of consecration? King Benjamin taught that we are "eternally indebted to [our] heavenly Father, to render to him all that [we] have and [are]" (Mosiah 2:34). I understand the "all that we have"; in the Church we often talk of consecrating our time, talents, and possessions to build up the kingdom of God on earth. But Mosiah goes further to teach that we must also render to God "all that we are." What does that mean? I think that it is what Abinadi was talking about when he taught, "the will of the Son [was] swallowed up in the will of the Father" (Mosiah 15:7). To render unto God "all that we are" we must ultimately subordinate our will to that of the Father.

Elder Neal A. Maxwell cautions us: "So many of us are kept from eventual consecration because we mistakenly think that somehow, by letting our will be swallowed up in the will of God, we lose our individuality. . . . What we are really worried about, of course, is not giving up self, but rather selfish things—like our roles, our time, our preeminence, and our possessions. No wonder we are instructed by the Savior to lose ourselves (see Luke 9:24). He is only asking us to lose the old self in order to find the new self. This is part of what Benjamin's sermon is all about—to put off the natural man in order to come into our spiritual inheritance. So, it is not a question of losing one's identity but of finding it."[7]

At Gethsemane we see Abinadi's prophecy fulfilled when the Savior pleaded, "O my Father, if it be possible, let this cup pass from me: nevertheless not as I will, but as thou wilt" (Matthew 26:39). At a point when fear *might* have set in, the Savior instead exerted his faith. His will was swallowed up in the will of the Father. Our Savior led a consecrated life. In both his thoughts and deeds he gave not just all that he had, but all that he *was* to the work of his Father. Allowing his will to be swallowed up in the will of the Father did not diminish who he was; rather it magnified him as it will also magnify us if we come boldly and move forward with faith.

The second Old Testament image in Hebrews that I would like to discuss that gives context to our verse is the image of the High Priest serving in the Tabernacle. While anciently the High Priest performed many functions, the most notable was that every year he represented Israel as he entered into the Holy of Holies on *yom kippur*, or the Day of Atonement. The Holy of Holies represented the place where God sat on his throne, sitting in judgment upon his people. The High Priest, therefore, was not just entering into the Holy of Holies; he was entering into the presence of God. This was a task he performed alone, as a representative of the people, because at Mount Sinai they had rejected the opportunity to enter God's presence. Hebrews 9 gives a description of the Tabernacle and then verses 7–10 read, "But into the second [veil; i.e., the Holy of Holies] went the high priest alone once every year, not without blood, which he offered for himself, and for the errors of the people: The Holy Ghost this signifying, that the way into the holiest of all was not yet made manifest [for the people], while as the first tabernacle was yet standing: Which was a figure for the time then present, in which were offered both gifts and sacrifices, that could not make him that did service perfect, as pertaining to conscience; which stood only in meats and drinks, and divers washings, and carnal ordinances, imposed on them until the time of reformation" (Hebrews 9:7–10). When Christ came, however, he became *our* High Priest who ministered, not in an earthly tabernacle "made with hands," but in the heavenly temple, of which Moses' tabernacle was merely a copy (Hebrews 9:24; see also 8:2). Hebrews 9 then continues in verses 11–12, "But Christ being come an high priest of good things to come, by a greater and more perfect tabernacle, not made with hands . . . Neither by the blood of goats and calves, but by his own blood he entered in once into the holy place, having obtained redemption for us." It is not unimportant that at the moment when Christ died on the cross the veil of the temple "was rent in twain from the top to the bottom" (Mark 15:38). The barrier which prevented Israel from the presence of God was removed because of our Savior's atoning sacrifice.

With this background in mind, let's now turn to Hebrews 4:14–15, the verses that immediately precede verse 16, "Seeing then that we have a great high priest, that is passed into the heavens, Jesus the Son of God, let us hold fast our profession. For we have not an high priest which cannot be touched with the feeling of our infirmities [or weaknesses—Greek *astheneia*); but was in all points tempted like as we are, yet without sin." These verses give us the reason that we can come before God's throne with boldness: because our High Priest knows what it is like to be tempted. We can come boldly because "in all things it behoved him to be made like unto his brethren, that he might be a merciful and faithful high priest in things pertaining to God, to make reconciliation for the sins of the people. For in that he himself suffered being tempted, he is able to succor [or "come to the aid of"—Greek *boēthēsai*] them that are tempted" (Hebrews 2:17–18). Likewise, Alma teaches, "And he shall go forth, suffering pains and afflictions and temptations of every kind; and this that the word might be fulfilled which saith he will take upon him the pains and sicknesses of his people. And he will take upon him death, that he may loose the bands of death which bind his people; and he will take upon him their infirmities, that his bowels may be filled with mercy, according to the flesh, that he may know according to the flesh how to succor his people according to their infirmities" (Alma 7:11–12).

Yes, as our High Priest, Jesus comes to our aid because he knows what it is like to be tempted, but he knows it even better than we do. As one New Testament scholar has noted, Jesus "does not merely contemplate our weakness from a safe distance. He knows what it is like, for He came where we are and underwent temptation just as we do. . . . His temptations were greater than ours because he did not yield. The only person who knows the full force of a given temptation is the one who resists it right to the end. The one who gives in at some point along the way does not know the fierceness of the temptation that would follow at a later point. But Jesus did not give in. He knows all the power and all the force of temptation, not only the small part that sinners who give way know."[8]

So what does all this mean for Hebrews 4:16? The invitation to come boldly is, in part, a response to Israel's fear to come into the presence of God at Mount Sinai. The writer of Hebrews pleads with the Christians in his day, and ours, to learn from the Israelite experience. The Greek word that is translated as "boldness" in the King James Bible is *parrēsia.* It can be translated as boldness or confidence, but it can also mean courage. In other words, no matter where we are in our personal spiritual journeys, the invitation to come is a call to have courage—courage to strive for something more, courage to not settle for spiritual mediocrity, courage to pay the price to be able to enter the presence of God. After all, our Heavenly Father sent us here to earth to become gods! For us to achieve that goal, it is important that we don't get stuck at the base of our personal Mount Sinai. The invitation to come boldly is also a recognition that we have an empathetic High Priest who not only acts as our advocate with the Father, but who has broken down the barriers which, in the earthly tabernacle, kept us out of his presence. It is true that we still must complete the spiritual journey, but because of Christ's Atonement we can move forward with confidence, knowing that he understands better than any other High Priest, the difficulties and challenges that we face along the way.

Hebrews 4:16 concludes with an explanation of why we should come boldly unto the throne of grace, "that we may obtain mercy, and find grace to help in time of need." *Mercy* and *grace* here seem to be near synonyms, although, as one scholar has noted, "it might be appropriate to see the first as relating to past transgressions and the second as relevant to contemporary and future needs."[9] Another way of translating the last phrase could also be that when we come boldly we will "find grace when we need it most" (Greek *eis eukairon boēthеian*). I love that thought! His grace is available when we need it most! That thought is what makes this verse so important to me.

Sisters, I love the gospel of Jesus Christ. I love what it teaches me about Christ and his role as *my* personal Savior. In Hebrews we find taught that there is a balance between our personal responsibility to respond to Christ's invitation to come unto him, and his infinite mercy and grace. The author of Hebrews implores his readers, and implicitly all of us, that we "cast not away therefore your boldness, which hath great recompence of reward" (Hebrews 10:35). Of this *I* testify.

NOTES

1. See Philip Edgcumbe Hughes, *A Commentary on the Epistle to the Hebrews* (Grand Rapids, MI: Eerdmans, 1977), 174.
2. See Dieter F. Uchtdorf, "Come, Join with Us," *Ensign*, November 2013, 23.
3. Jeffrey R. Holland, "A Prayer for the Children," *Ensign*, May 2003, 85.
4. The Prophet Joseph taught, "Moses sought to bring the children of Israel

into the presence of God, through the power of the Priesthood, but he could not" (*Teachings of the Prophet Joseph Smith*, comp. Joseph Fielding Smith [Salt Lake City: Deseret Book, 1938], 159).

5. William Shakespeare, *Measure for Measure*, in *Willam Shakespeare: The Complete Works, Second Edition*, ed. Stanley Wells and Gary Taylor (Oxford: Clarendon Press, 2005), act 1, scene 4, lines 77–79.
6. Thomas S. Monson, "Duty Calls," *Ensign*, May 1996, 44.
7. Neal A. Maxwell, "King Benjamin's Sermon: A Manual for Discipleship," in *King Benjamin's Speech: "That Ye May Learn Wisdom,"* ed. John W. Welch and Stephen D. Ricks (Provo, UT: FARMS, 1998), 13; available at http://publications.maxwellinstitute.byu.edu/fullscreen/?pub=1087&index=1; accessed 1 July 2014.
8. Leon Morris, *Hebrews: Bible Study Commentary* (Grand Rapids, MI: Zondervan, 1983), 50.
9. Harold W. Attridge, *The Epistle to the Hebrews: A Commentary on the Epistle to the Hebrews, Hermeneia*, ed. Helmut Koester (Philadelphia: Fortress Press, 1989), 142.

"The Dove of Peace Sings in My Heart, the Flowers of Grace Appear"

Amy H. White and Brad Wilcox

Some say members of The Church of Jesus Christ of Latter-day Saints don't believe in grace. Nothing could be further from the truth. The Book of Mormon is full of grace. General conference is full of grace. In fact, we checked a computerized corpus of general conference addresses and found that from 1990 to now the word *grace* has been used almost 400 times. In addition to scriptures and the words of living prophets and apostles, the hymns are also full of grace.

In "How Firm a Foundation," we sing, "My grace, all sufficient, shall be thy supply."[1] In "Abide with Me," we sing, "What but thy grace can foil the tempter's power?"[2] In "Come, Come, Ye Saints," we sing, "Grace shall be as thy day."[3] Over and over, the doctrine of grace is taught in hymns.

Amy Howells White has served as a teacher in the auxiliaries and the seminary program of the Church. She graduated from the University of Utah in photojournalism and served in the Italy South Mission. All her life she has enjoyed nature, especially on horseback. She served as a member of the Sunday School general board from 2009–2014. She and her husband, Karl, appreciate their eight children and their spouses and twenty-one adventurous grandchildren.

Brad Wilcox is an associate professor in the Department of Teacher Education at Brigham Young University, where he also enjoys working with such programs as Especially for Youth and Campus Education Week. Along with Amy, he served as a member of the Sunday School general board. He is the author of The Continuous Atonement, The Continuous Atonement for Teens, *and* Practicing for Heaven, *among other books. He and his wife, Debi, have four children and five grandchildren.*

Today we want to focus on three: "Come, Thou Fount of Every Blessing,"[4] "There Is Sunshine in My Soul Today,"[5] and "I Stand All Amazed."[6]

COME, THOU FOUNT OF EVERY BLESSING

"Come, Thou Fount of Every Blessing" was written by Robert Robinson. He was just a small boy in the 1730s when his father died and he had to go to work to help support the family. He soon fell in with a wild crowd and lived a worldly lifestyle. One day he and his rowdy friends heard that a well-known minister was going to preach in a nearby church and they decided to attend in order to heckle him. Instead of heckling, Robert was captivated by the message of the preacher and left the meeting determined to repent. At the age of twenty, Robert set out to become a minister himself. Two years later, in 1757, he wrote a hymn expressing his gratitude for divine grace: "Come, thou Fount of every blessing; / Tune my heart to sing thy grace; / Streams of mercy, never ceasing, / Call for songs of loudest praise."[7]

There is a phrase later in the hymn that is difficult to understand: "Here I raise mine Ebenezer; / Hither by thy help I'm come."[8] This comes from 1 Samuel 7:12, in which the prophet Samuel raises a stone as a monument, saying, "Hitherto hath the Lord helped us." The English transliteration of the name Samuel gives to the stone is *Eben-ezer*, meaning "stone of help." What a beautiful definition of grace: Divine assistance from Him who is the Rock of our Salvation.

How else can we define grace? We asked friends and here are some of their responses: Atonement, salvation, revelation, belief, peace, forgiveness, covenants, help, power, and strength. All of these are correct answers because they all describe some contact with the Lord. *Grace is basically every contact we have with the Lord in which He enables us to change.* This is what King Benjamin's people experienced when they cried, "The Spirit of the Lord Omnipotent . . . has wrought a mighty change in us" (Mosiah 5:2). This is what Alma experienced when he believed the words spoken by Abinadi, "And according to his faith there was a mighty change wrought in his heart" (Alma 5:12). This is what King Lamoni's father experienced when he prayed to God and said, "I will give away all my sins to know thee" (Alma 22:18). These are all manifestations of how grace *changed* people.

We cannot speak about grace in the Church without quickly quoting the scripture in 2 Nephi 25:23: "For we know that it is by grace that we are saved, after all we can do." This verse makes it sound like we have to do all we can before grace is provided, but perhaps we are not taking into account the context of the chapters around the oft-quoted verse. For example, in the very next chapter Nephi extends the invitation to "Come, . . . buy milk and honey, without money and without price" (2 Nephi 26:25). No time condition is mentioned. Perhaps this is why Elder Bruce C. Hafen has clarified, "The Savior's gift of grace to us is not necessarily limited in time to 'after' all we can do. We may receive his grace before, during, and after the time when we expend our own efforts."[9]

Grace is not a booster engine that kicks in once our fuel supply is exhausted. Rather, it is our constant energy source. It is not the light at the end of the tunnel but the light that surrounds us and moves us through the tunnel. Grace is not achieved somewhere down the road. It is received right here and right now.

At a youth conference in Fresno, California, a young woman named Marina was asked to speak on the theme: "Come unto Christ, and be perfected in him" (Moroni 10:32). She said, "I used to think that meant I had to be perfect *for* Christ. Now I realize that it means I can be perfected *in* or *with* Christ." That young woman gets it! Coming to Christ is not the end. It is the means to the real end of becoming like Christ.

The word *we* in the phrase "After all we can do" may refer to you and me, but we understand the sense of the verse better when we think of it referring to Christ and each of us.[10] C. S. Lewis put it this way, "We are now trying to understand, and to separate into watertight compartments, what exactly God does and what man does when God and man are working together."[11] In this greatest of all companionships, we must not see a ratio of His part and our part, but rather a relationship that is greater than the sum of the parts. Instead of speaking of His part and our part, let us speak of His heart and our hearts loving each other, working together, and being conformed to the same image.

We cannot see our works as somehow supplementing Christ's grace, or Christ's grace as somehow supplementing our works—as if we have to meet some sort of minimum height requirement to get into heaven. It is not about height. It is about growth. We don't reach heaven by supplementing, but by covenanting. And, as our friend Ann Madsen has said, a covenant is not a cold contract between party A and party B. It is a warm relationship between two friends who are—think of the temple—on a first-name basis.[12] When we recognize, value, and foster that relationship, we are changed forever.

Amy shares the following experience of when she felt changed by grace:

> On April 13, 1961, I arrived home from school and was surprised to find my grandpa at our house. He explained that there was a possibility that my father had crashed his plane while flying out to our sheep ranch. I was only eleven years old but I knew what to do when my world was coming to an end. I went to the bathroom, locked the door, knelt by the bathtub, and poured my heart out to God. Not only was I terribly worried about my dad, but deep inside I was also scared that this was all my fault. Earlier that day when I found out my dad would be flying to the ranch I asked him to bring me back a bummer lamb. Bummers are lambs that have been orphaned and need to be fed with a bottle if they are going to survive. In my eleven-year-old mind, I assumed my dad must have been flying low looking for a bummer lamb for me—so if he died it would be my fault.
>
> Before I even finished thinking that thought, I had the impression, *This is not your fault.* Again I tried to explain that it *was,* but again it was as if someone were stopping me from even thinking it. I began to feel like I was wrestling back and forth with God. When I finally stopped struggling, I felt a profound and complete peace pour over me. The peace remained with me even when I found out later that evening that indeed my dad had died in the crash. I was only eleven, but that day I learned that God is real and He loves me. He had gone to great lengths to bring truth, light, and peace to me. He knew exactly who I was and what was happening in my little world. He was very

concerned that I understood truth and was not confused with false assumptions. This was a manifestation of His grace. I was forever changed.

Brad shares the following experience from his life:

I remember being a young missionary in Chile and having a difficult transition. It was hard adjusting to the culture and learning Spanish. It was discouraging to find out that no one was lining up to hear the message I had come to share. I felt homesick. One day as my companion and I were climbing a hill in the hot sun I thought, *Why am I even doing this?* But I knew the answer. I was there for God. Then came a thought I had never considered before: *So where is God?* Growing up in a strong Latter-day Saint home had buffered me from such doubts, but now I was being hit full force. The question bothered me and over the next few months I grappled with the disequilibrium it caused. It was a time of doubt, but also a time of great study, learning, service, and growth.

Several months later, my mission president came to town for interviews. He asked all the usual questions and I gave all the usual answers. As I stood to leave my president said, "Do you have any questions?" Did I ever!

I asked, "Is there even a God?"

"Yes," he responded.

"Does He know me?"

"Brad Wilcox, He knows you by your first name."

"Does He love me?"

"Yes."

That was it. No scripture references or quotes from the Brethren. Just one word—*yes.* That's when the Spirit washed over me, confirming my mission president's words. That night I prayed, and my supplication soared. I prayed to a Heavenly Father I was at last beginning to know, in the name of a Redeemer I was finally beginning to comprehend. This was a manifestation of grace.

Often people say, "God doesn't talk to me. Others may get answers but I never do." It is important to remember that God speaks to each of us in our own language (Moses 6:46). How he speaks to us is different for everyone because He has a different relationship with each of us. We are His children and we are all unique in His heart. Some people need visual examples, some memories, or impressions, or distinct thoughts that come to mind. Some respond to dreams, some recognize His voice in the scriptures, some get His message through other people. God has spoken to you and He will continue to "tune [our hearts] to sing [His] grace."[13] However He chooses to reach out to us, we can come to know He is there and He will help us.

THERE IS SUNSHINE IN MY SOUL TODAY

Another hymn that teaches us of grace is "There Is Sunshine in My Soul Today."[14] This hymn not only helps us define grace but also teaches us how to receive and accept that grace. That acceptance starts as we turn to the Lord by being believing—full of optimism, hope, and faith.

Becky and Tim live in California and have an eleven-year-old son named Matthew. Check out this boy's recent journal entry:

"All my new year's resolutions are almost done. I have the dream of five years—an iPad mini. I've seen [and read] a ton of uplifting and just plain epic movies and books. I have a complete family. I have a house. We are debt free. I've made some friends here:

"Aidan, Anders, Tiago, Denver, and Jenna. I love my life. I'm a Mormon. I know it. I live it. I love it. This is my life: Perfectly mixed; good variety; happy, healthy, wonderful, epic. I know who I am, what I am, how I came here, why I came here. The world is corrupt, but there is definitely good in it. We have money. We're alive. I'm happy, healthy, and joyful. I've gone to Guatemala. I love my parents and honor them. I am wonderful, treasured by God who is my everlasting Father. I am. I can. I ought. I will. My life so far is epic."[15]

When was the last time we felt like that? For most of us it has been too long. Our lives go up and down, but we may be spending too much time feeling down. Readjusting our binoculars, microscopes, and reading glasses is required. Instead of focusing on the "oughts" in our lives, we will focus on our possibilities.

Think about what you ought to be. Perhaps you are thinking, *I ought to be smarter and more physically fit* or *I ought to be a better spouse or parent.* How do you feel? Focusing on the oughts usually makes us feel discouraged and overwhelmed because they represent ideals—images of perfection from which we usually fall short. Oughts never die. They just become more intolerable. Oughts are an obligation. The very word says that we are coming up short. Oughts are usually critical. Oughts make it easy to feel like failures.

Now think about what is possible. It is a different way of looking at life—a *choosing* way of life. It is empowering. We use our agency. Instead of thinking about the perfect ideal, choose a doable step in that direction. In the end, our ultimate goals may not be very different but our progress toward them will be greater and more satisfying. We are progressing instead of feeling guilty. We shed the discouragement that comes with oughts, put our hand in the Lord's, and go forward. Focusing on something that is actually possible makes us successful.

We don't tell a seed it ought to be a flower. Instead, we recognize the possibilities and nurture the growth one day at a time. We understand that all things are possible with our hand in the Lord's hand. When a father brought his fitful son to the Savior, the Savior tenderly told him, "If thou canst believe, all things are possible to him that believeth." And the father answered in anguish, "Lord I believe; help thou mine unbelief" (Mark 9:23–24). The apostles then asked the Lord why they were unable to help the boy and He said to them, "If ye have faith as a grain of mustard seed . . . nothing shall be impossible unto you" (Matthew 17:20).

When Mary asked Gabriel how she could possibly be with child, he answered her, "With men this is impossible; but with God all things are possible" (Matthew 19:26). When the disciples exclaimed distress about how to get into the kingdom of God, the Lord instructed, "The things which are impossible with men are possible with God" (Luke 18:27). Our "possibilities" dramatically increase when we understand the limitless power of the Savior's grace.

When we focus on *oughts*, we focus on attaining flawlessness immediately. When we focus on *possibilities*, we focus on self-improvement over time. When we focus on oughts, we focus on God proving us. When we focus on possibilities, we focus on God improving us. When we focus on oughts, we see Heaven as a prize for the perfect. When we focus on possibilities, we see Heaven as the future home of all who are willing to be perfected. Remember, the Savior calls for a broken heart and a contrite spirit, not a perfect heart and a flawless spirit.

That simple shift in focus is a wonderful step toward accepting and applying grace. It opens the door to faith and happiness. The hymn "There Is Sunshine in My Soul Today" is a happy hymn. We sing, "The dove of peace sings in my heart, / The flowers of grace appear."[16] Were these words written by somebody who had never experienced any trials? Not at all. The author, Eliza ("Lidie") Hewitt, experienced great trials. She graduated valedictorian in her class and started her teaching career with great optimism. One day a prankster in her class hit her in the back with a slate and injured her so badly she became bedridden and was placed in a body cast for six months.

On her first day out of the cast she went outside and wrote, "There is sunshine in my soul today, / More glorious and bright / Than glows in any earthly sky, / For Jesus is my light."[17] Later, Lidie became the superintendent of a Sunday school at an orphanage called "The Northern Home for Friendless Children." She taught them "There Is Sunshine in My Soul Today" because she wanted them to know that by being faithful despite difficult circumstances, by focusing on possibilities instead of oughts, we can begin to access Christ's grace and be happy: "When Jesus shows His smiling face, / There is sunshine in the soul."[18]

I STAND ALL AMAZED

In the hymns we learn what grace is and how to access it, but we also learn how to share it with others. Elder D. Todd Christofferson taught, "Jesus is said to have gone about doing good (see Acts 10:38), which included healing the sick and infirm, supplying food to hungry multitudes, and teaching a more excellent way. . . . So may we, under the influence of the Holy Spirit, go about doing good in the redemptive pattern of the Master."[19]

As Christian disciples we forgive others as Christ forgives us. We love others as He loves us. We serve others as He serves us—not in an effort to deserve grace, but in an effort to offer it to others as freely as it is offered to us. Each calling we fulfill, each mission we serve, each dollar we donate, each temple session we attend is not a "work" done in place of faith but an inevitable outgrowth of that faith. We are not trying to earn grace but to return grace for grace. Of what value is Christ's unearned gift if it goes unused by ourselves and unrecognized by others?

When people disagree with us, or make us feel stupid, or fail to live up to our expectations, the most human response is to resist and reject. Sometimes we do it with anger and often with silence. How do we respond to those who have chosen not to believe in the gospel? We all know someone who has made this decision. Think of your friend or loved one who now thinks differently about things you hold sacred. If you are the one distancing yourself from the Church, think of how your actions affect your loved ones. This is a time when grace is needed on both sides of those relationships. The enabling power of Christ can enable us to see others as people, not objects, special projects, or enemies. Grace given human to human is filled with respect and love. When we are angry or fearful or blaming, we disable relationships. When we see others as people we love and desire to help, we enable relationships.[20]

Amy shares this personal experience:

> A few months ago my son told me he no longer bought into the ideas he had been taught when he was growing up. He is not comfortable with many things in the Church and has decided to walk a different road. Needless to say, it was pretty devastating to me. Because he knows how I feel about the Church, I'm sure he expected a negative response from me. Preemptively and defensively he said to me, "If you have to judge my decisions and tell me that I am a bad person, you are not welcome in my life. And you can tell that to the rest of the family too." How would you reply?
>
> Because of my personal experience with the Savior giving me grace and my indefinable love for my son, my answer came as a gift, swiftly and gently, "You will always be welcome in my life and my heart. There is nothing you can do that would keep

me from loving you. You can tell me anything and I would hope that you would be open to me telling you anything." He believed me because it was completely true. I wasn't saying words while thinking something else. My son felt the truth of my statement and our relationship stayed intact. What if I had reacted defensively and *without* grace? What damage might have been done?

That inspired answer came easily to my mind because I have felt Christ whisper those same words to my heart at difficult times in my own life: "You will always be welcome in my life and my heart. There is nothing you can do that would keep me from loving you. You can tell me anything and I would hope that you would be open to me telling you anything." As Christ honors our agency, I must honor my son's agency. As Christ loves me intensely (which I don't understand), I will continue to love my son intensely (which I do understand). I am trying to return grace for grace.

The hymn "I Stand All Amazed" was written by Charles H. Gabriel, who was born in 1856. He was raised on a farm in Iowa, but developed an interest in music early because his father taught singing in their home. When Charles was a young boy he overheard his pastor ask if anyone knew of a good hymn to go along with the topic of his upcoming sermon. The next day this boy presented him with a song he had written himself. That was the start of an entire lifetime of composing and publishing sacred music. His hymn "I Stand All Amazed" is greatly loved by Latter-day Saints. In it we sing, "I stand all amazed at the love Jesus offers me, / Confused at the grace that so fully he proffers me."[21] In our day we usually think of the word *confused* as meaning not understanding something. However, in Charles Gabriel's day it also was used to express wonder and awe. Similarly, the word *proffer* is not one we hear often today, but it means much more than to give or offer. It means volunteering a gift with no strings attached. It means extending or holding out a gift—literally putting it someone's hands. So when we sing that hymn we are singing, "I stand all amazed at the love Jesus offers me, / Confused at [totally in awe of] the grace that so fully he proffers [he volunteers, extends, and holds out] to me."

When the Brigham Young University Museum of Art presented an exhibit titled *Sacred Gifts*, we wanted our families to see the beautiful paintings of the Savior. Amy decided to take some of her grandchildren. In the museum the lights were subdued and mothers encouraged their children to whisper. One of the moms was kneeling next to six-year-old Max and four-year-old Zoe explaining a painting. Zoe left that painting and stopped alone in front of Carl Bloch's *Christ on the Cross*. In this quietly subdued atmosphere, little Zoe broke into song (and not in a whisper): "I stand all amazed that for me he was crucified, / That for me, a sinner, He suffa'd, he bled and died. / . . . Oh it is wonderful, wonderful to me!"[22] Completely unaware of anyone or anything else, this little girl sang with her whole heart.

If anyone has ever wondered if Mormons believe in grace, that person should have been there to hear little Zoe sing as she stood before a picture of Christ on the cross. Yes—we believe in grace. We know it is any contact we have with the Lord in which He enables us to change. We begin to accept it by turning to the Lord, being believing, staying positive, and showing faith. We offer it to others as freely as it is offered—even proffered—to us.

As you consider what we have shared, we invite you to do the following: 1) Pay close attention to when the word *grace* appears in the hymns. Ponder those texts during the sacrament and share your thoughts with others. 2) Think of something you ought to do or be. Write it down, rip it up, and throw it out. Think instead of smaller goals that you can accomplish instead of what you *ought* to accomplish. These are all possible in the strength of the Lord. 3) Think of someone in your life who needs your approval or forgiveness. Pray for the ability to show grace to him or her.

Elder Bruce C. Hafen has taught, "We all need grace, both to overcome sinful weeds and to grow divine flowers in ways we cannot fully do alone."[23] We know this is true. We have experienced both these blessings personally. With Zoe, we proclaim: Oh, it is wonderful that God should care for us, enough to die for us, enough to live for us, and enough to help us in our quest to become more like Him.

NOTES

1. Attributed to Robert Keen, "How Firm a Foundation," *Hymns of The Church of Jesus Christ of Latter-day Saints* (Salt Lake City: The Church of Jesus Christ of Latter-day Saints, 1985), no. 85.
2. Henry F. Lyte, "Abide with Me!" *Hymns*, no. 166.
3. William Clayton, "Come, Come, Ye Saints," *Hymns*, no. 30.
4. Robert Robinson, "Come, Thou Fount of Every Blessing," *Hymns: The Church of Jesus Christ of Latter-day Saints* (Salt Lake City: The Church of Jesus Christ of Latter-day Saints, 1948), no. 70.
5. John R. Sweney, "There Is Sunshine in My Soul Today," *Hymns* (1985), no. 227.
6. Charles H. Gabriel, "I Stand All Amazed," *Hymns* (1985), no. 193.
7. Robinson, "Come, Thou Fount of Every Blessing," *Hymns* (1948), no. 70.
8. See, for example, "Hither by Thy Help I'm Come," *Music and the Spoken Word* (blog); available at fans.musicandthespokenword.org/2009/10/04/hither-by-thy-help-im-come/; accessed 30 July 2014.
9. Bruce C. Hafen, *The Broken Heart: Applying the Atonement to Life's Experience* (Salt Lake City: Deseret Book, 1989), 155.
10. See Joseph M. Spencer, "What Can We Do? Reflections on 2 Nephi 25:23," *Religious Educator*, vol. 15, no. 2 (2014): 25–39.
11. C. S. Lewis, *The Joyful Christian* (New York: Touchstone, 1996), 136.
12. Robinson, "Come, Thou Fount of Every Blessing," *Hymns* (1948), no. 70.
13. See Truman G. Madsen and Ann N. Madsen, "House of Glory, House of Light, House of Love," in Truman G. Madsen, *The Temple: Where Heaven Meets Earth* (Salt Lake City: Deseret Book, 2008), 69.
14. Sweney, "There Is Sunshine in My Soul Today," *Hymns* (1985), no. 227.
15. Personal correspondence in the author's possession.
16. Sweney, "There Is Sunshine in My Soul Today," *Hymns* (1985), no. 227.
17. Ibid.
18. Ibid.
19. D. Todd Christofferson, "Redemption," *Ensign*, May 2013, 110.
20. See C. Terry Warner, *Bonds That Make Us Free* (Salt Lake City: Deseret Book, 2001).
21. Gabriel, "I Stand All Amazed," *Hymns* (1985), no. 193.
22. Ibid.
23. Hafen, *Spiritually Anchored in Unsettled Times* (Salt Lake City: Deseret Book, 2009), 18.

Holding Ourselves in Readiness to Act on the Lord's Timing

Ginny U. Smith

For the Lord God is a sun and shield: the Lord will give grace and glory: no good thing will he withhold from them that walk uprightly.

Psalm 84:11

Whenever I attend a session at BYU Women's Conference, I always feel I must have something in common with every single sister because something in the title of the session drew us together to the same session. I wonder if we face similar challenges, seek insights into the same doctrine, or hope for the same blessing. Whatever your reason for being here today, it is my prayer that the Holy Ghost will reveal at least one truth during the time we share together that will sustain you as you "hold yourself in readiness to act on the Lord's timing" and seek to find answers to the following questions:

- How can we *trust* in the Lord's plan?
- How can we exercise *faith* in the Lord's timing for us?

Ginny U. Smith is currently the executive director of a private charitable-giving foundation. For over twenty-five years, she has enjoyed a career in nonprofit administration with a focus on children. She received her bachelor's degree from the University of Utah in business administration. She is a member of the Primary general board. Ginny and her husband, Douglas H. Smith, have three children and eight grandchildren.

- How can we be more *understanding* of the Lord's timing for others?

I wonder if the one thing we might have in common is that we are *waiting* for something. That is what women seem to do. We wonder, we worry, and we wait upon the Lord for our prayers to be answered—sometimes patiently and sometimes impatiently. I would like to ask you a few personal questions:

ARE YOU WAITING FOR AN ANSWER TO A SPECIFIC PRAYER?

Have you waited for a long time? Has it been weeks—months—a whole year? Have you been waiting for several years? For some, does it seem like you might even have to wait a lifetime before your prayer is answered?

Waiting upon the Lord is what we do when our hopes and dreams and our most fervent desires are put on hold. Waiting sits right in the middle of living. And life goes on while we wait. We may be waiting for something wonderful to happen or until something horrible is finally over; we may be waiting for the slightest something that will keep our hearts from breaking or for something miraculous to cause a loved one's heart or behavior to change.

CONSECRATE OUR WAITING

As I was preparing my talk, a thought came to me in the temple that simply would not go away. So I have prayerfully decided to share it with you today, as something you may wish to ponder and consider. As we wait upon the Lord for answers to our prayers—what if we consecrate our waiting to Him?

We have been counseled to consecrate everything we have to the Lord for the purpose of building up His kingdom here on earth. Why not consecrate our waiting? Waiting occupies so much of our time. I like to think of waiting as the sacred space between when our prayer is first offered and when it is finally answered.

Prayer Offered ⟶ Sacred Space ⟶ Prayer Answered

Think of the collective good we could do! *Consecrated waiting* is not passive, but can be filled with purpose. We would all be available to do the Lord's will, to be on His errand whenever He needed us, to answer His call joyfully with, "Here am I, just waiting, waiting. Please, oh, please send me! Let me serve Thee or others while I wait!"

If we choose to consecrate our waiting, it may redefine how we wait:

- From passively waiting for *our* prayer to be answered to actively becoming the answer to *someone else's* prayer.
- From an inward expression of waiting to *receive* to an outward expression of *giving.*

How we wait may have a great influence on who we can and will become. How we wait conveys much about our trust and faith in the Lord, and is evidenced in how we live, hope, and worship. Elder Neal A. Maxwell coined the phrase "graceful endurance" as more than just surviving or hanging on. He said, "Passing beyond breaking points without breaking takes the form of [graceful] endurance."[1]

I personally witnessed graceful endurance in my sister and her husband as they experienced a difficult time in their lives when he was diagnosed with ALS (also known as Lou Gehrig's disease). They chose to quietly consecrate their waiting as his disease progressed, and in so doing they gifted our family and their friends an inheritance of hope that all things would be made right through the Atonement and Resurrection of Jesus Christ, our Savior. We witnessed in their countenances, in what they did, said, and how they conducted their lives that by consecrating their waiting they were filled with the promised peace "that passeth all understanding" (Philippians 4:7). Together, we lived and waited in the sacred space they created for us for nearly five years until my sister's husband passed away.

We have been given patterns for creating a sacred space in the temple chapel as we wait for a session to begin, and every Sunday during the sacrament service as we wait to partake of the sacrament. By creating a sacred space in which to wait, we can feel a deep and personal connection to the Lord as we wait to know His will for us and wait upon His timetable.

Jesus Christ himself set a pattern of righteous behavior for us to follow as He waited unto death upon the cross, offering forgiveness to those who had sinned and extending love and compassion towards His mother, Mary.

Waiting and Agency

Elder Dallin H. Oaks gently reminds us that often our own happiness is subject to more than the Lord's timing. It is also subject to the agency of others. Thus we cannot bring to pass everything we desire in our lives because there are things over which we have no control.[2]

In a recent conversation with a friend, he shared how a sister in Montana consecrated her waiting but also understood the doctrine of agency. Her eighteen-year-old son defiantly announced that he was through with the Church, no longer believed, and was definitely not serving a mission. Heartbroken, this mother and her sister fasted and prayed for her son every week for seventeen years (844 weeks). At the age of thirty-five, her son returned to activity in the Church.

When asked how it all happened, she replied that she fasted and prayed weekly and when her son was ready to return, he did—and it worked! This faithful mother consecrated her waiting while her son regained his desire to return to Church.

One evening I mentioned the idea of consecrating our waiting to my daughter. The very next morning she sent me a text that read: "Mom, I am reading *The Alchemist*, an inspiring fable by Paulo Coelho, and I just read a passage that made me think about our conversation last night. In a chapter about our dreams and journeys, this is what it says, 'Every second of our search is a second's encounter with God and with eternity.'"[3] Sarah then concluded, "Every second of waiting we consecrate to the Lord is a second's encounter bringing us closer to Him." I thought that was such beautiful pondering.

Elder Neal A. Maxwell wrote, "This life is not really chronological but *experiential*."[4] I have found that it is really a series of vignettes, chapters or short stories.

The poet James Bailey eloquently bids us to be present, to be aware, to embrace and experience every singular moment that passes through our lives. He states:

We live in deeds, not years; in thoughts, not breaths;
In feelings, not in figures on a dial.
We should count time by heart-throbs.[5]

How Can We *Trust* in the Lord's Plan?

Look Back and Remember!

Sister Kristen M. Oaks shared this story of having trust in the Lord's plan at a Church Educational System devotional at Brigham Young University in 2011—just six months following the horrific 8.9 magnitude earthquake that set off a devastating tsunami in Sendai, Japan.

To put the disaster into perspective, thirty-foot waves washed over the coastal city, causing over $300 billion in material damage, sweeping away vehicles in its path, collapsing buildings and bridges at every turn, and claiming the lives of 15,884 people. Sister Oaks said:

"A Japanese sister driving her car felt the earthquake, had her car engulfed by water from the tsunami, and with quick thinking, an open car window, and knowledge of the terrain, she leapt from her car and began [to run] to safety. Her first thoughts were, 'Save yourself, and hurry.'

"Struggling to [find] safety, she glanced over to see another car with locked windows, sealed tight by the water pressure. Inside she could see small children and a grandmother who would surely drown because they could not escape. Her natural instincts told her to keep running if she wished to survive. There was no time; she had to save herself. Then a voice filled her mind, saying, 'You are a member of The Church of Jesus Christ of Latter-day Saints.' She looked back at the car and remembered who she was and what she should do. [Perhaps she even remembered the promises she made long ago.] She reacted quickly, grabbing a nearby floating desk, smashing the window of the car, pulling the little family to safety, and then helping them find shelter before she made her way home."[6]

This faithful sister held herself in readiness to do the Lord's will. What incredible faith! How did this woman find the courage and strength to do what she did? In Isaiah 40:31 we find the answer: "But they that wait upon the Lord shall renew their strength; they shall mount up with wings as eagles; they shall run, and not be weary; and they shall walk, and not faint."

"Have You Thought to Pray?"

As increasing numbers of church members respond to the prophet's call, hastening the growth of missionary work has become an exciting reality! Sister Rosemary M. Wixom, general Primary president, as busy as she is on a daily basis, had offered an earnest prayer that she, too, might have a personal missionary experience.

Not having time to give it much more thought, imagine her surprise when her missionary moment occurred because someone dialed a wrong number and left a message on her cell phone. The message was intended for someone in Utah from a woman living out of state. The caller was very distraught about the possibility of having to move to Salt Lake City. She definitely did not want to move to Utah, didn't know what to do, and needed advice immediately.

After listening to the message, Sister Wixom felt strongly that she should let the caller know that her intended message was not received by the person she thought she had called.

The woman was very surprised that Sister Wixom had taken the time to return her call. Still distraught, she started to repeat the same worries and concerns all over again and after a few minutes said, "Oh, I have no one to talk to . . . but why am I telling you all this? I don't even know you." There was a long pause. Sister Wixom was then prompted to ask, "Do you mind if I ask you a personal question? Have you thought to pray?" The woman responded "No," and said she didn't know how to pray. Sister Wixom was prompted again and asked, "Would you like to learn how to pray?" Surprisingly, the woman said, "Yes."

So over the phone with a complete stranger, Sister Wixom taught this woman to begin by kneeling down and saying, "Dear Heavenly Father."

"Then what?" the woman asked.

"First, thank him for your blessings. Then talk to Him just like you have been talking to me. Share with your Heavenly Father your concerns and ask Him for help in knowing what to do. Explain how you feel. Then close your prayer, "In the name of Jesus Christ, amen."

"That's it?" asked the woman.

Sister Wixom explained that now she must *wait* for an answer . . . that it may not be immediate, but she would begin to know what to do and would feel much better. She reassured the woman that Heavenly Father knew her, loved and cared about her, and wanted her to be happy. They said their goodbyes and ended their conversation.

While Sister Wixom may never know the final outcome of this woman's dilemma, she had held herself in readiness to act on the Lord's timing as she consecrated her waiting-for-a-missionary-moment to the Lord and trusted that He wanted her to teach a stranger how to pray.[7]

In 1 Nephi 11:17 we read, "I know that [God] loveth his children; nevertheless, I do not know the meaning of all things."

Elder Neal A. Maxwell once expounded upon Nephi's great faith:

"There have been and will be times in each of our lives when such faith [as Nephi's] must be the bottom line: We don't know what is happening to us or around us, but we know that God loves us, and knowing that, for the moment, is enough."[8]

This is precisely what Sister Wixom shared in her brief telephone conversation with a stranger she most likely will never see again . . . that God knows, cares, loves, and listens to all His children. As we begin to consecrate our waiting to the Lord, we will come to understand that "we are not saved in isolation. This life is not just about me [or you or the desires of our hearts]. We are placed on earth to bless the lives of those around us, to act as agents of righteousness, . . . to 'be anxiously engaged in a good cause' (D&C 58:27),"[9] even as we wait upon the Lord for answers to our own prayers.

How Can We Exercise *Faith* in the Lord's Timing for Us?

"Through the Window"

One of the most beautiful examples of "exercising faith in the Lord's timing for us" is that of Brother Moses Mahlangu, as shared by Elder Ulisses Soares during the October 2013 general conference. You may remember hearing it:

"[Brother Mahlangu's] conversion began in 1964, when he received a copy of the Book of Mormon. But it wasn't until the early '70s that he saw an LDS Church sign on a building in Johannesburg, South Africa. . . . [He] entered the building to learn more about the Church. He was kindly told that he could not attend the services or be baptized because the country's laws did not allow it at the time.

"Brother Mahlangu accepted that decision with meekness, humility and without resentment. . . . He asked the Church leaders if they could leave one of the meetinghouse windows open during the Sunday meetings so he could sit outside and listen to the services. For several years, his family and friends attended church regularly 'through the window.' One day in 1980, they were told that they could attend church and also be baptized. What a glorious day it was for Brother Mahlangu."[10] These good and humble people exercised faith in the Lord's timing for them and consecrated sixteen years of waiting by keeping their hearts fixed on the gospel of Jesus Christ until they received full fellowship into this Church.

Waiting upon Us

Consecrated waiting "gives us a priceless opportunity to discover that there are many who wait upon us"[11] as we wait upon the Lord. Sisters, I know there are many members who attend church regularly but, metaphorically speaking, they are waiting on the outside, feeling isolated and alone, looking and listening "through the window," desiring the full fellowship that the gospel of Jesus Christ can bring. They exercise faith in the Lord's timing for them as they enter church each week carrying, along with their scriptures, life's disappointments, plans that have not come to fruition, or expectations yet unfulfilled.

We may brush shoulders with them weekly, sit in front of or behind them in class or sacrament meeting, or exchange a quick hello in the hallway. They may include a single sister yearning for the blessing of eternal marriage; a young couple waiting for the blessing of parenthood; a single parent struggling to keep food on the table; parents of a child with disabilities trying to control a major meltdown in sacrament meeting; a young husband searching for employment after losing his job; a young wife yearning for financial security and a home of her own; a longtime member grieving for the loss of a loved one or overcoming the devastation of a heartbreaking divorce after thirty-five years of marriage.

Such members may also be a single adult trying to blend into a resident ward upon leaving the security of a singles ward; new members having just moved in or been recently converted; a recently returned missionary (or even mission president) trying to adjust to life back home; a military family missing a father who has been deployed; a teenager overcoming an addiction to drugs, alcohol, gambling, or pornography; an active member reeling from the loss of a loved one who has taken their life or who is imprisoned for making a wrong choice; an older member losing their memory, their sight, or their desire to live. And there may be many, many others whose sorrows "the eye can't see."[12]

How do I know these faithful members exist? Because they are real people—people in my own ward or stake, people in your ward or stake, people who are waiting upon the Lord for comfort and answers to their prayers—people who are waiting upon us for fellowship and friendship.

These good and faithful members keep their hearts fixed on the gospel of Jesus Christ and believe in God's plan of happiness, all the while living valiantly with the challenges and heartaches they face in this mortal life. While we cannot alter the Lord's timetable for them, we can develop friendships, embrace their gifts and offer them love, empathy, understanding, and inclusion. Sisters, can you see how much we need each other? Can you see the many opportunities we have to wait upon each other as we wait upon the Lord?

How Can We Be More *Understanding* of the Lord's Timing for Others?

Enlarging Our Hearts toward Others

Elder Neal A. Maxwell once said: "With increased understanding we see that, while enduring is more than simply waiting, it includes waiting. But even waiting can be used to facilitate our becoming more like Jesus. . . . Our [waiting and] enduring is easier if we see it as part of God's unfolding."[13] Such is the true story of Lisa and her sister Julie.

Both sisters had been diagnosed with the same medical condition that made bearing children very difficult. Theirs is a poignant story of how we can be more understanding of the Lord's timing for someone else. This short version of Lisa's story does not begin to capture all the sorrow, anguish, heartache, and resilience that she has experienced over the years, but it does capture a story of trust, faith, compassion, and the genuine love between two sisters. I will be quoting and retelling Lisa's story as she shared it with me.

After several years of waiting, Lisa received an e-mail that would change her life. She and her husband had finally been chosen by a young woman who had experienced an unplanned pregnancy to become her child's adoptive parents.

Lisa shared these thoughts:

"As excited as we were [to become adoptive parents], I couldn't help but feel a tinge of sadness, too. My older sister Julie and her husband, who live out of state, had also been hoping and praying to adopt a child. I wanted more than anything for them to experience the same joy and excitement but the days continued on for Julie without so much as a prospect [for adoption] on the horizon. As we waited for the day we would become parents, my husband and I continued to pour out our hearts in prayer that Julie and her husband would be granted this same blessing in their life."[14]

Lisa recounted that Julie never once uttered a word of jealousy, envy, or spite. She called frequently to see how things were progressing as the due date drew near. She was truly happy for Lisa and cheerful whenever they spoke on the phone. These remarkable sisters were both waiting upon the Lord for similar answers to their prayers while at the same time waiting upon each other by offering sisterly love. Lisa had created a space in her heart for Julie's sadness to reside right next to her own happiness. And Julie had created a space in her heart for Lisa's happiness to reside right next to her own sadness.

Whenever I think of Lisa and Julie's story, Colossians 2:2 comes to mind: "That their hearts might be comforted, being knit together in love, and unto all riches of the full assurance of understanding, to the acknowledgement of the mystery of God, and of the Father, and of Christ."

Lisa continued:

"Our adorable baby boy, Finley, was born on Saturday, April 27, 2013. . . . It was a sacred and beautiful experience. . . . Finn's birth mother was required by state law to wait forty-eight hours after giving birth to sign the adoption papers. . . . Our family had been waiting on pins and needles . . . until Monday around noon, all the paperwork was signed and our sweet baby boy was ours!

"Julie called just as we were leaving the hospital. We asked if she wanted to video chat so she could meet Finn online. She said, 'Yes, and there is something I want to show you.' Imagine my utter surprise as the video popped up on our screen and there was a perfect, healthy, beautiful boy nestled safely in the arms of my sister. After my initial screams of excitement, Julie explained that a baby boy had been born over the weekend and he was in need of a family to adopt him that very day. At almost the same hour that our adoption paperwork was being signed, Julie's paperwork was also being signed. We were both able to bring our sweet miracle babies home *on the very same day!*

"What a sweet blessing this experience has been. I will forever be grateful for a loving sister who lacked envy and displayed grace in this situation and so many others. We have watched the Lord's hand in our lives—in the details that we could not have planned if we had tried. We have seen prayers answered more perfectly than we thought possible.

"We know that we have a Father in Heaven who loves us and blesses us in so many ways [all in accordance with His plan and according to His timetable]."[15]

Lisa also shared these words of wisdom from Elder Jeffrey R. Holland:

" . . . Sisters, there are going to be times in our lives when someone else gets an unexpected blessing or receives some special recognition. May I plead with us not to be hurt—and certainly not to feel envious—when good fortune comes to another person? We are not diminished when someone else is added upon. We are not in a race against each other to see who is the wealthiest or the most talented or the most beautiful or even the most blessed. The race we are *really* in is the race against sin, and surely envy is one of the most universal of those."[16]

The adversary hovers over and around us as we wait for answers to our prayers. The adversary is hoping that we will lose hope, fretting that we will remain faithful, and taunting us when we trust in the Lord. It is the adversary that makes waiting difficult, that causes us to give up hope and feel that God has abandoned us in our time of need.

It is my prayer that we will fight back the darkness and despair when the answers to our prayers are delayed or not what we desired or expected. May we create a sacred space in which to consecrate our waiting to the Lord, trust in His plan, exercise faith in His timing for us, and come to better understand his timing for others. And may our lives reflect the Savior's will always.

In closing, I have asked my husband, Douglas, to sing, "May My Life Reflect Thy Will," accompanied by Ashley Hoyle.

May My Life Reflect Thy Will

When temptations of the world seem to beckon me
When with darkness crowding in I am slow to see
I plead for strength that righteousness will be my goal
That I may keep the promises made long ago

O Savior, may my life reflect thy will
May I overcome through faith in thee
Let thy light be a constant guiding star
To lead me, ever lead me to thee

When the pleasures of this world
Pull me from my course
When I yield in moments weak to an evil force
I yearn to feel the peacefulness that makes me whole
And helps me keep the promises made long ago

O Savior, may my life reflect thy will
May I overcome through faith in thee
Let thy light be a constant guiding star
To lead me, ever lead me to thee
Ever lead me to thee

O Savior may thy purpose be fulfilled
May my life be used in serving thee
Let thy light guide my efforts from afar
And lead me, ever lead me to thee.[17]

NOTES

1. Neal A. Maxwell, *Not My Will, But Thine* (Salt Lake City: Bookcraft, 1988), 115.
2. See Dallin H. Oaks, "Timing," Brigham Young University devotional address, 29 January 2002; available at http://speeches.byu.edu/?act=viewitem&id=229; accessed 1 July 2014.
3. Paulo Coelho, *The Alchemist* (New York: HarperCollins, 1993), 132.
4. Neal A. Maxwell, *Not My Will, But Thine* (Salt Lake City: Bookcraft, 1988), 115; emphasis added.
5. James Bailey, "We live in deeds, not year; in thoughts, not breaths"; available at http://www.poets.org/poetsorg/poem/we-live-deeds-not-years-thoughts-not-breaths; accessed 2 July 2014.
6. Kristen M. Oaks, "To the Singles of the Church," CES BYU devotional, 11 September 2011; available at https://www.lds.org/broadcasts/ces-devotionals/2011-09-to-the-singles-of-the-church?lang=eng; accessed 2 July 2014.
7. This story is shared with the kind permission of Rosemary M. Wixom.
8. Neal A. Maxwell, *Not My Will, But Thine* (Salt Lake City: Bookcraft, 1988), 119.
9. Kristen M. Oaks, "To the Singles of the Church"; accessed 2 July 2014.
10. Ulisses Soares, "Be Meek and Lowly of Heart," *Ensign*, November 2013, 10–11.
11. Robert D. Hales, "Waiting upon the Lord: Thy Will Be Done," *Ensign*, November 2011, 73.
12. Susan Evans McCloud, "Lord, I Would Follow Thee," *Hymns of The Church of Jesus Christ of Latter-day Saints* (Salt Lake City: The Church of Jesus Christ of Latter-day Saints, 1985), no. 220.
13. Maxwell, *Not My Will, But Thine*, 123–24.
14. Personal correspondence in author's possession.
15. Ibid.
16. Jeffrey R. Holland, "The Parable of the Laborers in the Vineyard," *Ensign*, May 2012, 31.
17. K. Newell Dayley, "May My Life Reflect Thy Will," © 1974 Sonos Music. Used by permission.

The Powerful Privilege of Women

Heidi S. Swinton

In 1842, Joseph Smith, beloved and honored by the Saints as the prophet of God, stood before the sisters of the Female Relief Society of Nauvoo and made this promise, "If you live up to your privilege, the angels cannot be restrain'd from being your associates."[1]

These were women who had left homes—and even families—to join the Lord's Church in preparation for His Second Coming. Some had suffered degradation, privations and unthinkable horrors for having chosen to follow Him. Strong in the gospel, they were sure of their faith and humble in their worship of God the Father and Jesus Christ.

But Joseph wanted them to recognize that the Lord had more in store for them. "If you live up to your privilege," the Prophet said, angels will come, you will be connected to the heavens, you will be divinely directed in what the Lord will have you do. Such is our promise today.

Without question we, as daughters of God, are entrusted with privileges that exceed any honor or opportunity the world pushes our way. As

---

Heidi S. Swinton is the author of President Thomas S. Monson's biography, To the Rescue. *She is an award-winning author and screenwriter whose works include the PBS documentaries* American Prophet, Sacred Stone, Sweetwater Rescue, Trail of Hope, *and* America's Choir. *She has served on the Relief Society general board and as a member of Church writing committees. She served with her husband, Jeffrey C. Swinton, as he presided over the England London South Mission from 2006 to 2009. They are the parents of five sons, four living, and have four daughters-in-law and six grandchildren.*

disciples of Jesus Christ, we have precious privileges on earth that reach far beyond here and now, privileges that are attended by Godly manifestations of His mighty power. The priesthood of God is not elusive nor is it a commodity to be bartered for or bantered about. It is the Lord's and it is holy.

Today I want to focus on three things, all relating to the priesthood of God:

- First, the privilege to exercise faith in God the Father and in His Son, Jesus Christ, and in the Holy Ghost.
- Second, the privilege to understand, seek, and feel the power of the priesthood in our lives.
- And third, the privilege to draw upon and act with authority given us by those holding priesthood keys.

Let's begin with faith, for it enables and underscores all blessings. By our faith in the Lord Jesus Christ, buttressed by our willingness to follow His example and live—truly live—His commandments, we draw closer to living up to our privileges. We become, quite simply, faithful disciples of the Savior and are blessed for following Him.

By faith the woman with an issue of blood was healed as she reached out to touch the garment of the Lord. She believed in Him. She counted it a privilege to be in His presence and she stretched out her hand exercising faith in His power, priesthood power that permeated the very folds of His clothes. Such is the faith underpinning our privileges.

Are we the kind of women whom the Lord can count on to reach for righteousness, to live his ways, to be worthy of treasuring and bearing witness that He lives—the testimony of His divine power? Are we learning from the disciples of old who watched the Lord perform miracles—and were healed as well—healed from the ways of the world? Do we accept the Lord's plan for our lives as did Mary when she said, "Be it unto me according to thy word" (Luke 1:38)? Do we heed His counsel to Emma Smith to "lay aside the things of this world, and seek for the things of a better" (D&C 25:10)?

Consider the faith exemplified by a young girl in the Biblical account of Naaman, a heroic warrior—and a leper. Leading the Syrian army, he had brought captive out of Israel a little maid—we don't even know her name but we know she was a believer in the power of God; she knew in whom she trusted to do God's bidding. "She said unto her mistress, 'Would God my lord were with the prophet that is in Samaria! for he would recover him of his leprosy'" (2 Kings 5:3).

You know the story: Naaman comes with his horses and chariot to the door of Elisha expecting some great reception, some fire from the sky as a demonstration of priesthood power. The prophet Elisha, instead, has his servant tell Naaman, "Go and wash in Jordan seven times, and thy flesh shall come again to thee, and thou shalt be clean" (2 Kings 5:10).

Naaman was aghast. A servant, not the prophet receiving him? Wash in a river? He was hoping for a big splash, not a dip in the common, muddy Jordan. Another of Naaman's servants boldly suggested to his master, "If the prophet had bid thee do some great thing, wouldest though not have done it?" (2 Kings 5:13). Finally, Naaman goes down into the Jordan and is healed.

What has the Lord said? "My thoughts are not your thoughts, neither are your ways my ways" (Isaiah 55:8). Naaman was a man of the world with power to conquer armies, but Elisha was a man of God who had been given priesthood power that could cleanse the body and the soul. That power opens the gates of heaven. That demonstration of priesthood power began with the quiet testimony of a young woman whose faith was sure.

In 1846, Bathsheba Smith, young wife of Apostle George A. Smith and my great-great-great-grandmother, left Nauvoo with the early companies. This woman born to mortal privilege on a plantation in Virginia wrote of the experience:

"We left a comfortable home, the accumulations of four years of labor and thrift and took away with us only a few much-needed articles such as clothing, bedding and provisions. We left everything else behind us for our enemies. My last act in that precious spot was to tidy the rooms, sweep up the floor and set the broom in its accustomed place behind the door. Then with emotions in my heart . . . I gently closed the door and faced an unknown future, faced a new life, a greater destiny as I well know, but I faced it with faith in God."[2]

Do we have that profound faith in God? Are we "steadfast and immovable" (Alma 1:25; see also D&C 49:23), pressing forward with "a perfect brightness of hope" (2 Nephi 31:20)? Or are we standing by the side of the Jordan asking for a bigger river, clearer water, and a grandstand of onlookers who think power is theirs to demand?

Elder M. Russell Ballard said: "When all is said and done, each of us has the *privilege* of choosing whether or not we will believe that God is our Father, that Jesus is the Christ, and that They have a plan designed to help us return home to Them. This, of course, requires faith, which is why faith is the first principle of the gospel. Our testimonies and our peace of mind and our well-being begin with the willingness to believe that our Father in Heaven does indeed know best."[3] What our Father knows, sisters, is that grassy plains, treacherous caverns, and rocky mountains are ahead on our journey home. All the way home. Like Bathsheba Smith, the key is to face them with faith in God.

Our second privilege as women is to seek greater understanding of the priesthood and its profound blessing in our lives. This is one of the "ifs" Joseph Smith was talking about. "If" points us to look for the hand of God around us, feel His strength and His peace, and rely on His promises. And in so doing, "angels cannot be restrain'd from being [our] associates."

I was raised in a single parent home with a mother of incredible faith and charity. Not until I was married did I experience the blessing of having a righteous priesthood holder in my home. But my mother understood the gospel; she was a woman of great faith and reverence for God's almighty power. Elder Ballard has said, "The power of a converted woman's voice is immeasurable, and the Church needs your voices now more than ever."[4] Where do you voice your conviction? Do you speak with the tongue of angels, bearing witness of Jesus Christ in your homes and to your family, friends, and associates? Do we live up to that privilege?

I will always remember when my uncle Jon baptized me just days before he left on his mission to the Central States. He and I share an eternal connection that reaches back to the Salt Lake Tabernacle when he pronounced, "Having been commissioned of Jesus Christ, I baptize you in the name of the Father, and of the Son, and of the Holy Ghost. Amen" (D&C 20:73). It was my privilege to be his first baptism.

Elder Neil A. Andersen has taught: "All of the ordinances invite us to increase our faith in Jesus Christ and to make and keep covenants with God. As we keep these sacred covenants, we receive priesthood power and blessings."[5]

With each priesthood ordinance we receive, we are drawn closer into the family circle of our Father in Heaven. And we are changed, both by the love of God and by our love for Him.

Every one of us has moments in our lives where we must choose to be believers in the power of God or to be skeptics turning our hearts away. If you wrestle with feelings of being overlooked or lonely, humbly reconsider the love of God in your life. President Thomas S. Monson, our living prophet, has reminded us:

"Your Heavenly Father loves you—each of you. That love never changes. It is not influenced by your appearance, by your possessions, or by the amount of money you have in your bank account. It is not changed by your talents and abilities. It is simply there. It is there for you when you are sad or happy, discouraged or hopeful. God's love is there for you whether or not you feel you deserve love. It is simply always there."[6]

Priesthood ordinances are an expression of God's love, for they bring us back into his presence. "The Lord will give grace and glory: no good thing will he withhold from them that walk uprightly" (Psalm 84:11). Are we worthy of those promised blessings? Worthy by living the commandments? Worthy by prayerful use of our agency? Worthy by receiving and living up to our covenants?

It isn't always easy to walk uprightly.

I always prayed in my pregnancy with twins that they would be born with all their fingers and toes. I never imagined that one would die. Christian Horne Swinton lived only twenty-two hours. I remember standing at his graveside, his tiny little casket being readied to lower into the hard winter ground. It was a wrenching moment that to this day—thirty-eight years later—is still fresh in my heart and mind and soul.

At the same time Cameron, the younger of the two by just minutes, fought valiantly for his life in newborn intensive care—all three-plus pounds of him. His journey there with tubes and monitors and daily frightening experiences lasted for weeks that turned to months. But Cameron lived; he and Christian both received priesthood blessings at birth. The Lord chose to let Cameron stay and he is a daily reminder of the power and love of the Lord.

I remember slipping into the back of my ward sacrament meeting after the twins were born and Christian was gone. The opening song was "Come, Come, Ye Saints" and the congregation was singing, "And should we die, before our journey's through, / Happy day! All is well!"[7] Happy day? Not yet and in some ways, not ever, but "all is well" was true.

"All is well" is an eternal perspective that draws upon the power of the priesthood. Christian was born under the covenant, sealed to us, forever. I now had a son who was all the way home with our Father in Heaven. For me and my husband, Jeffrey, everything changed. I came to treasure the sealing power on earth, the blessings and covenants in the temple, because my family now straddled the veil.

The power of the priesthood of God did not take away the pain or the loss that still surfaces, even today, usually when I least expect it. But the Lord's promise that we will be together for eternity was and is a privilege that prompts me, my husband, and our four sons every day to live true to the ordinances we have received and the covenants we have made.

That expression of love is our privilege as daughters of our Father in Heaven. When we visit the temple and come out into the world we are renewed with the strength and power born of sacred covenants. Do we realize what has just happened in our lives—the manifestation of priesthood power? And not just for us but also for those waiting—who knows how long—for those profound blessings in their lives! When we raise a hand to sustain and support the prophet of God who holds all the priesthood keys for the work of the kingdom of God on earth—right now—we are exercising great power. We are bearing witness that Jesus Christ lives, this is His Church, and we have a significant place in moving it forward. When hands are placed on our heads to call down the power of heaven we feel "angels round about" to lift us, bring comfort and sometimes, even heal. When we accept a calling and are set apart by the power of the priesthood, we go forward with authority.

And that is the third message.

Elder Dallin H. Oaks taught recently at general conference, "Priesthood ordinances and priesthood authority pertain to women as well as men." Elder Oaks then quoted in part from a message delivered more than forty-five years ago by President Joseph Fielding Smith: "'While the sisters have not been given the Priesthood, it has not been conferred upon them, that does not mean that the Lord has not given unto them authority. . . . to do some great and wonderful things, sacred unto the Lord, and binding just as thoroughly as are the blessings that are given by the men who hold the Priesthood.'"[8] The Joseph Fielding Smith address that Elder Oaks quoted also says: "Authority and Priesthood are two different things. A person may have authority given to him, or a sister to her, to do certain things in the church that are binding and absolutely necessary for our salvation, such as the work that our sisters do in the House of the Lord."[9]

I sustain prophets, seers, and revelators—President Monson, Elder Oaks, Elder Ballard, Elder Andersen, and President Smith—whose words give us added insight to the power of the priesthood in our lives. They have explained not only what the practice of the church is, but also what the doctrine of the Lord is. As a woman sealed in the temple in the new and everlasting covenant, I know I share in priesthood power with my husband that is best understood by grasping the significance of that blessed, holy ordinance. My responsibility here and now is to continue to live up to that precious privilege.

Sisters, we have been given authority under the direction of priesthood leaders. And with it comes a sacred trust. So what does that mean for us? Are we taking seriously what the Lord has asked us to do in our own little patch in the vineyard? Are we casual about being called, set apart, and serving? Or are we like Naaman, wanting a bigger playing field? Do the words "not my will, but thine, be done" (Luke 22:42) clearly define our service?

The Lord bore our burdens in the Garden of Gethsemane with drops of blood oozing from him, the very life-blood of mortality. He asks us to find strength beyond our own, to lift and encourage and bear witness of His saving power. Shall we not count it an honor to be in His service?

Every time we partake of the sacrament, we are exercising privilege as members of His Church. We say "amen," promising to "always remember Him" and live worthy of His spirit. The sacrament is holy and filled with power. I think of the time I was sitting in sacrament meeting preparing to receive the sacrament and my heart was heavy. I was distressed by something really difficult that had happened in the life of someone I dearly loved. I couldn't imagine how I was going to handle it and not be contentious, as the scriptures so clearly counsel, and not be just plain mad. As the priest said those sacred words of the sacrament prayer, I heard the Lord say to me, "You have to forgive. You have to show love, my love."

That was not easy to do, but drawing upon the power of the Atonement, I did forgive. And it became a sweet experience.

Those words, "to always remember Him," hold such meaning for each one of us. Yes, we remember that 2,000 years ago a wicked mob belittled Him, scourged Him, beat Him, and hung Him on a cross. But why did this Son of God, who raised the dead and healed the blind, allow it to happen? Because He counted it a privilege to serve God and He concluded his ministry with those stirring words, "It is finished" (John 19:30).

He sacrificed His life for every one of ours—our sins, our disappointments, yes, even our very bad days. He loves us so much that He is willing to pick up our burdens so that we will not harden our hearts and turn away.

It is sobering to remember the Lord's words, "Not every one that saith unto me, Lord, Lord, shall enter into the kingdom of heaven; but he that doeth the will of my Father who is in Heaven" (3 Nephi 14:21).

So there I was, in that sacrament meeting, on the precipice of hardening my heart with anger and resentment. As a young man, probably with a crooked tie, said the sacrament prayer, I heard in my mind the words, "that which the Spirit testifies unto you . . . that ye should do in all holiness of heart, walking uprightly before me" (D&C 46:7).

Humility, honor, duty, service, charity—these are the workings of authority within us. We raise our hands to sustain the prophet, the Twelve Apostles, the general officers of the Church, including our sisters who lead the Primary, Young Women, and Relief Society auxiliaries. They have committed to serve us; we count it a privilege to receive that service. We sit in councils, men and women called of God to further his work, and we seek ways to bless the lives of those in our care. What a privilege it is for us to join together in service to God. We attend the temple, serve in the temple, and feel the priesthood blessings promised us in the Lord's house. We pray for one another that the Lord might intervene with blessings and comfort. All of these we do within our spheres of authority, privilege, and assignment.

I have circled and underlined and written in the margins around the response of the Nephites to Jesus Christ when He prayed for them:

"The eye hath never seen, neither hath the ear heard, before, so great and marvelous things as we saw and heard Jesus speak unto the Father; . . . no one can conceive of the joy which filled our souls" (3 Nephi 17:16–17).

Not all was well with them. Cities had sunk into the ground and pillars had fallen and those who had mocked—even dear ones, I imagine—were swallowed up. This was not a time of general calm. But it was heavenly in its manifestations and they were "good enough" to receive such privileges.

The question is: "Are we?"

I know that my Redeemer lives. I know that he has placed in my path and yours privileges far beyond our own capacities that remind us who we are and why we are here. I have felt angels round about (as have you); the angels Joseph Smith promised could "not be restrain'd from being [our] associates." We are in good company. We stand with the Lord; we feel His spirit; we are blessed by His power, infinite and immeasurable.

It all comes down to having faith in Jesus Christ and trusting in His ways, seeking the blessings of the priesthood in our daily lives and exercising with courage and commitment the authority given to us to serve by those with priesthood keys. Said President Joseph Fielding Smith, "It is within the privilege of sisters of this Church to receive exaltation in the kingdom of God and receive authority and power as queens and priestesses, and I am sure if they have that power they have some power to rule and reign. Else why would they be priestesses?"[10]

When we hope for more in this life may it be as the song says, "More holiness give me, / More strivings within." May we plead for more of the things that the Lord loves—more patience, gratitude, meekness, purity, strength, and wisdom to fulfill the work given each one of us that we might be "More fit for the kingdom," and in the end, "More blessed and holy— / More, Savior, like thee."[11]

And then we will feel it a privilege as did Nephi when he said, "Rejoice, O my heart, and cry unto the Lord, and say: O Lord, I will praise thee forever; yea, my soul will rejoice in thee, my God, and the rock of salvation" (2 Nephi 4:30).

NOTES

1. Relief Society Minute Book, 17 March 1842–16 March 1844, 35; available at http://josephsmithpapers.org/paperSummary/nauvoo-relief-society-minute-book?p=35; accessed 8 July 2014.
2. Bathsheba Smith, "Autobiography," ed. Alice Merrill Horne, typescript, 14–15, in author's possession.
3. M. Russell Ballard, "'Let Us Think Straight,'" Brigham Young University Education Week devotional, 20 August 2013; available at http://speeches.byu.edu/?act=viewitem&id=2133; accessed 9 July 2014.
4. Ibid.
5. Neil L. Andersen, "Power in the Priesthood," *Ensign*, November 2013, 92.
6. Thomas S. Monson, "We Never Walk Alone," *Ensign*, November 2013, 123–24.
7. William Clayton, "Come, Come, Ye Saints," *Hymns of The Church of Jesus Christ of Latter-day Saints* (Salt Lake City: The Church of Jesus Christ of Latter-day Saints, 1985), no. 30.
8. Dallin H. Oaks, "The Keys and Authority of the Priesthood," *Ensign*, May 2014, 49, 50.
9. Joseph Fielding Smith, "Relief Society—An Aid to the Priesthood," *Relief Society Magazine*, vol. 49, no. 1 (January 1959): 4.
10. Ibid., 5–6.
11. Philip Paul Bliss, "More Holiness Give Me," *Hymns*, no. 131.

The Atonement Heals, Comforts, Consoles, and Enables Us

Linda K. Burton

Years ago, I was touched as President James E. Faust related the following story of a little boy whose mother purchased tickets to a concert featuring the great Polish concert pianist Paderewski. Our son had recently returned from his mission to Poland, so of course my ears perked right up as the Polish composer's name was mentioned. President Faust explained:

"'The night of the concert arrived and the mother and son found their seats near the front of the concert hall. While the mother visited with friends, the boy slipped quietly away.

"'Suddenly, it was time for the performance to begin and a single spotlight cut through the darkness of the concert hall to illuminate the grand piano on stage. Only then did the audience notice the little boy on the bench, innocently picking out "Twinkle, Twinkle, Little Star."

"'His mother gasped, but before she could move, Paderewski appeared

---

Linda K. Burton was born and raised in Salt Lake City, Utah. She was studying elementary education at the University of Utah when she met Craig P. Burton. They were married in the Salt Lake Temple and are the parents of six children and are grandparents to twenty-four grandchildren.

Before her call as the sixteenth Relief Society general president, she served for a short time as a member of the Relief Society and Primary general boards. She served with her husband as he presided over the Korea Seoul West Mission. She has been blessed to serve in various callings in Relief Society, Young Women, Primary, and Sunday School.

on stage and quickly moved to the keyboard. He whispered to the boy, "Don't quit. Keep playing." And then, leaning over, the master reached down with his left hand and began filling in the bass part. Soon his right arm reached around the other side, encircling the child, to add a running obbligato. Together, the old master and the young novice held the crowd mesmerized.'"

President Faust then summed up the story with this lesson:

"'In our lives, unpolished though we may be, it is the Master who surrounds us and whispers in our ear, time and time again, "Don't quit. Keep playing." And as we do, He augments and supplements until a work of amazing beauty is created. He is right there with all of us, telling us over and over, "Keep playing."'"[1]

The Apostle Paul bore his own powerful witness that the Lord's grace strengthens us in our weakness, as we read in 2 Corinthians: "And he said unto me, My grace is sufficient for thee: for my strength is made perfect in weakness. Most gladly therefore will I rather glory in my infirmities, that the power of Christ may rest upon me" (2 Corinthians 12:9).

As I pondered that scripture, I found personal application as I reflected on some of my own experiences with the divine gift of grace. I wish I could report that, like Paul, I have always "gloried in my infirmities." I would have to honestly admit that my faith has sometimes resembled the wavering faith of Sariah, Lehi's wife, *before* her sons returned with the plates of brass. However, just as the Lord patiently tutored Sariah in her afflictions, He has also tutored me and continues to do so.

One of those tutoring times happened about thirty years ago. At that time, my husband was serving as a bishop. We had four small children—a young baby, a two-year-old, a five-year-old, and a seven-year-old, and we had gone without income for almost a year. The national economy was weak, and we had recently built a home. Because interest rates kept climbing, we were advised by well-meaning and trusted family members and friends to keep our home financed on our construction loan until the interest rates went down. But interest rates just kept climbing. As you might suppose, it wasn't long until we were on the brink of losing our home.

To make matters worse, Christmas was coming and our sweet little children had visions of sugarplums dancing in their heads, which only added to my discouragement, for I knew that those expectations would go unfulfilled. We tormented ourselves with regrets and self-doubting thoughts that began with phrases like "If only we had . . ."; "Why didn't we . . ."; "We should have . . ."; or "We shouldn't have . . ."; and similar thoughts and self-condemnation.

During this time, my cousin gave my father a copy of my great-great-grandmother's autobiography, and my father, in turn, loaned it to me. Each night after the children were in bed, I would stay up late reading about Mary Lois Walker Morris while waiting for my husband to get home from his bishopric responsibilities. I came to know and love her, and I wept over her life, which was filled with challenges much greater than my own. I will name just a few.

At age fifteen, Mary and her parents left their beloved England to sail to America to join the Saints. They suffered homesickness, seasickness, cramped quarters, and faith-testing ravaging ocean storms. When Mary was sixteen, her mother died. As a seventeen-year-old newlywed, Mary crossed the plains on foot with her husband's family but without her husband. There wasn't enough money for both her and her husband to pay the price required to join the wagon train. He had to stay behind to work until he was able to earn enough to join them later, which he did.

During their first winter in the valley together, Mary and her husband were so poor that they suffered from hunger, freezing temperatures, and sickness. When Mary was nineteen, her first baby was born, but the baby became very ill and died three months after birth. Three weeks after the death of her baby, Mary's husband died, leaving her not only childless, but a teenage widow. Her trials did not end there. Though she was blessed to marry again and bear more children, at age thirty-three her five-year-old boy, Conway, burned to death as the result of an accidental fire in the chicken coop. By the time Mary saw the flames, heard her son's screams, and ran to his rescue, he was perishing right before her eyes. At age forty-seven, she bore a fifteen-pound baby who died the same day he was born.

Although her life was filled with one major trial after another, Mary's autobiography surprisingly reflects sweet expressions of faith and testimony. As I share a couple of excerpts, notice how the Lord not only blessed her to bear her burdens but, through His grace, healed her heart in the midst of her sorrow. He comforted and consoled her and enabled her to let go of her regrets or self-condemning thoughts.

Following the deaths of her first baby boy and her husband, Mary recorded: "As we sat by the firelight after our return from the cemetery I looked back upon my life, and though in deep sorrow, I was able to see where the hand of the Lord had been over me and felt how thankful I should be that he had sent me to parents who had taught me to serve Him in all things, and to count all things as dross, compared with the wisdom that God gives to His faithful children."[2] "I felt that I had served God to the utmost of my ability, that I had His approval, and that He would stand by me."[3]

Later, in her autobiography she wrote: "I have my Heavenly Father to thank for His assistance, through the inspiration of His Holy Spirit. No matter was too small for me to [raise] a petition to Him for help, and my prayer was always answered."[4]

I have long held that Heavenly Father is the Divine Economist. As we are willing, He helps us learn through the experiences of others in order to help us overcome our own trials and tribulations. Such was the case with me as I read Mary's story. I realized that her faith in the Savior and His "amazing grace" enabled her to surmount heartache after heartache and challenge after challenge. As I read, I felt my own heart soften and I felt that I too could trust our Savior, who is "full of grace and truth" (D&C 93:11), to do the same for me if I were willing to do my part.

As you can imagine, our financial trial, which seemed overwhelming before I read about Mary's experiences, became easier to bear as I saw how the Lord had enveloped her in His loving arms during her adversities. I felt the assurance that if I placed my faith and trust in Him, He would do the same for me. And I can bear fervent witness that He did just that.

I am slowly learning that as we move along life's path, the Lord gives us burdens to carry so that we might yoke ourselves to Him. Yoking ourselves to Him not only helps us develop the spiritual muscle needed to get us through our current trials but also blesses us with His enabling power, which helps us face the future trials that surely await us. It is the weight of the load, Elder David A. Bednar reminded us, that gives us the needed traction to move forward.[5]

Remember how Alma's people found themselves in bondage, bearing heavy burdens placed upon them by Amulon? Here is the beautiful promise given to Alma's people by the Lord while they were suffering: "Lift up your heads and be of good comfort, for I know of the covenant which ye have made unto me; and I will covenant with my people and deliver them out of bondage. And I will also ease the burdens which are put upon your shoulders, that even you cannot feel them upon your backs, even while you are in bondage; and this will I do . . . that ye may know of a surety that I, the Lord God, do visit my people *in* their afflictions" (Mosiah 24:13–14; emphasis added). But that was not all He did. Because Alma's people were submitting cheerfully and patiently to the burdens that were upon their backs, the Lord strengthened them and spoke to them again, saying, "Be of good comfort, for on the morrow I will deliver you out of bondage" (Mosiah 24:16). And He did!

The world would have us believe that trials are unfair and that we are entitled to only blue skies and sunshine. Who of us has not heard people raise their hands against heaven and say, "If there really were a God, He would not allow such-and-such to happen." You fill in the blank. Maybe in our darkest hours, we have even said or been tempted to say or feel something similar. We may forget in the heat of our trials that God is aware of us and that He has a plan for us. He knows us individually and perfectly and customizes our mortal experiences to help us grow into our very best selves—if we will let Him. He is the ultimate personal trainer! I find that as I look back on the tests and trials the Lord has customized for me, I realize that some of my greatest joys have followed my darkest moments. Sometimes we just have to tie a knot in our rope and hang on! At other times we might have to tie a knot on top of a knot on top of another knot and just keep hanging in there one minute at a time, one hour at a time, and eventually one day at a time. It can happen as we yoke ourselves to the Savior and draw upon His enabling power.

In February 2014, it was my privilege, along with Sister Carol McConkie, to visit the Philippines. As you will recall, in November 2013 the super typhoon Haiyan hit the Philippines, the strongest typhoon ever recorded in the Philippines. We spent one day in Tacloban, the hardest hit of all the areas. As we witnessed the aftermath of the storm for ourselves, we were deeply moved with compassion for those affected by it. We had the privilege of attending Church meetings with the Saints in Tacloban and hearing their stories of faith, embracing them in our arms, assuring them that the Lord was aware of them, and reminding them of the continued prayers of their brothers and sisters throughout the world in their behalf. On our way to the airport to return to Manila, we stopped by to see the remains of a house where sister missionaries had lived. We had heard the miraculous story of the escape of the ten sisters and wanted to see for ourselves where the story took place. Let me give you a brief summary of their story.

The sisters living in areas close to the shore were advised to move further inland, where other sisters were located. As a result, ten sisters had gathered in one small house. As the super typhoon hit, it brought with it not only winds of up to 200 miles per hour, but a storm surge, which caught everyone by surprise. Black murky water began filling the cinder block home of the sister missionaries. The sisters retreated to what they thought was the safest place—a room on the second floor—but even there, the water rose as they sang hymns and recited scriptures in an effort to remain calm. Because the windows were barred, they were trapped in the house and could not find a way to get out.

Finally, they were able to escape by kicking away the plastic sheeting in a skylight in the ceiling and the sisters huddled together in a tight well-formed group under a short eave on the roof. They watched as parts of the roof and houses were torn away and felt they were being protected as the storm raged about them. Fearing they would be washed into the ocean, as the waters continued to rise, the sisters prayed that the waters would subside. They testified that as soon as they finished praying, the waters stopped rising.

As we stood outside the missionary home, I remembered the lyrics to the hymn we had sung earlier that morning with the surviving Saints in Tacloban: "When dark clouds of trouble hang o'er us / And threaten our peace to destroy, / There is hope smiling brightly before us, / And we know that deliv'rance is nigh."[6] And then I thought of the Primary children who had sung these words as the closing hymn that morning: "Heavenly Father, are you *really* there? / And do you hear and answer every child's prayer?"[7] As we looked at the sisters' home and thought about those precious missionaries and the other 194 missionaries who all survived, I knew the answer to that question was indeed, "Yes! I do hear!"

As we turned to leave the house, I took a photo of a pink shoe that we guessed must have belonged to a sister missionary. At first I entitled it "Faith in Every Footstep." However, I have since renamed it "Amazing Grace." To me it is symbolic of the grace of the Lord and what is required of us in order to receive that enabling power. I love the fact that the shoe is pointing away from the house—moving forward and not retreating or giving in to the overwhelming adversity of the moment. It is as if the Master is whispering, "Don't quit. Keep playing"—or in this case, "Keep faith-ing!" I know that these sister missionaries have built spiritual muscle as a result of their experience that will help them weather the trials they face in the years to come and continue to rely on the grace of the Lord.

No matter how thorny our path may seem, as we look unto the Lord "in every thought," doubting not and fearing not (D&C 6:36), "His arm is sufficient, though demons oppose."[8] That includes physical, financial, emotional, mental, and spiritual demons.

"Sister [Eliza R. Snow's] personal expression of faith and optimism can serve as a guide for all [of us]. 'I will go forward,' she said. 'I will smile at the rage of the tempest, and ride fearlessly and triumphantly across the boisterous ocean of circumstance . . . and the *'testimony of Jesus'* will light up a lamp that will guide my vision through the portals of immortality.'"[9]

I invite each of us to pay attention to the unseen arms surrounding us and to listen with faith to the reassuring whisperings in our hearts saying, "Don't quit. Keep playing." Let us remember always that the Savior is "full of grace and truth" and that He will comfort, console, heal, enable, and magnify us. He helps us to forgive ourselves in our times of need. Of this I am a humble witness.

NOTES

1. James E. Faust, quoting a talk given by Ann Woodland, Idaho Falls, in "What It Means to Be a Daughter of God," *Ensign*, November 1999, 101.
2. *Before the Manifesto: The Life Writings of Mary Lois Walker Morris*, Melissa Lambert Milewski, ed. (Logan, UT: Utah State University Press, 2007), 117.
3. Ibid., 12.

4. Ibid., 193.
5. See David A. Bednar, "Bear Up Their Burdens with Ease," *Ensign*, May 2014, 87–90.
6. William Fowler, "We Thank Thee, O God, for a Prophet," *Hymns of The Church of Jesus Christ of Latter-day Saints* (Salt Lake City: The Church of Jesus Christ of Latter-day Saints, 1985), no. 19.
7. Janice Kapp Perry, "A Child's Prayer," *Children's Songbook* (Salt Lake City: The Church of Jesus Christ of Latter-day Saints, 1989), 12; emphasis added. Used by permission.
8. Eliza R. Snow, "The Time Is Far Spent," *Hymns*, no. 266.
9. *Daughters in My Kingdom: The History and Work of Relief Society* (Salt Lake City: The Church of Jesus Christ of Latter-day Saints, 2011), 59; see also Eliza R. Snow, *Poems: Religious, Historical, and Political* (Liverpool, UK: F. D. Richards, 1856), 148–49; available at https://ia700200.us.archive.org/12/items/PoemsReligiousHistoricalAndPolitical/poemsreligioushi01snow.pdf; accessed 7 July 2014.

Taking the Time to Talk: Communication in Marriage

Mardi Townsend

A few months ago my husband, Matt, and I attended a planning meeting with all the other presenters of this BYU Women's Conference, and they warned us that the very topic we have been asked to speak about would be greatly needed and we would be tested as the conference got closer. I can't tell you how true that is! The closer this conference has gotten, the more we have needed the skills and blessings I'm hoping to address today.

As a relationship coach, Matt is often asked to speak at firesides on the topic of relationships and communication. Since people don't like to admit having their own relationship or communication problems, he usually starts out by trying to put everybody at ease by saying something like, "Brothers and sisters, I know that none of *you* have relationship or communication issues . . . ," then he pauses for about three seconds and says, ". . . but the person on your right does—they're seriously messed up!" He then encourages people not to look at each other, and says, "*You* know who they are. Many of you brought them with you today!" He then pleads with everyone by saying, "So let's just all be good sports and help out the person to your right today. Let's learn what we can about relationships

---

Mardi Townsend has a degree in elementary education from the University of Utah and worked previously as a teacher; she works as a substitute teacher and manages the speaking schedule for her husband, Matt. She also helps care for her mother, who has Alzheimer's disease. She serves as a counselor in her ward's Primary and enjoys hiking and biking. She and her husband are the partents of six children.

and communication—let's do it for them!" What's even funnier is when it's your partner who is sitting to your right!

Although we like to think that the problems we see are not ours but everyone else's (the person to our right, our partner, anybody but us), let's agree today that we are *all* a part of the problems in our lives, and, more specifically today, a part of our communication problems.

Marion and Ida Romney

An excellent example of our tendency to see communication problems as "outside of us" is found in a great story told by Elder F. Burton Howard about Marion G. Romney and his wife, Ida. Elder Romney was confident that his wife's hearing was going. He even went to the doctor and asked him about it. When the doctor asked Elder Romney how bad the situation was, he said that he wasn't sure. So the doctor told Marion to go home and find out. The doctor told him to go into a room as far from his wife as he could and then talk to her. If there was no answer, he should move closer and closer to her until she could hear him. Following the doctor's instructions, Elder Romney did just what he was told. He went into their bedroom while she was in the kitchen: "Ida!" There was no answer. He then moved a little closer and spoke again: "Ida!" Still no answer. He then went right up to the door of the kitchen and a little frustrated, said, "Ida, can you hear me?" She responded, "What is it, Marion—I have answered you three times."[1]

I love this story. There's such a great lesson to be learned here: It's probably best to worry about our own communication issues first and not our spouses' problems. Odds are by doing that, we'll fix at least half of our misunderstandings.

Take Responsibility

I've found that the sooner I take some responsibility for *my* contribution to poor communication and misinterpretation in my relationships, the sooner I can become a major contributor to solving those problems and finding the peace that accompanies healthier relationships. I've also found that the sooner I let my Savior into my communication with my spouse, the sooner peace will arrive.

It was exciting for Matt and me when we found out that our topic, "Communication in Marriage," came from a great quote by one of our favorite people, Elder Marvin J. Ashton. Elder Ashton and his wife were good friends of my grandparents and helped build our extended family cabin before I was even born. I also worked at a tennis club where Elder Ashton and his friends would play tennis; I often saw him there. He also performed our wedding ceremony in the Salt Lake Temple twenty-three years ago. I'm sure that his counsel to us in the temple that wedding day had something to do with communication in our marriage, but unfortunately we don't have a record of what he told us that day.

The quote from Elder Ashton says: "If we would know true love and understanding one for another, we must realize that communication is more than a sharing of words. It is the *wise* sharing of emotions, feelings, and concerns. It is the sharing of oneself totally."[2]

Many people may believe that communication is taking place when we are talking, when words are being transferred back and forth, but to "know true love and understanding for one another, we must realize that" it is so much more than that. Instead—and I repeat—communication is the "*wise* sharing of emotions, feelings, and concerns. It is sharing of oneself totally." With your spouse, do you feel like you have learned the art of wise sharing of emotions, feelings, and concerns? Or does it feel more like the opposite . . . the unwise battle of our shared fears, grievances, and unmet expectations?

WHAT GETS IN THE WAY?

Communication is known to be one of the leading causes of marital problems in couples. So what gets in the way of us communicating in a wiser fashion, as Elder Ashton is talking about? What gets in the way of us effectively sharing our emotions, feelings, and concerns?

Take a minute right now and think about the issues and concerns that are most difficult for you to communicate about with your spouse. Maybe it's the topic of money? Or in-laws that are outlawed? Perhaps you disagree on how you discipline the kids? Notice that there are topics you know are not safe to bring up with your husband or others, and notice how those concerns make you feel.

Is Conflict Normal?

Is this normal to have these issues in our marriages? Is having some conflict normal? Research in the field of marriage and family relationships shows that all couples have issues that they struggle with. In fact, some research even states that having conflict can be healthy for relationships. The real problem is not the fact that you *have* conflict, or even how much conflict you have—the real problem is our inability to talk through our problems with each other and to find, as Elder Ashton has taught us, the love and understanding that accompanies real communication.

In 3 Nephi 11:29–30, we are taught, "He that hath the spirit of contention is not of me, but is of the devil, who is the father of contention, and he stirreth up the hearts of men to contend with anger, one with another. Behold, this is not my doctrine, to stir up the hearts of men with anger, one against another; but this is my doctrine, that such things should be done away."

So let's begin to do away with contention in our lives and marriages by starting where the real communication problems lie. We need to understand where these problems come from. As mentioned before, we often put the blame on someone else. Human nature is to think, *If only he was better at communicating*, or *If only she were more understanding, our lives would all be so much better.* Or *If only my partner could understand the real me—my real feelings, concerns and thoughts—our lives would be so much easier.*

As Elder Ashton has taught, we must find a way to exercise wise communication skills to share our innermost feelings, thoughts, and concerns with our partner. *Wise* means "informed . . . having or showing a good sense of judgment."[3] *Wise* might also mean that our difficult conversations are driven more from eternal perspective than from moral insecurity. Perhaps *wise* also means that we use more of our Savior's example to meet the basic needs of those we love, instead of simply fighting for *our* needs to be met.

Our Savior Is Our Best Example

Our best examples of being wise come from the wisest of them all—our Savior. Our Savior's communication was always wise and incredibly informed. His love for us beautifully informed him on how to handle the prickly needs of us humans.

An excellent example of the Savior's wise communication took place one early morning as Jesus sat at the temple teaching a group of people. The scribes and Pharisees brought a woman to him who had been caught in adultery, and the angry crowd wanted her stoned. (See John 8:1–11.) Our Savior, instead of reacting to the emotion that existed in that setting, patiently and calmly knelt on the ground and drew with his finger in the dirt, perhaps to distract and redirect the thoughts and feelings of her accusers. Jesus said, "He that is without sin among you, let him first cast a stone at her" (v. 7). With their thoughts altered, their feelings changed, they willfully left the scene. Perhaps too, the accused woman was also humbled and changed. The Savior then, assuming nothing, asked the woman, "Where are those thine accusers?" They had left. He then told her to "go, and sin no more" (vv. 10, 11). Notice the emotion had dissipated, no lecture was given (or needed), no rebuffing, no judgment, but just understanding and love. His involvement in this potentially catastrophic situation was as the theme of this year's Women's Conference suggests: "For the Lord God is a sun and shield" (Psalm 84:11). The Savior brought light to the minds of all involved, and a shield for the woman who so desperately needed Him.

SMOKE AND FIRE

In an effort to follow our Savior's example and become a wiser participant in our conflicted conversations in our homes and lives, let me explain a metaphor that Matt often uses to teach the couples he works with about their communication patterns, and to help them understand where these problems originate.

Imagine for a minute a blazing campfire with a nice plume of smoke rising out of it. The smoke in the metaphor symbolizes any and all of the issues where we tend to have disagreement with our partners. Your smoky issues may vary depending on your relationships. Remember a few minutes ago when you thought about those issues that are so difficult to talk about with your spouse. These issues might also include things like addictions, differences, hobbies, communication, your children, time and scheduling issues, and so forth. Matt calls these the smoke because these are the concerns in our marriages where things get a little hazy. As with smoke, they tend to irritate you and make your eyes water and make you feel like you're suffocating. They make you feel like you need to either run away or sit and fan the smoke away—which just gives new life to the fire.

Matt calls these concerns the smoke also because these are the issues, feelings, and concerns that, if not dealt with wisely, could end up consuming the air necessary to keep your relationship alive. These smoky issues alone can kill a marriage, just as the smoke from a house fire can be a bigger killer than the flames themselves.

In Matt's book *Starved Stuff: Feeding the Seven Basic Needs of Healthy Relationships*, he teaches us a way to share the feelings of our heart more wisely by getting out of the smoke and down to the fire—to the real issues that are causing all the smoke.

In this analogy, the fire represents the seven basic needs of healthy relationships. There are seven basic needs that every human being looks for in a happy and healthy relationship. Each of the words build upon each other, forming an acronym that spells out the word STARVED. The basic needs are Safety, Trust, Appreciation, Respect, Validation, Encouragement, and Dedication. When these needs are being met, we feel loved and content in our relationships, and we feel safe to share "oneself fully," as Elder Ashton has taught us. When these needs are not met, we feel, as the acronym states, STARVED! And when *we* are feeling starved, the tendency is to starve others. "You not meeting my needs" justifies *my* need to not meet *your* needs and we both end up starving each other—and downward goes the spiral. Doesn't that sound like the perfect plan of the adversary?

Let's take a closer look at each of these seven basic needs and see how the Savior and other righteous communicators douse the fire and eliminate the smoke of conflict. As you're listening, try to figure out what the fire behind all *your* smoky issues is.

The Seven Basic Needs

The first letter in our acronym is S, which stands for Safety.

Imagine in the premortal world how safe we felt in the presence of our Heavenly Father. Then imagine the lonely and unsafe feeling that Adam and Eve must have had when they left the Garden of Eden and headed out into the lone and dreary world. That was the beginning of our Safety issues.

All of us want to feel safe in many different ways. In our marriages, we desire and deserve to feel *physically* safe, knowing we won't be harmed; *socially* safe, knowing we won't feel embarrassed; *emotionally* safe, able to share what's in our hearts; *financially* safe, having enough money to meet our needs; and *spiritually* safe, feeling that we share the same moral values with our partner.

When couples fall into an argument about money—which is one of the things couples argue most about—they really are struggling with financial safety issues. The smoke is the money and the budget, and financial safety is the fire, or the real issue. When you're concerned about something you saw on the computer when you walked in on your spouse, we could argue about Internet filter software or the pictures that were up on the screen (the smoke), but perhaps the wiser communication might be to express our feeling of a lack of emotional or spiritual safety, and begin the discussion there.

So here are some questions to ask yourself:

- Does your partner feel *safe* with you?
- Do you feel safe with your partner?
- Do you feel safe financially, socially, physically, emotionally, *and* spiritually?
- Do any safety topics tend to separate you?

T stands for Trust. In Stephen M. R. Covey's book *Speed of Trust*,[4] he teaches that in order to trust somebody, you must be able to trust two basic things. You must trust their character (their decency and their honesty) and their competency (their skills and abilities) to be able to talk about the issues you've got to talk about. Nobody would trust a doctor that had a lot of character but no competency, nor would you trust a physician that had no character but a lot of competency.

When we can't trust our doctors, we have to get second opinions, and that makes our lives more complicated and costly. The same is true in our marriages. When we can't trust either the character or competency of our partners, then our communication is going to be affected. Think about it—how do you end up communicating with a person that you don't trust? You hold back and don't talk at all—or you blow up. Basically, the lower the trust, the smokier the conversation, and the more difficult the relationship will be. If you are arguing with your partner about something inappropriate you saw on his computer screen, you probably have a trust issue.

When trust issues emerge and we seek second opinions about our problems, may I suggest in our marriages that we first turn to our Heavenly Father to influence our understanding about each other. Although friends are also very important to have and to confide in, turning to our Father in Heaven, who is the source of all light and knowledge, is always a more reliable source. There is no better guide to truth than the gift of the Holy Ghost.

In Proverbs 3:5–6 we are taught: "Trust in the Lord with all thine heart; and lean not unto thine own understanding. In all your ways acknowledge him, and he shall direct thy paths."

So ask yourself these questions: Does your spouse trust you, your character and competency? Do you trust your spouse?

A stands for Appreciation. William James said, "The deepest principle of Human Nature is the *craving to be appreciated.*"[5]

Everyone's need to be loved and appreciated is different. When conflicts arise about marital intimacy, or about who is doing more around the house, then we are probably dealing with appreciation issues. Matt teaches that humans feel love through different senses. Some of us sense love through our eyes (we see it), others hear it through their ears, and some feel it through their hands or hearts.

Matt calls them "see-ers," "hearers," "touchers," and "sensers." Matt and I are complete opposites when it comes to this. I am a "see-er," so I like to see Matt vacuuming and doing dishes. I also like to see notes, text messages, surprise gifts, help around the house, and a clean house. I am also a "senser," meaning I feel loved when I feel appreciated. We "sensers" like time and undivided attention and can sometimes get offended when our partner gets preoccupied with their phone or computer or when they are seemingly not paying attention to the family.

Matt is a "hearer," and so he feels loved by the words people say and by the tone they use. Matt is also a "toucher," so he feels love through the sense of touch. He likes hugs, cuddling, pats on the shoulder, hand-holding, kisses, and all that other stuff!

The key to learning your partner's preference is to notice what they complain about or what they respond positively to. For example, "You never have time for me!" indicates a "senser." "I like it when you sit next to me when we're watching TV and tickle my back" indicates a "toucher." Our natural tendency is to love others using our own loving preferences, but it's important that we learn to love our partner *their* way. How do *they* feel loved? Do you know what your partner's preference is?

R stands for Respect. *Respect* comes from the Latin root "*specere*," which means "to look."[6] *Respect* means that you have the ability to *see* the other person with reverence, with esteem, honor, value, and admiration. Many times in our marriages we feel that our partners do not respect our opinions, our ideas, or our feelings.

A fairly common pattern that evolves in marriages is when a woman feels unsafe or afraid, she'll tend to say something about it, which in turn sets off the man's need for respect, causing him to erupt and get mad. A funny example of this pattern often takes place when we drive somewhere with Matt in the driver's seat. He claims I have no depth perception whatsoever and can't understand why I'm so jumpy when he drives. He says that even when we are nowhere near getting into any kind of accident, I startle easy, throw my leg over my head, turn my head so I can't see what's about to happen, and scream loudly, thinking my life is in danger. This does not sit well with him, as you can imagine, and apparently he feels disrespected when I do this. I just don't understand it.

Long-term relationships are not going to last if we don't respect the person we're married to. When you struggle to respect your partner because of some past issue, it helps to remember that in the end we are all sons and daughters of our Heavenly Father and we all make mistakes. That alone should earn your partner some respect.

So ask yourself: Does your partner know you value and admire him? Do you feel valued and respected by your partner?

V stands for Validation. Validation is the simple idea that two people's ideas and points of view can both be valid at the same time, even if those points of view are different. Have you ever expressed an opinion about something only to have it shot down or ignored? That's the opposite of validation. Invalidation is the most basic cause of most of our communication problems. As human beings, we want to feel that our thoughts and feelings are seen by others as valid, good enough, and understood. When someone validates us, it doesn't mean that they agree with everything we are saying, but that they have tried to understand us from *our* frame of reference, and not from *their* frame of reference.

One of the most beautiful examples of validation in the scriptures comes from the woman who had been suffering from a blood disorder for twelve years (see Mark 5:25–34). She knew that if she could just touch the hem of her Savior's robe, she would be healed. This woman who was afflicted probably felt safer in a social sense not approaching the Savior face-to-face. She instead opted simply to touch his garment. When the Lord was within her reach, she extended her arm and touched her Master's clothes. The Lord, in tune with the Spirit, felt "virtue [go] out of him" and knew exactly when she touched him. He then turned toward the woman and asked the simple question, "Who touched my clothes?" (v. 30). I'm sure her heart was racing as she was exposed and as their eyes connected. Then, in the warmest way I can imagine, the Lord validated her act of pure faith by saying, "Thy faith hath made thee whole" (v. 34).

Do you validate the thoughts and concerns of your partner? Do you hear them out and try to find where you agree, instead of immediately arguing about where you disagree? Do you feel validated by your partner?

E stands for Encouragement. Hidden in the word *encouragement* is the word *courage*, which comes from the French word for heart, *coeur*. Encouragement is getting to the center of your partner's feelings to see what is really in his heart—his interests and deepest dreams—and then being supportive and interested, and encouraging him to press forward. Research shows that the healthiest couples are each other's best cheerleaders. Does your partner feel encouraged by you? Do you feel encouraged by your partner?

The final letter of our STARVED acronym is D, which stands for Dedication. Do you feel that your partner is more dedicated to you than to any other person, place, or thing? If we sent investigators into your home to gather all of the evidence of what you and your spouse are most dedicated to, would there be enough evidence to prove that your partner is your number-one interest? Or would they find more evidence that your computer, social media, your children, hobby, or church calling are far and away more important things in your life? Dedication means you put your partner first—over friends, parents, coworkers, phones, computers, and even kids!

Matt used to teasingly question my dedication to him in relation to our children when they were young. He says I was under the influence of oxytocin, the brain chemical that reinforces bonding. He used to say that if we were to ever have a house fire and I had the choice of choosing between him or the kids, he knew he'd be a crispy critter!

Anytime couples are arguing about time, schedules, or priorities, odds are you have a dedication issue. Elder Russell M. Nelson has said: "Taking time to talk is essential to keep lines of communication intact. If marriage is a prime relationship in life, it deserves prime time! Yet less important appointments are often given priority, leaving only leftover moments for listening [and talking] to precious partners."[7] Does your partner feel like they're your number one priority? Do you feel dedication from your partner?

So there you have it! There are the seven basic needs of healthy relationships. When those needs are met, we feel loved, cared for, listened to, connected, and fed. When those needs are not met, we tend to feel STARVED—and we fight about a lot of smoky issues. Sadly, when people are feeling starved, it's a fairly common trigger for the natural man to settle in.

So look at yourself and your relationship. Are you starving? Or do you just have the munchies? Obviously we didn't get married to starve each other, so the solution is to start to get more wise by allowing our Savior into our communication. Cut through the smoke by following Elder Ashton's admonition of wisely sharing your emotions, feelings, and concerns; share all of yourself with those you love. Let's also be willing to create a space of Safety, Trust, Appreciation, Respect, Validation, Encouragement, and Dedication, where others will feel free to share all of themselves. Remember, you are not alone in your marriage covenant. We are the Lord's covenant daughters and there is a reason why, in our marriages, the Lord has placed us in a covenant together with Him. We have the rights, power, and privilege to God's grace and glory. He will be our sun to lighten the sometimes dark paths that we find in our marriages. He is also our shield to protect us and to watch over us during those times when we feel starved.

I testify that His grace is sufficient. I know if we can wisely slow down our conversations and get out of the smoke and down to the fire, we will learn how to feed our partners. More importantly, we will learn to become like Him, our Savior. May we always remember that He is there and so desperately wants us to feed one another. May that always be our goal, I pray.

NOTES

1. See F. Burton Howard, *Marion G. Romney: His Life and Faith* (Salt Lake City: Bookcraft, 1988), 144–45.
2. Marvin J. Ashton, "Family Communications," *Ensign*, May 1976, 52.
3. *Merriam-Webster's Collegiate Dictionary, Eleventh Edition* (Springfield, MA: Merriam-Webster, 2003), s.v. "wise."
4. Stephen M. R. Covey, *The Speed of Trust: The One Thing That Changes Everything* (New York: Free Press, 2008), 30.
5. William James, *The Letters of William James*, Henry James, ed., 2 vols. (Boston: Atlantic Monthly Press, 1920), 2:33.
6. *Merriam-Webster's Collegiate Dictionary, Eleventh Edition*, s.v. "respect."
7. Russell M. Nelson, "Listen to Learn," *Ensign*, May 1991, 23.

Communing Like Jehovah

Matt Townsend

Our topic of "Taking the Time to Talk: Communication in Marriage" was influenced by the words of Elder Marvin J. Ashton, who I'll always feel eternally connected to, as he was the one who officiated over our marriage in the Salt Lake Temple twenty-three years ago. Elder Ashton says:

"If we would know true love and understanding one for another, we must realize that communication is more than a sharing of words. It is the *wise* sharing of emotions, feelings, and concerns. It is the sharing of oneself totally."[1]

True love is the understanding of one another, the communication, or "wise sharing of emotions, feelings, and concerns. It is sharing oneself totally!" Isn't that what we all want in our lives? Isn't that what every human being longs for, to be able to truly share oneself with another totally, and in the process of sharing, to be able to truly find oneself? Such "wise communication" is something most of us probably haven't felt since we left our heavenly home. That dissonance is possibly the reason why so many of us feel, as the popular hymn mentions, "Ofttimes a secret something / [Whispers], 'You're a stranger here.'"[2]

Matt Townsend has a PhD in human development from Fielding University and an MA in communications from Brigham Young University. He is a relationship and life coach, an author, a regular contributor to the KSL-TV program Studio 5, *and the host of* The Matt Townsend Show *on BYU Radio. He serves as the gospel doctrine teacher in his ward. He and his wife, Mardi, are the parents of six children.*

If we truly desire to have a wiser sharing of ourselves in our relationships, then each of us must align our interactions more closely to the ultimate source of wisdom, love, spirit, and peace. For most of us, the thought or ability to implement such intimate communication seems so foreign, even awkward to us. I've found it easier to bridge the gap by understanding that we're really talking about two different types of communication. Merriam-Webster's dictionary tells us that *communication* is simply "an act or instance of transmitting."[3] *Communion*, on the other hand, is defined as "intimate fellowship or rapport."[4] It seems like communion may be the best way to describe Elder Ashton's thought of "wise communication that includes understanding, true love, and the sharing of oneself totally." So, the goal of our limited time together is not only to better understand how to commune (as the Prophet Joseph did) *with* Jehovah, but also how to commune *like* Jehovah with those we love.

In my own professional work with couples and in private work in my own marriage, I've found that there are three basic distortions that consistently impede our progress toward communion. They are: (1) our natural differences, (2) the confusion of paradox, and (3) the natural man.

The Mate and Switch

Sisters, I'm going to shoot straight with you today because I don't have a lot of time. Here are the facts—men and women are different! (Profound, huh?) Have any of you noticed that? Interestingly, the differences aren't noticed initially while dating because we're all so flooded with chemistry. Instead, the differences kind of sneak up on you once you're together for a while and some of that initial chemistry starts to fade. It's what I call the "Mate and Switch." It's a lot like the illegal marketing "bait and switch" technique, but mine is the dating version. The Mate and Switch is nature's way of getting you excited to marry a person you really know very little about. Then, after a while, once you're married, your chemistry normalizes and it's time to discover who you are really married to.

For some, the switch seems drastic, even scary, and yet for others it's not a big change. A typical unveiling of the "mate and switch" usually goes something like this: Let's say it's a normal evening with your hubby of six months or so. You are arriving home later than usual because of a meeting at work and you're excited to see what your cute hubby has thrown together for dinner. You're also hoping for a relaxing night together, maybe a walk, and to watch some of your favorite shows cuddling with your man. You walk in your apartment and it's dark. The only light is coming from the television set. You see dishes in the sink, clothes on the floor, and your stress level begins to rise. As you enter the living area, you see your eternal mate lazily lounging in his recliner, watching his favorite cable TV show about wrangling gators. As he waves hello, you notice his fingertips are brightly covered in orange dust from the hundreds of Cheetos he has consumed. You can see that he has emptied the entire family-sized bag and discarded it on the floor next to him, and yet somehow he's also overlooked the dozen or so stray snacks that are still clinging to his sweater. Shocked, you ask, "What's for dinner?" And he replies, "Nothing for me, babe, I've eaten—but could you grab me a drink? I'm parched." A cold chill shoots up your spine, a feeling of anger spreads over you, and your heart rate races upward. *Oh boy*, you think to yourself, *how will I ever make it forever?* Sound familiar? Some version of that experience happens to every person and couple at one time or another. Although the details may differ, the principles are the same. Just as it was for Adam and Eve, eventually all of our eyes need to be opened—and that's when the real test begins.

THE SAME SOCIALITY

As with all things from God, our job is to use our spirituality to improve our mortal experience, and nowhere is that more important than in our most important relationships. In D&C 130:2, we learn that the "same sociality which exists among us here will exist among us there, only it will be coupled with eternal glory, which glory we do not now enjoy" (D&C 130:2).

The same sociality you have here you will have there, only coupled with God's glory. *Sociality*, although a fairly rare word, is footnoted in this verse to the topics of "Eternal Family; Love within Family; and Continuing Courtship in Marriage" (D&C 130:2*a*). So the same love and courtship you have in your marriage here on earth you will have there in heaven. Isn't that great? Did you notice that little word *same*? The same courtship you have here, you will have there. The same love within your family that you have here, you will have there. The same Cheeto surprises you have here, you will have there—assuming there will be Cheetos there. Is that a comforting thought, or were you hoping that all of your relationships would just grow much richer and deeper once your mortal worries were erased in the Resurrection? Were you hoping that once your husband was "twinkled" that you would both magically be able to talk and appreciate each other more effectively? I don't think it works that way. King Benjamin explained the principle perfectly when discussing our relationship with our Heavenly Father: "For how knoweth a man the master whom he has not served, and who is a stranger unto him, and is far from the thoughts and intents of his heart?" (Mosiah 5:13).

So how could we expect to get closer to our spouses, or even want to live with them in heaven, if they really are strangers to us while here on earth? Communing with our spouse will help us to bring our thoughts and the intents of our hearts closer together, and the estrangement will disappear.

So let's get on the road to communion by better understanding the three mortal distortions that keep us from communion: our natural differences, the confusion of paradox, and the natural man.

Our Natural Differences

Obviously one of the biggest problems we face with communing with our spouses is the fact that we are all so completely different from the person we married. These differences aren't only gender specific, but can come down to basic preferences, expectations, and things we've learned from the families in which we grew up.

In my own marriage, my wife and I are very different, yet still in love. My wife seems to bond through talking, and in fact she usually does connect with any human being within a five-foot radius. I, on the other hand, prefer to bond with much less talking and a lot more activity.

I can be totally fine just going to a movie with Mardi (especially if it's an action movie) and yet she gets frustrated because we aren't able to talk. Another example of these differences was very obvious to both of us after the birth of every one of our six children. With each new child, Mardi would take the infant in her arms and, after counting the baby's fingers and toes, would turn the baby to her face. Face-to-face, she would talk to our new baby: "Who-da-baby?" she would say in a baby voice. I would think to myself, *Does she think that baby is going to answer her?* You may notice that your husbands don't always spend hours looking into your baby's eyes talking to them to bond like you do. But if they're anything like me, I'm confident that your husband does spend considerably more time tossing your baby into the air than you do. Right?

I'm sure they also spend more time on the ground wrestling, tickling, and roughhousing with your children than you do, don't they? I've found that I bond through playing with my children more than I do by talking with them, and yet my wife bonds through talking more than wrestling. Even though we bond differently, I've found those differences can make a huge difference in our family's life.

Instead of lamenting our differences, we need to learn to celebrate them. We're different and we're supposed to be. Many of those differences may be designed to help us fulfill our specific roles in the family.

"By divine design, fathers are to preside over their families in love and righteousness and are responsible to provide the necessities of life and protection for their families. Mothers are primarily responsible for the nurture of their children. In these sacred responsibilities, fathers and mothers are obligated to help one another as equal partners."[5]

Obviously none of us are perfect in fulfilling our roles. I consistently stumble while trying to magnify my responsibilities to protect, provide, and preside. In fact, to be honest, in my own life, I've seen my wife do a much better job in some of those roles than I ever could. Gratefully though, this isn't a competition but simply a partnership, and the partnership is not just between the two of us. We must not forget that the senior partner in this covenant is a loving, perfect member of the Godhead.

Sometimes in my inadequacy in certain roles as a father, I'll compensate by using my strength of "finding the funny" to try to balance things out. I remember one time when I valiantly announced to Mardi which of the three roles of protect, provide, and preside was my favorite. I announced that of the three, my personal favorite was the role of presiding. She then quickly tried to take advantage of my declaration and enrolled me to use my skills in that area and said, "Great, let's have family home evening tonight!" I quickly concurred, saying, "Excellent, let's do that," and then looked right back at her. After a very awkward pause, where neither of us seemed to know what to do next, she said, "So, do you want to get on that?"

I calmly replied, "No, not tonight, honey. I'm just going to be presiding." She just sat there stunned, and I quickly added with a smile on my face, "But I do want to be recognized." Sadly, one of our most obvious differences is that she didn't find that as funny as I did.

Remember that our roles are not mutually exclusive, meaning that men can also be nurturing—and, in fact, should—and women can be excellent protectors, providers, and presiders. Our roles, even if they don't come easily or naturally to us, are divinely assigned from a loving Father in Heaven, for us to learn and grow and to become more like Him. (See Moroni 7:48.)

The Confusion of Paradox

Another mortal impairment that affects our goal to commune with our partner is the confusion that paradox creates in our lives. According to Merriam-Webster, *paradox* is "a statement that is seemingly contradictory or opposed to common sense and yet is perhaps true."[6] The most popular example we see in the scriptures comes from the Lord, who said, "He that findeth his life shall lose it: and he that loseth his life for my sake shall find it" (Matthew 10:39). Or how about the popular paradox that tells us we need to be "in the world, but not of the world"? (See John 15:19.)

In our marriages we constantly deal with paradoxes that can confuse us, and that sometimes will even turn us against each other. For example, what might happen to two people who believe deeply in the proclamation on the family, but the father is by far a better nurturer than the mother, and the mother is a better provider than the father? Perhaps even more confusing might be the scenario where one parent we'll call the "doer" seems to be good at everything and the other parent, the "bystander," struggles doing anything very well. Is it possible that the doer is justifiably frustrated when he or she never gets any help with the kids? Is it also possible that at the same time the bystander is justifiably frustrated with helping because all he or she hears from the doer is that everything he or she does is wrong? That is the confusing standoff that can be created by the paradox of our lives. Do you see how that very paradox could, without communion, create lasting damage and problems in *their* marriage? The ability to create close communication, where we can all wisely share our emotions, feelings, and concerns, can help us cut through the paradox and minimize the confusion. Here are a few more examples of paradox you may see in your life:

- Have you ever loved your children with all of your heart, and at the same time felt like they were driving you crazy?
- Have you known you weren't supposed to yell at your children and yet you still did, regularly?
- Can you love a child so much that you impede his or her chance to grow?
- Can you give a child growing experiences that are so difficult that he or she questions if you love him or her at all?

Paradox can be seen everywhere in our lives, and if we cut through it peacefully, in communion, the Spirit will dissipate the confusion. One of my favorite examples of paradox actually does not create any tension in my marriage, but it is fun to share anyway. It's called "The Prayer Fight." (I've asked my wife's permission to share this.)

THE PRAYER FIGHT

In our home, we have a beautiful paradox called "The Prayer Fight." Every night, at about 8:30 P.M., my faithful wife tries to gather the family together for family prayer. I would've given this up years ago because getting our children to do what is right should not be this hard (that's a paradox). It goes pretty much like this: At about 8:30 P.M., with the most angelic, beautiful voice I have ever heard, my wife will have a call to prayer, "Children, come pray," she says. Her voice even has a little vibrato . . . and our children just sit there. No one moves.

So again, Mardi will call the children to prayer, but this time she won't call them children. Now she increases the volume and states,

"Kids [so now they're baby goats], okay, goats, come pray!" Still nothing! Nobody moves. Even I don't move.

And she says, "Why aren't you moving?"

I say, "I'm not a kid. Don't call me a kid."

Now, getting tired of compelling righteousness, she takes it up a notch: "Kids . . . *now* . . . come *now!* We are praying *now*! Get down here and kneel! Kneel down, kneel up [to the child sprawled over the floor], give me that ball or you're going to *need* this prayer . . . and I mean it! Is that your phone? Give. Me. Your. Phone. Okay now, stop, freeze! [Long pause.] Who wants to pray? [Long silent pause.] None of you want to pray? Seriously? [To the always-eager eight-year-old:] Not you? You always want to pray. Okay, *you* pray [pointing to the teenager], and you mean it! You mean this prayer and you [pointing to the pre-teen], shut your eyes! You shut them because I'm watching you. Don't wonder how Mama watches you when her eyes are closed. That's how mamas are. Give me the ball [gesturing to the boys playing catch again]! Give me the ball! Give me your phone! Freeze. You guys, now I want you to feel the Spirit . . . Hurry, mama needs to Facebook!"

Isn't that beautiful? You're laughing because you can't get *your* kids to pray, can you? How do you think Heavenly Father feels trying to get *you* to pray? And we do it every night . . . because we're faithful! Faithfully, we pray and fight every night as a family. Weaker families would have given it up by now, but not us! We will pray and fight if it kills us! Do you see the paradox oozing out of that story—and the irony? We need to figure out a way to negotiate this chaos. We need to figure out how we can talk through it, understand both sides of the paradox, and find the peace that exists somewhere in between the two sides.

The third and final distortion that impacts our ability to commune is the natural man. Such communion can't happen when our body and our mind and our spirit are at odds with each other. If our goal is to connect on a different level spiritually with one another, then we need to start focusing on having spiritual conversations. In order to understand the natural man, we must first understand who we really are as spiritual beings.

The Spirit

Let's have a quick review in order to set the foundation for how we're going to truly commune. Before we came here to earth we lived in the premortal world with our loving Heavenly Father. While we were there, we felt an incredible peace and we were perfectly protected, provided for, and presided over. Our Heavenly Father nurtured us and assured us of our most important roles as His sons and daughters. His infinite love created a safe space for us, a place where we could experience abundant joy, acceptance, and hope in our desire to become more like Him. Paradoxically too, we weren't perfect while living with Him. We had much more we needed to learn, a body we needed to receive, and yet we understood that our growth would take time. The power of our Father in Heaven is the power to balance the paradox of being imperfect and also being perfectly loved and peaceful. So the fruits of being in the Spirit are the same fruits we enjoyed when we were in His presence. Those fruits are "love, joy, peace, longsuffering, gentleness, goodness, faith, meekness, [and] temperance" (Galatians 5:22–23).

You are His daughter and He knows your name. Think of your love for your earthly children. That is but a glimpse of the love your Heavenly Father has for you. We were spiritual beings long before we were mortal beings and so our most natural state truly is spiritual (see D&C 29:32).

We should never forget that we lived spiritually much longer than we have lived as mortals. The natural man is a fairly new thing to us. Teilhard de Chardin said, "We are not human beings having a spiritual experience; we are spiritual beings having a human experience."[7] The same is true with our Heavenly Father, who says, "Wherefore . . . all things unto me are spiritual" (D&C 29:34).

I am convinced that as spiritual beings we are completely capable of handling the natural differences, the confusion of paradox, and the pulls of the natural man that keep us from communion (see 1 Nephi 3:7).

The Natural Man

As you come down to this earth, that beautiful spirit that was filled with so much peace, love, and confidence in the first estate is somehow squeezed into the body you now possess. So what makes us feel like a stranger in our own world and even in our own body? I would suggest it is the natural man. Remember, it is an enemy to God, which means it's an enemy to our spirits as well.

"For the natural man is an enemy to God, and has been from the fall of Adam, and will be, forever and ever, unless he yields to the enticings of the Holy Spirit, and putteth off the natural man" (Mosiah 3:19).

I once heard that it takes about one trillion cell divisions to create a human being. Think about that for a minute. If you were to do anything one trillion times, what are the odds that it would come out perfect every time? Not very high, right? Perhaps that lower quality of existence is one reason why mortality immediately separates us from our very perfect Heavenly Father. When it comes to all of us, sisters, we are all somewhat messed up. I'm not trying to be rude or sensational, but honestly, we're all battling with something, aren't we?

The random game of roulette that we play here on earth leaves us with different challenges to face while here in mortality. Some of us were born with anxiety, some with depression, and others struggle with attention deficit disorder. Sadly some of you can't get a good night's sleep and yet others feel like all they can do is sleep. Others have physical impairments or deformities. Some experience other body-based and psychological challenges which can be equally confusing, like same-sex attraction, addictive personalities, eating disorders, and Asperger's, to name just a few. Others in life will be diagnosed with other afflictions, like multiple sclerosis, Alzheimer's, or Parkinson's disease. Some of you have a cancer gene that is lying dormant in your system right as we speak, while others are valiantly battling that very active gene.

Whether it's a disease, a disorder, a defect, a deformity, or a dysfunction, the mortal body is designed to be the perfect testing ground for your spirit. It also seems to be the perfect testing ground for your relationships as well. Many of these physical challenges affect our ability to effectively relate to our spouses and family members.

The Carnal Mind

Another part of the natural man that needs to be pointed out is the carnal mind. The body may create the chemistry to go out and party as a teenager, but the mind creates the justification for the act when it argues, "Everybody is doing it!" or "What's so bad about a little alcohol?" Remember that the Lord specifically said, "For my thoughts are not your thoughts, neither are your ways my ways" (Isaiah 55:8). The carnal mind was born during the fall of Adam and Eve.

Immediately upon partaking of the fruit, we're told that their eyes were opened (see Genesis 3:7). Those new eyes began to see things that they had never seen or done before. They noticed their nakedness, and because of their shame and fear, they began running and hiding, fearing, blaming, guilting, and shaming. And this new carnal mind had them running from whom? From their Father in Heaven, the most loving being they had ever known. Why would they run from their God? Because the "natural man is an enemy to God," remember? So instead of "yielding to the promptings of the Holy Spirit and putting off the natural man," they turned their entire relationship with God over to their carnal bodies and minds, which left them colluding with Lucifer instead of communing with Jehovah. Anyone who follows the natural man will feel as Alma did, ensnared by the adversary, "that he might chain you down to everlasting destruction" (Alma 12:6).

The chains of hell are the patterns and reactions that keep you and your partner from creating communion. So ask yourself: are you receiving the fruits of the spirit of communion with your spouse, or are you feeling more like you're in a pattern of running, hiding, fearing, shaming, and blaming?

So how do we cast off the natural man and commune with those people closest in our lives? We must learn to "[yield] to the enticings of the Holy Spirit . . . and [become] a saint through the atonement of Christ the Lord, and [become] as a child, submissive, meek, humble, patient, full of love, willing to submit to all things which the Lord seeth fit to inflict upon him, even as a child doth submit to his father" (Mosiah 3:19).

THREE PRINCIPLES OF COMMUNION

As Elder Jeffrey R. Holland concisely confirmed in the April 2013 general conference, "Except in the case of His only perfect Begotten Son, imperfect people are all God has ever had to work with. That must be terribly frustrating to Him, but He deals with it. So should we."[8] In order to more effectively relate with even the hardest among us, here are three principles of communion that Christ modeled in his perfect journey through life. They are, (1) staying in the "now," (2) yielding to the enticings of the Holy Spirit, and (3) looking to God to live.

STAY IN THE "NOW"

The first principle of communion to practice in our marriages is to stay in the "now" with your spouse. The only time you can ever connect with the heart and mind of another person is in the current moment, in the "now." The "now" is only place one can actually be in the Spirit. An excellent example of this took place the morning after the Savior had been laid to rest in the tomb. Mary Magdalene, eager to be by the side of her beloved Savior, went "early" in the morning, "when it was yet dark, unto the sepulchre" (John 20:1). When she arrived at the tomb, she realized that the stone had been rolled away and her Savior's body wasn't there. Can you imagine how distraught she was? She ran to Simon Peter and John and said, "They have taken away the Lord . . . and we know not where they have laid him" (John 20:2).

So as a fellow human being, what do you think most concerned Mary at this very sad time in her life? I'm sure all of the beautiful memories (from her past) that Mary had shared with the Lord were flooding back to her mind. The thought of not having his body to properly anoint and bury (in the future) undoubtedly overwhelmed her. I'm sure she worried what had been done to his body as well as how she would effectively mourn her loss without a place to go to be near him (also in the future). Perhaps some of her thoughts were caught up in how different her life would be without him (in the future). She realized, I'm sure, that her source of peace was missing and perhaps had some regrets that she hadn't done more while he was with her. As humans, it is so easy for us in times of distress, contention, and fear to do as Mary did for that short moment—to lose ourselves in the regrets of the past or the fears of the future, worrying ourselves endlessly about things we really can't control or change.

The problem in these moments of tension, where we follow our natural tendencies to live in the past and fret about the future, is the sad truth that we're not being present in the "now." The same is true when we're into ineffective fight-or-flight moments in our marriages. We, just like Mary, may find ourselves running around to find the other apostles, frantically looking for peace everywhere but in the now.

Mary was finally brought back to the present moment by the Savior himself, after she made her way back to the tomb. As she looked in and saw that her master was missing, then weeping, Mary was peacefully engaged by two angels who asked her, "Woman, why weepest thou?" She answered, "Because they have taken away my Lord, and I know not where they have laid him" (John 20:13). Notice she's still preoccupied with the past. After answering, "She turned herself back, and saw Jesus standing, and knew not that it was Jesus" (John 20:14). Can you see how much our natural man tendencies affect our ability to be present, even while mourning? The Lord then patiently and lovingly attempted to bring Mary to the "now" by asking, "Woman, why weepest thou? whom seekest thou? She, supposing him to be the gardener, saith unto him, Sir, if thou have borne him hence, tell me where thou hast laid him, and I will take him away" (John 20:15).

Mary's concern was making it very difficult for her to hear the voice of her Savior. How many times in our own conversations with our spouses are we incapable of hearing what they are actually saying, because we're too focused on what *we* want, what *we* need, or how *we* think things should be going?

Again, the Lord patiently tries to help Mary to hear his voice, making it more intimate by calling her by name. Mary, finally in the now, "turned herself, and saith unto him, Rabboni; which is to say, Master" (John 20:16).

Can you fathom the communion that took place between those two in that very intimate conversation? What a beautiful example of how we should interact with one another during times of stress, and how we, like the Savior, can patiently invite the people we love into the now. Let's be clear that the *only* time that we can actually feel the Spirit on this earth is in the now. The Spirit is the essential source of communion with God and another person. When we commune with God through His Spirit, it's not in the past and it's not in the future—it's always in the now.

By the way, "When is the time to prepare to meet God?" *Now* is the time to prepare to meet God. If you're going to want the Spirit in the conversation, you need to stay present in the conversation. You need to keep your head in the moment, in the "now."

"Yield to the Enticings of the Holy Spirit"

The second principle that will improve our ability to commune with our spouse, especially after our first step has taught us to stay in the "now," is to "yield to the enticings of the Holy Spirit" (Mosiah 3:19).

Think about your most difficult communication moments with your spouse. Do you feel that in those tense moments you are actively yielding to the enticings of the Holy Spirit? Or are you being overwhelmed and overtaken by the natural man and mind?

A humbling example of our Lord showing the power of communion with His followers is found in 3 Nephi 17. The Lord was finishing His first full day of ministering to the faithful Saints in the Americas. They were exhausted and "edified out" from all that they had experienced that day. The Savior, recognizing that they could not handle much more, announced:

"I perceive that ye are weak, that ye cannot understand all my words which I am commanded of the Father to speak unto you at this time. Therefore, go ye unto your homes, and ponder upon the things which I have said, and ask of the Father, in my name, that ye may understand, and prepare your minds for the morrow, and I come unto you again" (3 Nephi 17:2–3).

Notice how present the Savior is in the moment with those with whom He's interacting. He could see that they were exhausted and were physically unable to "understand all [the] words which I am commanded of the Father to speak . . . at this time." Have you ever been in a confusing conversation with your spouse where you could tell that he just wasn't understanding you? Perhaps he was too tired or something was distracting him. The Savior could see the talk wasn't working as well as it could be and so He changed the plan. He wasn't offended or frustrated with their inability to focus, and He didn't follow His natural man tendencies to either fight or flee. Instead He just stayed in the now and yielded to the promptings of the Holy Spirit.

"And it came to pass that when Jesus had thus spoken, he cast his eyes round about again on the multitude, and beheld they were in tears, and did look steadfastly upon him as if they would ask him to tarry a little longer with them" (3 Nephi 17:5).

Their sadness and love for Him could not be contained and was effectively communicated through the tears that flowed down their cheeks. Notice how our most loving Savior was open to that sincere communication. He let their emotion into Him, it penetrated Him so deeply that He described it by saying, "Behold, my bowels are filled with compassion towards you. Have ye any that are sick among you? Bring them hither" (3 Nephi 17:6–7). Such beautiful words for the ears of the faithful! Their Lord was staying! He had made a plan to leave because they physically couldn't take any more learning and yet our Lord was willing to feel compassion and to yield to the enticings of the Holy Spirit and, in turn, changed His plan to leave (see 3 Nephi 17; D&C 121:45).

Sisters, are you willing to yield to the enticing of the Holy Spirit in your conversations? Are you willing to change your plans, your ideas, your need to win an argument, your preconceptions of your spouse? Are you willing to change some of your mind-based conversations to your spirit-focused communions? Numerous times I've heard clients share how they were prompted in the middle of the night to get up to go check on their husbands who weren't in bed with them. Those promptings eventually led some to take a closer look at a phone, finding inappropriate texts or pictures, or even to find him in the grasp of temptation on the computer. Although startling, I've seen such yielding to the Spirit by faithful spouses literally save marriages, I've seen it save families, I've seen it save communities, and I've seen it save souls!

When we put the promptings of the Lord before our own needs of the flesh, the Lord's most abundant blessings are ours, including and especially communion with our Heavenly Father. Examples of those blessings followed the Savior's willingness to stay with the exhausted Nephites. Not only were their children and the afflicted blessed by the Savior, they were also given the opportunity to "bathe his feet with their tears." Not only were they given the opportunity to be present in the communion between the Savior and His loving Heavenly Father, but they also received the fruits of that communion:

"And after this manner do they bear record; The eye hath never seen, neither hath the ear heard, before, so great and marvelous things as we saw and heard Jesus speak unto the Father; and no tongue can speak, neither can there be written by any man, neither can the hearts of men conceive so great and marvelous things as we both saw and heard Jesus speak; and no one can conceive of the joy which filled our souls at the time we heard him pray for us unto the Father" (3 Nephi 17:16–17).

Are you willing to yield to the promptings of the Holy Spirit and do what needs to be done to save souls? Remember that you can't experience a true communion with another being without also experiencing some sense of closeness and affection with your God.

President Dieter F. Uchtdorf tells us: "As we extend our hands and hearts toward others in Christlike love, something wonderful happens to us. Our own spirits become healed, more refined, and stronger. We become happier, more peaceful, and more receptive to the whisperings of the Holy Spirit."[9]

You can't experience the sharing of oneself totally without feeling blessed in the process. Jesus himself was also profoundly affected by His experience with the Nephites, which He witnessed by saying, "Blessed are ye because of your faith. And now behold, my joy is full. And when he had said these words, he wept" (3 Nephi 17:20–21). In the end, when we yield to the enticings of the Holy Spirit, all will be edified (see D&C 88:122).

Look to God and Live

The final principle we can use to increase communion with our spouses is to "look to God and live" (Alma 37:47). After years of coaching couples on how to improve their communications and relationship problems, I've come to one simple truth. Our partners will never be the permanent source of peace and comfort in our lives. They can't be—because they're humans. Nor will our promises, properties, popularity, prestige, or profits. The only true and lasting source of peace in our mortal life will not come from our bodies or our minds, our spouses or our children. True and everlasting peace only comes from our God when we live His principles.

I learned this principle while studying about the life of our Savior, Jesus Christ. Can you imagine being such a perfect and pristinely spiritual being who has to live day-to-day with a bunch of spiritually challenged mortal misfits? None of those around Him—even those who knew Him best—really understood exactly who He was. Regularly they would declare their loyalty; yet minutes later, they would fall incredibly short, leaving Him to feel more alone with a much greater load to bear. Most of the time, their abandonment was not intentional but simply came from ignorance.

Remember that while in Gethsemane, Christ carried the burden alone. When He was on bended knee offering up the infinite sacrifice, His faithful apostles disregarded His plea to "watch with me" and slept (Matthew 26:38). Where was the loyalty after that long and tedious night when He was betrayed by Judas? Where was Christ's rest who, despite not sleeping all night while in Gethsemane and being arrested by Malchus, still lovingly healed His arresting officer's ear that was injured by the now-protective Peter? Those that Christ had surrounded Himself with were not trying to make His life difficult; their "spirit indeed [was] willing, but the flesh [was] weak" (Matthew 26:41).

Where else could the Savior "turn for peace" when He was forced to stand and be humiliated before the Jewish hierarchy of Caiaphas and his father-in-law, Annas? Where was the justice when He was forced to face Herod Antipas, whose father tried to kill the Savior as a child? Or Pontius Pilate, who was the only mortal left that could free an innocent God, but feared the mortals more. Amazingly, Jesus was calm during those visits because He chose to take His direction from heaven and not from the politicians. Christ knew His peace would come only from above. His example of how to survive the trials of mortality and the abundant aloneness that can accompany human relationships is inspiring. Christ taught us a very important lesson about dealing with the mercurial mortals of this earth. In Alma 37, it reads, "Yea, and cry unto God for all thy support; yea, let all thy doings be unto the Lord, and whithersoever thou goest let it be in the Lord; yea, let all thy thoughts be directed unto the Lord; yea, let the affections of thy heart be placed upon the Lord forever.

"Counsel with the Lord in all thy doings, and he will direct thee for good; yea, when thou liest down at night lie down unto the Lord, that he may watch over you in your sleep; and when thou risest in the morning let thy heart be full of thanks unto God; and if ye do these things, ye shall be lifted up at the last day. . . .

"For behold, it is as easy to give heed to the word of Christ, which will point to you a straight course to eternal bliss . . . If we follow their course, [the words of Christ will] carry us beyond this vale of sorrow into a far better land of promise.

"O my son, do not let us be slothful because of the easiness of the way; for so was it with our fathers . . . that if they would look they might live; even so it is with us. . . .

"And now, my son, see that ye take care of these sacred things, yea, see that ye look to God and live" (Alma 37:36–37, 44–47).

Each of us battles our own earthly missions and challenges. In a much more insignificant way than the Savior, each of us too must deal with loneliness and the abandonment of those people closest to us. We also, like the Savior, need to find someone who can help us to drink the bitter cup and not shrink (see D&C 19:18–19). That source, who will carry us through our trials and will facilitate the peace of communion, is our God. Unlike our Savior who had to take a solo journey through the pain of mortality and who cried unto His father, "My God, my God, why hast thou forsaken me?" (Mark 15:34), we are promised that our Father in Heaven will never turn His back on us: "I will go before your face. I will be on your right hand and on your left, and my Spirit shall be in your hearts, and mine angels round about you, to bear you up" (D&C 84:88).

Just as our Savior's marvelous Atonement was accomplished by looking to God to live, then so too can our mission with our spouse be accomplished by looking to our God and living.

The Eyes of Christ

A powerful way to connect to your purpose with your spouse and children is by creating your own vision and purpose as to why you are here on this earth. My wife, Mardi, talked about feeling STARVED in your relationships.[10] Think about when you are most exhausted or tired. Imagine when you've felt most alone in your marriage over the past year of your life. Truly imagine those loneliest feelings. Imagine you are in your bedroom alone, crying, empty, and wishing your Father in Heaven would remove this cup from you. In that lonely moment, imagine you feel a peace come over you, a peace that envelops your entire body, mind and spirit. You open your eyes and standing there in your room is your Savior, Jesus Christ. He approaches you, reaches His hands out to you, and holds you in His arms.

Notice what you are feeling right now as you think about that moment. Do you feel peace? Love? Hope? That is the spirit of Christ telling you in that moment that He has you. Notice, though, He still hasn't taken away your burdens or trials. You still have laundry to do, you still have a husband that doesn't understand you, and yet those problems are evaporated when you're in the arms of the Lord.

I want you to think about your husband or somebody you want to improve your communication with. I want you to imagine a scenario where they are struggling and your Savior appears to them and embraces them. You have the privilege of sitting back and watching your husband or friend in the arms of their Lord. What will your Savior do to your husband when they have a chance to meet and commune? What will the Savior say to him? What will happen when his inadequacies and weaknesses from this mortal world disappear? And what happens to you as you watch your husband or someone else you love dearly in the arms of the Savior? What would happen to all of us if we could bring that sweet spirit of peace and understanding into our conversations with those we love?

CONCLUSION

I testify that you truly are spiritual beings here on earth having a human experience. I am convinced that our relationship trials—including our natural differences, the confusion of paradox, and the shackles of the natural man—can be minimized if we would focus on communing. I have seen the powerful presence that comes by staying in the "now." I have seen the dramatic insights afforded when we yield to the enticings of the Holy Spirit, and I have felt the peace and love distilled when we are looking to God to live.

As the theme of this conference affirms:

"For the Lord God is a sun and a shield: the Lord will give grace and glory: no good thing will he withhold from them that walk uprightly" (Psalm 84:11).

The Lord will be our sun and will provide the light and knowledge we need in our sometimes dark and shadowy world. The Lord will also be our shield, protecting us, watching over us, and shielding us from some of the painful experiences we sometimes foist upon each other here on earth. You are His daughters! I testify that when we commune with Jehovah and learn to commune *like* Jehovah, He will not withhold anything from you. Just as Lehi reassured Jacob in a blessing, "Thou hast suffered afflictions and much sorrow, because of the rudeness of thy brethren. Nevertheless . . . thou knowest the greatness of God; and he shall consecrate thine afflictions for thy gain" (2 Nephi 2:1–2).

Sisters, please use your nurturing gifts to touch the spiritual lives of those around you. And never forget that there is a reason you are in a marital covenant with our God and King, and not just with your partner. God will never let you down and He will never turn His back on you. This is my promise and witness that the path to communion is real and it is worth it!

NOTES

1. Marvin J. Ashton, "Family Communications," *Ensign*, May 1976, 52.
2. Eliza R. Snow, "O My Father," *Hymns of The Church of Jesus Christ of Latter-day Saints* (Salt Lake City: The Church of Jesus Christ of Latter-day Saints, 1985), no. 292.
3. *Merriam-Webster's Collegiate Dictionary, Eleventh Edition* (Springfield, MA: Merriam-Webster, 2003), s.v. "communication."
4. Ibid., s.v. "communion."
5. "The Family: A Proclamation to the World," *Ensign*, November 2010, 129.
6. *Merriam-Webster's Collegiate Dictionary, Eleventh Edition*, s.v. "paradox."
7. Pierre Teilhard de Chardin, quoted in Stephen R. Covey, *The Seven Habits of Highly Successful People* (New York: Simon and Schuster, 1989), 319.
8. Jeffrey R. Holland, "'Lord, I Believe,'" *Ensign*, May 2013, 94.
9. Dieter F. Uchtdorf, "'You Are My Hands,'" *Ensign*, May 2010, 75.
10. See Mardi Townsend, "Taking the Time to Talk: Communication in Marriage," in *The Lord Will Give Grace and Glory: Talks from the 2014 BYU Women's Conference* (Salt Lake City: Deseret Book, 2015), 75–86.

The Holy Ghost and the Hand of the Lord

Richard Neitzel Holzapfel

In the Book of Mormon, we read, "And by the power of the Holy Ghost ye may know the truth of all things . . . that by his grace ye may be perfect in Christ" (Moroni 10:5, 32). As we consider this scripture, we might ask ourselves three questions:

1. How can I invite the Holy Ghost to be a constant companion?
2. How can the Holy Ghost help me reach out to the Savior and rely on His divine help?
3. How can I develop the ability to hear the Holy Ghost more clearly?

In answering those questions for myself, I considered some experiences my wife and I had between 2010 and 2013 when we served in the Alabama Birmingham Mission. That mission covers most of Alabama, some of the southern counties of Tennessee, northeastern Mississippi, and a slice of Georgia. It is in the Deep South and is part of the Bible Belt that crosses the American Southeast.

Richard Neitzel Holzapfel is a professor of Church history and doctrine at Brigham Young University and recently served as president of the Alabama Birmingham Mission of The Church of Jesus Christ of Latter-day Saints. He holds a PhD from the University of California—Irvine and is the author of numerous published articles on Latter-day Saint history and ancient history as well as the author, co-author, or editor of more than forty books.

According to a recent Gallup poll, our mission contained three of the five most religious metro areas in the United States.[1] No one should be surprised to learn that Provo-Orem, Utah (where Brigham Young University, the Missionary Training Center, one of the largest LDS institute programs in the world—the Orem Institute of Religion adjacent to Utah Valley University—and two temples, one dedicated and another under construction, are located), is the most religious metro area in the United States—with 77 percent of the residents classified as "very religious."

The next four religious areas on the list are all found in the South, and are all either part of the Alabama Birmingham Mission or adjacent to it. Following Provo-Orem, second on the list is the Montgomery, Alabama, metro area, the state capital of Alabama and at the southern end of our mission. Third on the list is the Jackson, Mississippi, metro area, practically next door. Number four is the Birmingham-Hoover area, where the mission home and office are located. And number five is the Huntsville, Alabama, metro area, in the northern section of our mission.

So no one should be surprised that this specific region is also known as the Buckle of the Bible Belt, a deeply religious area where small and large churches, Christian private schools, numerous Bible colleges, and gigantic crosses dot the landscape.

The first year and a half of our mission went very much as expected. But something dramatic happened in the second half of our mission. The United States held a presidential election. As the campaign revved up, America's citizens began to realize that a Latter-day Saint would likely win the Republican presidential nomination.

Because those states within the boundary of the mission—Alabama, Tennessee, and Mississippi—generally vote for the Republican candidate in the general election, many people living in the Deep South began to realize they faced a dilemma.

For generations, many Evangelicals had been taught to demonize the Latter-day Saints. Though some religious leaders among the Protestant denominations tried to teach their people to love Mormons but hate our doctrine, practices, and leaders, lay members of those churches sometimes struggled to separate their animosity of the Church of Jesus Christ from how they felt and treated individual Latter-day Saints who lived in their neighborhoods, worked with them at their places of employment, or attended the same schools.

The election raised a question: How could Southerners support a Mormon in the upcoming general election, given their unfavorable views of the Church? Obviously, they found themselves in a quandary. Certainly, some chose not to vote in the 2012 presidential election. However, the vast majority chose to vote, and that is where our story became most interesting.

As the election season began, I received a call from a pastor of a large Protestant church in our mission, inviting me to speak to his congregation. My inclination was to decline the invitation, knowing by personal experience that such requests generally were no more than a request to engage in a heated debate.

Instead of engaging those antagonistic to our missionary purpose, we focused our efforts on the unchurched—those people who did not attend or financially support a particular church. We never focused on finding pastors or priests. In fact, as directed by the Missionary Department, we did not proselyte near any church.[2] We were, after all, looking for "the lost, the least, and the last."

Although we invited everyone to hear our message, our work was primarily among those who were searching for the truth instead of those who assumed they already possessed it.

As this pastor pleaded with me to accept his invitation to speak to his congregation, he said something like, "You don't understand, President. I have been taught my whole life that you are Satan. And now my congregation has to vote for one of you. So please come and convince us that Mitt Romney is not the devil!"

That got my attention! I instantaneously saw a golden opportunity for us to set the record straight in his church, and from his own pulpit. The occasion would also provide us an opportunity to teach the restored gospel in an atmosphere that was neither hostile nor combative but was open and friendly. I certainly did not expect to convert anyone, but I hoped to make some friends—closing the immeasurable gap that existed between us somewhat.

That first call turned into countless other calls over the next several months with requests for us to share our beliefs. We became busier in our outreach efforts with other faith traditions that we had witnessed previously in our mission.

These opportunities to share our beliefs expanded to include interviews on radio and in newspapers, visits to religious schools and local universities, and involvement at various church youth groups for their meetings and venues. Along with requests to speak in other churches, we also had congregations ask to visit us in our own buildings. This turn of events was very surprising. I will never forget the first time I saw several Protestant church buses in one of our stake centers' parking lot! These tours ended up being friendly, enjoyable, and positive. I was impressed with the questions and insights these visitors had because the change was so dramatic from our previous experiences. Most people left visiting us feeling like they knew us better and appreciated our dedication, commitment, and passion to Jesus Christ, even though they did not agree with our interpretations of the scriptures or of Christian history. This time had a most remarkable outcome!

On one occasion, our area Church public affairs director asked me to accept an invitation to be interviewed on a local talk show, a well-known political talk show in the South. When some people learned that I would be on the air, a few concerned individuals warned me that this talk-show host was well known for his hard-hitting questions and combative personality. They also felt he had not always been friendly toward the Church as evidenced by some comments he had made on the air over the years.

I had a delightful experience meeting him, going into the studio, sitting down in front of a microphone, putting on the headset, and looking across at him as the show began.

The half-hour invitation to be on the air turned into two hours, which provided a wonderful opportunity to share the gospel with a large number of people in the South. At some point, I noticed that as we were getting ready to come back online, he seemed to be less jovial. I thought, "Well, here it is. Get ready. He's going to start playing hardball."

I do not remember his exact words as we came back on the air, but he said something like this: "Now, President, let's get things straight here. You have a PhD from a major university in California, you were a university professor before you came here, and so now just please help me understand. How can you really believe that silly story of gold plates and a young boy?"

I responded something like this: "Well, I'm a simple man of faith. I've never seen the stone tablets upon which God wrote His law with His own finger, yet I still believe in the Ten Commandments!" And then I followed up with something like, "So I guess the story of a young boy and plates doesn't require a very big leap of faith for me."

Later, someone said, "That was a brilliant answer! Did you prepare what you were going to say ahead of time?"

I said, "No!"

The questioner responded inquisitively, "Then how did you come up with that great response?"

I have been asked that question many, many times since as I have shared this story. The appropriate answer has always seemed self-evident to me: "It was the Holy Ghost!"

Those words bring me back to the three questions mentioned earlier: (1) How can I invite the Holy Ghost to be a constant companion? (2) How can the Holy Ghost help me reach out to the Savior and rely on His divine help? (3) How can I develop the ability to hear the Holy Ghost more clearly?

I will now provide some suggested answers to those questions when we view them together as a composite trilogy.

We discovered a way to increase the opportunity to have the Holy Ghost help our missionaries. The insight came from a section in *Preach My Gospel.*

In connection with *Preach My Gospel*, I feel the need to share an important invitation with you. You may be familiar with it. Elder M. Russell Ballard at the Sunday session of the general conference in April 2014 asked members of the Church to obtain a copy of *Preach My Gospel*, read it, and share what they learned with their missionary children and with the missionaries who labor in their area.[3] I have committed to follow his counsel and direction.

In that spirit, I am pleased to share something that will help in answering the question of "How can I invite the Holy Ghost to be a constant companion?" It is a quotation from *Preach My Gospel* and is found under the heading of "Study Journal": "*Preach My Gospel* frequently asks you to use a study journal to help you understand, clarify, and remember what you are learning. Elder Richard G. Scott taught, 'Knowledge carefully recorded is knowledge available in time of need. Spiritually sensitive information should be kept in a sacred place that communicates to the Lord how you treasure it. This practice enhances the likelihood of your receiving further light.'"[4]

We learned that the study journal does not have to be fancy or expensive. We saw missionaries who had simple spiral-bound school notebooks. What is important is that you record the promptings of the Spirit in your life. In so doing, you demonstrate to the Lord that what the Holy Ghost teaches you is important. Like Nephi, who recorded the Lord's words on golden plates, you demonstrate through your efforts to preserve the revelation and inspiration you receive that you love His words and cherish them.

By recording the inspiration received, we are like Samuel the prophet, about whom the scriptures record, "And Samuel grew, and the Lord was with him, and did let none of his words fall to the ground" (1 Samuel 3:19).

Because holy men and women have often recorded the words of the Lord, He knew those words were precious to them, and He invariably gave them more of His word. This is the same principle that Elder Scott taught us in *Preach My Gospel*. When we record promptings from the Holy Ghost—or when we record what we have learned and the insights we have received—we show the Lord that our associations with the Holy Spirit are precious to us. In response, the Lord will freely give us more: "The doctrine . . . shall distill upon thy soul as the dews from heaven. The Holy Ghost shall be thy constant companion" (D&C 121:45–46).

My wife began keeping a study journal the very first day we met with Elder Robert D. Hales of the Quorum of the Twelve Apostles in November 2009 to discuss the possibility of going on a mission. She continued to add to it when we met with President Henry B. Eyring and he called us to serve in December of that year and then later when he set me apart to preside in the mission.

We took time to thoughtfully record what we learned through the Holy Ghost as we "sat at their feet." The practice of keeping a study journal since those visits with Elder Hales and President Eyring has yielded numerous and invaluable study journals that my wife and I refer to often and from which we often find what we are looking for when we need some insight, scripture, or teaching. Those study journals have become a priceless treasure as we go back and reread what was recorded earlier. They are, to us, our own copies of the brass plates or the golden plates.

We taught our missionaries to do the same. Their study journals helped them see how the Holy Ghost spoke to them, guided them, and taught them, which in turn allowed them to see the hand of the Lord in their lives.

As part of our training, we regularly invited our missionaries to "open their mouths" (see D&C 24:12) and to follow the promptings of the Spirit without question.

One elder wrote, "I was on an exchange with a young missionary, and we were driving back to the chapel after knocking on an investigator's door to see if he was still planning on coming to church. Driving south on Lorna [a street in Hoover, Alabama], we passed a woman walking north. I felt prompted to turn around and talk with her. But I knew we had only a few minutes until sacrament meeting started. I thought it would be best to get back to the chapel, but the prompting persisted. I flipped around at the light where the branch building was and started driving north. My companion was confused, but I explained the situation to him. I parked at a mechanic's shop about fifty yards in front of where the woman was walking and told my companion we were going to 'check the air pressure' until the woman reached us when we could talk to her. We both got out of the car. As she approached, I said, 'Good morning, Ma'am.' She replied, 'Stay away from me you devil worshippers. You are both going to hell!' I was shocked and instinctively said, 'Have a nice day.' She yelled back, 'I don't want to hear that,' and she then continued walking.

"I was stunned, and my companion was even more confused. As we drove to church, my companion asked me why in the world I had been prompted to stop and talk with the woman. I tried to come up with some things that would make him feel better. Honestly, however, I was as bewildered as he was.

"In that moment, I felt the Spirit teach me a valuable lesson. I had recently promised my Father in Heaven that I would follow *any* divine prompting I was given—no matter how insignificant it seemed to me. At the time, my assigned companion and I were on exchanges, and we both were acutely aware that we should be missionaries the Lord could trust. I told this new missionary with whom I was working on that particular day that God sometimes asks us to do things without our understanding why—even after we obey. He tests His servants to see if He can trust them with the revelation He gives them. Even though the woman did not show any signs of coming unto Christ after we tried to talk to her, we understood that maybe the encounter did have a positive impact on her later. We had shown God that we valued the revelation He gave us and that we would always act upon it."[5]

Because this missionary had learned to follow the Spirit through experiences he recorded, he became a great missionary and witnessed much success in the vineyard.

Another story involves President Thomas S. Monson. At a very young age, he was called to serve as a bishop in Salt Lake City. His biography states: "On the evening of a stake leadership meeting, Bishop Monson took his seat with the other bishops in attendance. Earlier in the day, a classmate from the University of Utah had asked him to visit his uncle, a less-active member of the Sixth-Seventh Ward, who was gravely ill and in the hospital. Bishop Monson indicated that he had a stake priesthood meeting that evening but would pay a visit when it concluded.

"As the session dragged on, he kept watching the clock, trying to balance a growing sense of urgency with the uneasiness of leaving in the middle of the meeting. During the closing song, he bolted. Arriving at the hospital, he hurriedly checked at the desk for the room number and then raced up the stairs to the fourth floor. As he came down the hallway, he could see a cluster of people and activity at the door of a room—his ward member's room. The nurse looked at him and said, 'Are you Bishop Monson?'

"'Yes,' he replied heavily, concerned that perhaps he was too late.

"'The patient was asking for you just before he died,' she said.

"Remorse consumed him. He had not responded immediately to the prompting of the Spirit, had let his obligation to attend a meeting take precedence over the needs of one of his people. From this experience Thomas Monson learned a lesson and a truth that has defined his life:

'Never postpone a prompting.'"[6] And, as we all know, President Monson is now rather famous for following the promptings of the Spirit.

Recently, I attended a viewing for Paul Christofferson, a dear friend who had died a few days earlier, in Draper, Utah. President Monson also attended the viewing to pay his respects to Paul's family, which includes Elder D. Todd Christofferson of the Quorum of the Twelve Apostles.

As I stood in the doorway waiting in line to greet the Christofferson family, I noticed President Monson was about to leave. Those accompanying him were trying to gently help him exit the room. I thought that he must have had another engagement and could not stay to greet all those who would have loved to shake his hand.

As they moved forward to leave the room, most of us standing in line simply stepped aside because we knew he was trying to leave. As he approached the door, I heard him say, "I always do what I'm supposed to do." He then told those accompanying him, "We're going to be waiting here a few minutes." And then he walked down the line and shook the hands of everyone, including my hand, as he left the room. I gazed into his kind eyes and thought to myself that he had learned his lesson well from that earlier experience when he was a young bishop.

Returning back to the study journal, I counsel you that as you begin to record *your* spiritual experiences, you will see a pattern—you will see how the Lord speaks to you personally. The Holzapfel family study journals are filled with miraculous stories, and we have come to know how the Lord speaks to us individually.

We found an analogy that helped us teach our missionaries this specific principle. Each fall, countless numbers of Cloudless Sulphur butterflies migrate from Canada through the South on the way down to the coast of the Gulf of Mexico. Unlike the famous Monarch butterflies in California, these midsized butterflies do not migrate in large groups and are easily missed. During our first fall in the South, we did not notice them. During the next fall, my wife discovered them and showed me. Once I knew what to look for, I started seeing them everywhere—literally. I saw them at stop signs, I saw them along the road, and I saw them in fields and around houses and barns. It was rather remarkable how I had missed them when they were everywhere!

My wife taught our missionaries that following the promptings of the

Spirit and looking for the hand of the Lord are like looking for those butterflies. Once you start noticing them, you will see more and more of them. Our missionaries began reporting that they *saw* the butterflies—because, like us during our first year in the mission, none of the missionaries had ever noticed them.

In the following weeks and months, a great groundswell arose in the mission as more and more of our missionaries followed the promptings of the Spirit and saw the hand of the Lord in their lives. My wife received hundreds of letters from our missionaries recounting how they saw the hand of the Lord in their lives as they followed the promptings of the Holy Spirit.

Here is one more story from our mission. As some of you may know, a new missionary is always assigned a trainer, a more experienced missionary who helps teach the new missionary how to become a great missionary. The trainer is a new missionary's first companion and holds a special position of trust from the Lord and the mission president. The trainer can be a great blessing to a new missionary if the senior missionary is diligent, dedicated, and kind. My first trainer, Elder Chris Meacham, was a perfect trainer. Over the years and through my recent experiences in the Alabama Birmingham Mission, I have come to discover how remarkable he really was and what a blessing I experienced to have him assigned as my trainer so many years ago in Lugano, Switzerland, in my first mission assignment.

In some instances, trainers can become a little overbearing. They mistakenly think that the new missionary knows nothing, so they may say, "I'm in charge. Just listen and observe what I do."

We wanted to create a mission culture where the best missionaries became trainers so that our new missionaries were trained and nurtured in the way the Lord intended. We were always happy when our trainers rose to the standards the Lord had set for them. In one instance, we had a young missionary from Southern California assigned to a small branch in the mission. At the same time, he was assigned to be a trainer. It was his first opportunity to serve in this important capacity. His companion, fresh from the MTC, was a bright, dedicated, and enthusiastic new missionary. Like most, this elder was really excited about beginning his missionary labors. He was worthy and ready to serve.

Shortly after this elder arrived in the mission, I called him and his companion and, as was my tradition, said, "I'm coming down, and we're going to work together. Please be prepared to teach by arranging some appointments."

When I arrived at their apartment a few days later, they jumped into my car and directed me to the first appointment. We routinely taught our missionaries to proselytize around the local Latter-day Saint chapel: "Don't go way out of town because it's too difficult for investigators to come to church. Additionally, if they join, it'll be a burden on them for the rest of their lives to travel fifty or sixty miles to church. So stay around the chapel or around other members. Build from centers of strength."

I was quite surprised when we drove some distance from town. I think they could tell that I was starting to get worried about how far we were going that evening because they tried to reassure me, "We have somebody we need to teach, and it's going to be great. Don't worry!"

At a certain point, they told me to pull off to the side of the road. It was a dark evening. As I recall, it had been raining, so it was wet. We could smell the wet soil in the air—nothing compares outside the South. We started walking down a muddy, narrow road. I was really surprised and said, "How did you find this place?" They didn't really respond but continued walking toward a clearing with a dim light.

As we continued to walk, I heard dogs barking. In the South, our missionaries avoid dogs because many dogs are rabid. No missionary wants to get rabies shots, so most missionaries go out of their way or simply turn around when dogs are present. Missionaries who had to get rabies shots were well known and were always pointed out by other missionaries at our meetings. But these two missionaries were determined and kept walking. I was surprised and thought, *Even with the dogs barking, we are still walking forward!*

Eventually, we came to a clearing, and there was the most unsightly trailer I had ever seen in my life. Trust me—I have seen some very battered trailers. The South has some of the poorest communities in America. And within our mission was one of the top five poorest, so we had been in some extremely run-down trailers. But this one may have been the worst of all. I do not remember if there was a step into the trailer itself. As one of my missionaries knocked on the door, it opened. It was dark inside, but I saw a woman's face, etched with the problems and burdens of a hard life. I could tell she had experienced some of the harshest aspects of life—they had made her appear much older than she was, in fact. When we got inside, I noticed that the interior of the trailer was as bad as the outside—cluttered, dirty, and disheveled.

The woman took her seat at a little desk with a small lamp sitting on the edge of it, the only light, as I recall, in that dark and dingy trailer. Oblivious to their surroundings, these fine young missionaries started teaching her. I sat on the floor because there was no other place to sit and I thought to myself, *I'll have to get my suit cleaned because the floor is so dirty.*

I then witnessed the Holy Ghost manifest himself in that dingy old trailer. The light of Christ was glowing in the face of the missionaries, and I was absolutely moved by it. And then one of the missionaries said what all mission presidents love to hear, the invitation to embrace the gospel, "Will you follow the example of Jesus Christ and be baptized by someone who has authority? We're holding a baptism." He then gave a date. "Will you prepare yourself to be baptized?"

Of course I immediately looked at the woman. By the light of the one little lamp in the trailer, I looked at her face and saw tears. She responded, "Yes. This is what I've been waiting for."

Her face was truly glowing with newfound hope. The entire trailer seemed to glow with the light of the Holy Spirit and the revelations and grace of Jesus Christ.

Following the short but powerful lesson, we left. As we made our way back to my vehicle along the muddy lane, I put my arms around those two remarkable missionaries. I was so proud of them on that night. I said, "How did you find this woman? She obviously needed the gospel. This is what she's been looking for. This will change her life. How did you find her?"

The trainer turned to me and said, "President, it was my companion. He said he was prompted by the Spirit to stop as we were driving along."

First, I was impressed that this trainer was willing to listen to his young companion. Second, I was impressed that this new missionary had already become familiar with the promptings of the Spirit. Later, the woman responded to the message of hope found in the restored gospel of Jesus Christ and was baptized. Her life began to improve with a new job and a new place to live.

As we consider the role of the Holy Ghost, let us consider what we can learn from the book of John. First, the Holy Spirit will "guide you into all truth" (John 16:13). Second, he will "shew you things to come" (John 16:13). Third, he will glorify Jesus Christ (see John 16:14). Fourth, he will show the disciples the things of God (see John 16:15). For these reasons, the Spirit here is often called the *Paraclete* ("helper" or "advocate").[7] The Holy Ghost's role is that of a revealer and teacher who offers assistance.

The scripture preserves Jesus Christ's promise, "I will not leave you comfortless" (John 14:18). The Greek word here is *orphanous*, from which we get our modern English word *orphan*. As we reread John with this linguistic insight, we realize that Jesus is actually saying, "I will not leave you as orphans."

To help us, the Lord sends the Comforter (see John 14:16). The Greek noun used in the King James Version for "comforter" actually allows a variety of possible English translations, all of them reasonable. As a result, various translations have provided different nouns in addition to "Comforter" (Tyndale/KJV), including "Advocate" (NRSV/TNIV) and "Counselor" (NIV/RSV). The original Greek-speaking audience would most likely have understood the various nuances of the word that today's Bible readers do not obtain with a single English noun.

To take advantage of this precious gift more fully, the Lord has provided us important insights on how we will be successful in having the Holy Ghost as our companion more often and for longer periods of time, how the Holy Ghost will help us reach out to the Savior, and how we will develop the ability to hear the Holy Ghost as he leads, guides, and helps us. Following the promptings of the Holy Ghost will become "second nature" to us, and we will begin to see the hand of the Lord in our lives more often. As we keep a study journal and record these promptings, we learn how the Lord speaks to us and how He will graciously give us more of His word.

Notes

1. See Frank Newport, "Provo-Orem, Utah, Is Most Religious U.S. Metro Area," available at http://www.gallup.com/poll/161543/provo-orem-utah-religious-metro-area.aspx; accessed 5 August 2014.
2. *Missionary Handbook* (Salt Lake City: The Church of Jesus Christ of Latter-day Saints, 2006), 41.
3. M. Russell Ballard, "Following Up," *Ensign*, May 2014, 80.
4. *Preach My Gospel* (Salt Lake City: The Church of Jesus Christ of Latter-day Saints, 2004), x; see also Richard G. Scott, "Acquiring Spiritual Knowledge," *Ensign*, November 1993, 86.
5. Personal correspondence in author's possession.
6. Heidi S. Swinton, *To the Rescue: The Biography of Thomas S. Monson* (Salt Lake City: Deseret Book, 2010), 135–36.
7. See Bible Dictionary, s.v. "Paraclete," 741–42.

Show Mercy and Grace unto Ourselves

Rosemary M. Wixom

Forty years ago, President Ezra Taft Benson told us, "Nothing is going to startle us more when we pass through the veil to the other side than to realize how well we know our Father and how familiar his face is to us."[1] I cannot repeat that quote enough—for each time I do, I feel at home. I can only imagine the joy of also recognizing the face of the Savior and feeling the warmth of His embrace. He promises us, "Draw near unto me and I will draw near unto you" (D&C 88:63).

In our weaknesses, we do draw near unto Him, and each time we do, He shows mercy and grace unto us. Let me share an example.

Soon after I was called as the Primary general president, I was assigned to speak at a regional conference in the Salt Lake Conference Center. In my talk, I spoke about the importance of talking and listening to our children. I told a story of Sister Susan Heaton from Elgin, Illinois. I used her very words as they were printed in the October 1998 *Ensign*. I quote:

"One busy evening I heard a little voice coming from our youngest daughter's bedroom: 'Mom, could you come here? . . . You forgot to talk me in!' . . . 'Talk me in' really made a great deal of sense.

Rosemary M. Wixom was sustained as Primary general president in general conference April 2010. She served with her husband as he presided over the Washington DC South Mission. She and her husband, Jack, have six children and twelve adorable grandchildren.

"At one point when our children were small, I got into the habit of watching a few favorite television programs—in fact, they were quite important to me. I looked forward all day to sitting in front of the TV to watch them. Unfortunately, the programs came on at the same time the children went to bed.

"I don't remember exactly when it happened, but at one point I realized I had put my programs at the top of my list and my children farther down. For a while I tried reading bedtime stories with the TV on, but I knew in my heart it wasn't the best way."[2]

Now let's push pause in Sister Heaton's story.

We could stop right here and say, "Exhibit number one: Obvious weakness of mother watching TV over caring for her children." Oh, we could easily point our fingers at Sister Heaton and shake our heads. But wait, there's more to her story. She goes on to say:

"As I pondered about the days and weeks I had lost to my TV habit, I began to feel guilty and decided to change. It took a while to convince myself that I could really turn off the TV.

"After about two weeks of leaving the television off, I felt a burden somehow lifted. I realized I felt better, even cleaner somehow, and I knew I had made the right choice. The subsequent months and years of 'talking children in' have been valuable to me."[3]

I love Sister Heaton's story. I love it because it is an inspiring story about talking and listening to children, and I love it for another reason.

In the days and weeks that followed my telling of her experience in my talk, I received numerous comments and notes from people who had heard my talk and related to the experience, but thought Sister Heaton's story was *my* story because I told it in first person, in her very words. Some missed my reference to her as the storyteller. Many of them expressed surprise that a general officer of the Church would be so open as to admit to a TV habit in a regional conference talk. At first I was dismayed, but then I thought: "No. Thank you, Sister Susan Heaton. You are not the only one who has character flaws. I'm right there with you. I could tell a story similar to your story about myself. How many times have I felt the remorse of repetitive choices I have made when I lacked the courage to change? If there are those who interpret your story, Sister Heaton, as mine, so be it. If just one person besides myself feels not alone in admitting to a weakness and finds hope through your example, I celebrate! Your story is an example of how through the grace of Jesus Christ a desire to change begins in our hearts, and that desire gives us the strength to draw upon the enabling power of the Savior's Atonement.

"Sister Heaton, you give us hope that we too can find the courage to change and be obedient. It requires humility to seek change in our lives, and then only with the Lord's grace, as you put it, we feel a burden lifted, we feel better and 'even cleaner somehow.'"

Moroni said, "If men [and women] come unto me I will show unto them their weakness. I give unto men [and women] weakness that they may be humble; and my grace is sufficient for all men [and women] that humble themselves before me; for if they humble themselves before me, and have faith in me, then will I make weak things become strong unto them" (Ether 12:27).

Moroni teaches us a principle when he begins with the phrase, "If men [and women] come unto me," meaning that it's not about being a certain person, it is about coming unto Him and becoming His. Elder Bruce C. Hafen said, "If you're seeing more of your weaknesses, that just might mean you're moving nearer to God, not farther away."[4]

We come unto Him when we say, "I give. I'm yours. I do need Thee every hour. Here is my heart, take all that I have and let everything else slough off."

King Benjamin said that possibility to change occurs when we "[become] as a child, submissive, meek, humble, patient, [and] full of love" (Mosiah 3:19). Like a child, we turn to our Father and we put our trust in Him and we "[yield] to the enticings of the Holy Spirit" (Mosiah 3:19).

We need the Atonement of Jesus Christ in our lives—as it heals, comforts, consoles, and enables us to show mercy and grace unto ourselves. How many times have we stood at our kitchen sinks and whispered, "Lord, please give me the strength to endure. Please give me the strength to forgive, to move on, the strength to embrace a child who is wayward, the strength to accept my circumstances and have hope for the future. Lord, please give me strength to simply expand my time, to curb a habit, or elevate my thinking. I need the strength to draw closer to Thee and to be better than I can be on my own." It's true—because of Him, we can have a fresh start.

President Ezra Taft Benson taught us that we do know our Heavenly Father.[5] Here on earth we are in the process of remembering what we once knew. At the same time, we are learning that He knows us and loves each one of us personally.

The Lord knew Samuel, a five-year-old boy. He called him by name three times in the night before Eli helped the young boy recognize the voice of the Lord. We read, "And Samuel grew, and the Lord was with him, and did let none of his words fall to the ground" (1 Samuel 3:19).

The Lord knew Joseph Smith. At age fourteen, Joseph knelt and prayed to the Father. He said, "I saw two Personages, whose brightness and glory defy all description, standing above me in the air. One of them spake unto me, calling me by name" (Joseph Smith–History 1:17).

The Lord knew Emma Smith. We read, "Hearken unto the voice of the Lord your God, while I speak unto you, Emma Smith, my daughter" (D&C 25:1). The Lord knew Emma so well the He spoke to her strengths, her fears, and her weaknesses. He said, "Lay aside the things of this world and seek for the things of a better" (D&C 25:10).

The Lord knows each one of our names. His love for us is beyond our comprehension. When we recognize His hand in every detail of our lives, it is similar to hearing Him call us by name. The Lord said to Emma, "Thou art an elect lady, whom I have called" (D&C 25:3). Would He not have the same message for each one of His daughters?

He knows us like He knows Georgia Marriott, a twenty-two-year-old vibrant young woman, a senior in violin performance attending Indiana University. Georgia delighted in the goodness of people and in her love for the Savior, Jesus Christ. Her goal was to testify to someone each day of Him and His restored gospel. Georgia was riding her bike to class one September morning in 2002 when she was hit by a truck. She left this mortal existence knowing and loving her Savior, Jesus Christ. She knew that He loved her. She wrote these words in her journal just one week before she died:

"[I] hold triumphantly the torch of Christ! I want that faith always and I want that hope always. I want to *be* that light. Christ makes it all possible for me because He's been showing me little by little that I am of worth. He is the definition of what I am truly inside and want to become. As I see that, I forget my worries and realize that I am founded on Him, and I have no fear because He is with me! I forget myself. . . . I am secure on His rock, and then I can focus on *others*, on the *gospel*, on *exerting* myself to good and building on *Him*. Then I progress, then I feel joy! Life holds no chains for me because I am liberated by that inherent Light given to me before this world. I know the Light is there because of Christ's Atonement. He gave [His] all to serve us and let us be like Him."

Georgia continues: "Let us have joy! Oh, don't you see, can't everyone see that He is our God and Savior? He is the Christ, and those words are finally becoming real and moving to me."[6]

Georgia now knows how familiar His face is.

There is a Primary song entitled, "I Know That My Savior Loves Me" with the words, "I did not touch Him or sit on His knee, / Yet, Jesus is real to me. / I know He lives! / I will follow faithfully. / My heart I give to Him. / I know that my Savior loves me."[7]

My testimony is that I know that He lives. He is real. As we look for His hand in our lives, our love for Him will increase. We won't let our weaknesses discourage us; instead, we will look forward to the opportunities to change and become better. We will seek a new level of hope and understanding. Only through the Atonement of Jesus Christ may we become better than we can even imagine we could become. Humbling our hearts and submitting our will to His opens the door to a world of serenity away from the storms. Through His mercy and grace, He welcomes everyone to enter that door. It begins with our desire. We will feel ourselves drawing nearer to our Heavenly Father and His Son, Jesus Christ. It's simply about living the gospel the best we can and looking for small and simple ways to be more obedient. Then "when he shall appear we shall be like Him, for we shall see him as he is" (Moroni 7:48).

Notes

1. Ezra Taft Benson, "Jesus Christ—Gifts and Expectations," Brigham Young University devotional, 10 December 1974; available at http://speeches.byu.edu/?act=viewitem&id=90; accessed 7 July 2014.
2. Susan Heaton, "Talk Time Instead of TV Time," *Ensign*, October 1998, 73.
3. Ibid.
4. Bruce C. Hafen, "The Atonement: All for All," *Ensign*, May 2004, 97.

5. Benson, "Jesus Christ—Gifts and Expectations."
6. Personal correspondence in author's possession.
7. Tami Jeppson Creamer and Derena Bell, "I Know That My Savior Loves Me"; available at https://www.lds.org/music/library/music-for-children?lang=eng#d; accessed 7 July 2014.

Got Oil? Replenishing and Fortifying Our Spiritual Reserves

Mary Ellen Edmunds

For the Lord God is a sun and shield: the Lord will give grace and glory: no good thing will he withhold from them that walk uprightly.

Psalm 84:11

It is sometimes hard to find time to replenish our spiritual reserves when we have so many demands on our time. Yet finding time to rejuvenate and fill our souls can provide opportunity for stress relief as well as time for self-evaluation. What things can we do to fortify our spiritual reserves—even with demanding schedules? How can we make time for these important spiritual priorities as we develop a personal relationship with our Savior?

It's been a wonderful experience to ponder on the theme of this year's conference and the theme for this session: "Replenishing and fortifying our spiritual reserves."

I've thought so much about having a spiritual reserve. I've wondered what that means. I have come to feel that it's having "enough and to spare" of spirituality.

And what is spirituality?

Mary Ellen Edmunds is the author of several books, including Buck Up, Little Buckaroo *and* Tug of War. *Trained as a nurse, she is also a former director of training at the Provo Missionary Training Center and a former member of the Relief Society general board.*

Years ago I had been invited to participate in a Sunday evening fireside. When I arrived, the woman who had invited me—the only one I knew in this area—hadn't come yet, so I just sat at the back and waited. Two older sisters were sitting right in front of me, and in a loud whisper the one asked the other: "Who did you say is speaking?"

The response went something like this:

"Her name is Mary Ellen Edmunds, and I hear she's really spiritual . . ."

Well, that got me thinking. What did she mean? That I attend meetings regularly? I do. Pay my tithing? Yes. Go to the temple often? Yes. Did I have a *glow* about me? No. I think spirituality is a whole lot more than what someone may have thought.

Simply stated, I think spirituality is the desire (and the increasing ability) to seek, recognize, and respond to the Spirit. It's doing what we need to do to have the Spirit—the gift of the Holy Ghost—with us always. Spirituality leads to godliness, to holiness, to personal goodness, to a mighty change of heart—to a sweeter relationship with our Heavenly Father and our Savior (as well as with each other).

I love the way Alma speaks of spiritual rebirth as an awakening. He tells us that with some, God "awakened" them—they "awoke unto God" (Alma 5:7). This awareness of God and a sensitivity to what is sacred with the help of the Holy Ghost is the essence of spirituality.[1]

The guidance of the Holy Spirit, the Holy Ghost, can sometimes lead us to life-saving actions—for ourselves as well as others—both temporally and spiritually. A friend who avoids going to doctors had a strong prompting a few years ago to do just that; she'd been experiencing unusually strong dizzy spells. It was discovered that she had a life-threatening cerebral aneurysm. If she hadn't responded to the prompting and received treatment—surgery—she might not be with us today.

Years ago, a Primary chorister followed a strong prompting to visit a little girl who had stopped coming to Primary, mostly because she was the only one in her family who was participating in the Church in any way. The chorister told her she missed her. She said "We don't have anyone to sing the high notes." The little girl came back, and she never left again. Her life was changed for the good—and she eventually sang the high notes as a member of the Mormon Tabernacle Choir!

Spiritual growth comes from spiritual sources. Each time we respond to the Spirit—to promptings from the Holy Ghost—we increase our spirituality. We replenish our spiritual reserve.

From the Bible Dictionary: "The gift of the Holy Ghost is the right to have, whenever one is worthy, the companionship of the Holy Ghost. More powerful than that which is available before baptism, it acts as a cleansing agent to purify a person and sanctify him from all sin. Thus it is often spoken of as 'fire.'"[2]

And Elder Bruce R. McConkie said: "Men are born into mortality with the talents and abilities acquired by obedience to law in their first estate. Above all talents—greater than any other capacities, chief among all endowments—stands the talent for spirituality."[3]

If we think of spirituality as a talent, it likely means we can improve our ability to recognize and respond to the Spirit, rather than demonstrating how spiritual we are in a talent show.

Jacob teaches, "Remember, to be carnally-minded is death, and to be spiritually-minded is life eternal" (2 Nephi 9:39). And from the Apostle Paul, "to be spiritually minded is *life* and *peace*" (Romans 8:6; emphasis added). Part of what being "spiritually minded" means is to follow the Savior's admonition to "look unto [Him] in every thought" (D&C 6:36).

Elder Dallin H. Oaks wrote: "The first of the Ten Commandments—'Thou shalt have no other gods before me' (Exodus 20:3)—epitomizes the nature of spirituality. A spiritual person has no priorities ahead of God."[4] Nothing comes before Him—there are *no* priorities ahead of God. This can be a very helpful key to keep in mind as we strive to prioritize the many responsibilities we have in our busy lives.

President Ezra Taft Benson said: "We must put God in the forefront of everything else in our lives. . . . When we put God first, all other things fall into their proper place or drop out of our lives."[5]

One thing that came to my mind as I pondered about having a spiritual reserve was the reservoirs which hold in reserve the water we need. When we speak of reservoirs of water, we worry when there is a drought. With our personal spiritual reservoirs, we should worry even more when there is doubt. As President Dieter F. Uchtdorf taught in the October 2013 general conference, "Please, first doubt your doubts before you doubt your faith."[6] Avoid *drought* in your spiritual reservoir—avoid *doubt* in your spiritual life.

Our personal spiritual reserve is compared to oil in the scriptures. We're familiar with the parable of the ten virgins—five had a "reserve" of oil for their lamps, and five did not. So what is the oil? What does it represent? The oil is the Spirit—it's the Holy Ghost. It represents the depth and strength of our testimony of Jesus Christ—the "condition" of our spiritual reserve.

The five wise virgins had prepared themselves carefully for the coming of the bridegroom (Jesus Christ). They had filled their lamps with oil to provide light (and maybe also some warmth)—they had fortified their spiritual reserve with good works, love, obedience, with being true and faithful. In this parable, the Lord uses oil to represent spiritual preparation, something which cannot be borrowed at the last minute.

President Spencer W. Kimball wrote: "I believe that the Ten Virgins represent the people of the Church of Jesus Christ. . . . [The five who were foolish] had the saving, exalting gospel, but it had not been made the center of their lives."[7]

President James E. Faust said: "Spirituality is like sunlight: it passes into the unclean and is not tainted. May our lives be such, that the spiritual within us may ascend up through the common, the sordid, the evil, and sanctify our souls."[8]

Elder Dallin H. Oaks said: "We should seek after spiritual gifts. They can lead us to God. They can shield us from the power of the adversary. They can compensate for our inadequacies and repair our imperfections."[9]

We seek the best gifts of the Spirit and use them in kindness and service to others. President David O. McKay wrote: "The development of our spiritual nature should concern us most. Spirituality is the highest acquisition of the soul, the divine in man."[10]

There are no limitations to our faith when we build it upon spirituality—when we add oil to our lamps and our lives, one drop at a time. (Talk about essential oil!) How do we keep oil in our lamps—how can we replenish our spiritual reserves? By keeping the commandments of God. By living our religion with all our hearts. Wilford Woodruff said, "When we are laboring for the kingdom of God, we will have oil in our lamps, our light will shine and we will feel the testimony of the spirit of God."[11]

Here are a few suggestions as to how we might replenish and fortify our spiritual reserves, how we might add oil to our lamps and to our extra supply of oil. As I share some ideas, I sincerely hope the Spirit will prompt you to choose even one thing which will make a difference in your life. As always, you'll learn so much more from the Spirit—from the Holy Ghost—than you will from me. These ideas are not necessarily in any order, so, for you, the last may be first!

1. THINK DEEPLY

Ponder and meditate more. These are significant, wonderful ways to increase spirituality. Find a time and a place where you can do this, even for short periods of time. Maybe it will be while you're driving, or walking, folding laundry, rocking a baby—make time for a longer-than-usual moment by just letting your mind be quiet as you welcome promptings from the Holy Ghost. These can be refining experiences.

President David O. McKay said: "We pay too little attention to the value of meditation, a principle of devotion. . . . Meditation is the language of the soul. It is defined as 'a form of private devotion, or spiritual exercise, consisting in deep, continued reflection on some religious theme.' Meditation is a form of prayer."[12]

Often, meditating becomes a time when we can do more listening, when we can give our Heavenly Father a chance to communicate with us through His Spirit. My personal times of meditation and pondering have brought me sweet spiritual experiences.

2. PRAY EARNESTLY

Do what you need to do to make your communication with your Heavenly Father matter more and be more enjoyable. Communicate honestly and often. There is a huge difference between "saying your prayers" and "communicating with your Heavenly Father," or counseling with Him. (Which means we give Him a turn! We allow Him to tell us what's on His mind, not just the other way around.)

The most meaningful experiences with prayer happen when we allow the Spirit to help us know what to pray about. Prayer is the opportunity to turn to the spiritual things in life, and to discover a sweeter, deeper relationship with our Heavenly Father, the Savior, and the Holy Ghost.

3. Search the Scriptures

Put these meaningful, wonderful thoughts and reminders into your heart often, and you will have oil for your lamps—you will have the light you need in your life. Studying the scriptures increases our spirituality, and this helps us to see our way more clearly to gain the inspiration from the Lord for our challenges and problems. The law of the fast is a source of spiritual strength—read Isaiah 58 again to be reminded of some of the sweetest blessings in all of scripture! Feast on the scriptures, and you'll have plenty of things to think and ponder about.

4. Follow the Prophet

Most, if not all of us, had the opportunity (the blessing) during the April 2014 general conference to raise our hands to sustain President Thomas S. Monson as not just the President of the Church, but the current living prophet. And we sustained him and fourteen others as "prophets, seers, and revelators." What does it mean to sustain them? Elder David B. Haight said: "When we sustain the President of the Church by our uplifted hand, it not only signifies that we acknowledge before God that he is the rightful possessor of all the priesthood keys; it also means that we covenant with God that we will abide by the direction and the counsel that come through His prophet. It is a solemn covenant."[13]

If you want an incredible resource for things to ponder, go to the talks from these fifteen and other General Authority and general auxiliary speakers at the recent general conference. This is an opportunity for great spiritual refreshment and renewal. President Marion G. Romney said at the conclusion of the April 1954 general conference: "We have heard enough truth and direction in this conference to bring us into the presence of God if we would follow it. We have been taken on to the spiritual mountain and shown visions of great glory."[14] President Howard W. Hunter said: "Our modern-day prophets have encouraged us to make the reading of the conference editions of our Church magazines an important and regular part of our personal study. Thus, *general conference becomes, in a sense, a supplement to or an extension of the Doctrine and Covenants*."[15]

5. EXPRESS GRATITUDE OFTEN

Being thankful (and expressing thanks) is a healthy thing to do. Psalm 92:1 says, "It is a good thing to give thanks unto the Lord." President Ezra Taft Benson wrote: "The Prophet Joseph said at one time that one of the greatest sins of which the Latter-day Saints would be guilty is the sin of ingratitude. I presume most of us have not thought of that as a great sin. . . . sometimes I feel we need to devote more of our prayers to expressions of gratitude and thanksgiving for blessings already received. We enjoy so much."[16] President Marion G. Romney said: "It is perfectly evident from [Doctrine and Covenants 59:5–7] that to thank the Lord in all things is not merely a courtesy, it is a *commandment* as binding upon us as any other commandment."[17]

6. COME TO THE TEMPLE!

This can be like jumping in a reservoir full of water, except that it's a reservoir of spirituality. Even if we can just be on the grounds of a temple, or sit in the foyer for a little while, get your soul filled as often as possible. The temple provides a unique setting for understanding spiritual things. President Ezra Taft Benson said, "I promise you that, with increased attendance in the temples of our God, you shall receive increased personal revelation to bless your life."[18]

He also said: "There is a power associated with ordinances of heaven—even the power of godliness—which can and will thwart the forces of evil if we will but be worthy of those sacred [covenants made in the temple of the Lord]. . . . Our families will be protected, our children will be safeguarded as we live the gospel, visit the temple, and live close to the Lord."[19]

President Gordon B. Hinckley asked, "Who in these times of stress would not welcome an occasional opportunity to shut out the world and enter into the Lord's house, there to ponder quietly the eternal things of God?"[20] He also said: "I am satisfied that if our people would attend the temple more, there would be less of selfishness in their lives. There would be [more] love in their relationships. . . . [and] more of love and peace and happiness in [their] homes."[21]

President Boyd K. Packer wrote: "Our labors in the temple cover us with a shield and a protection, both individually and as a people."[22] "Blessings there will not be limited to our temple service. We will be blessed in all of our affairs . . . both spiritual and temporal."[23]

7. Let Your Heart Be Filled with Love!

Pray with all the energy of heart to be filled with this love, this charity. Without charity—pure love—we are nothing. Charity never faileth! It sometimes getteth tired, and maybe even getteth frustrated and impatient . . . but it *never* faileth! I call Matthew 25:34–40 the "inasmuch" miracle: "Inasmuch as ye have done it unto one of the least of these my brethren, ye have done it unto me" (v. 40). It seems that the Savior is teaching us that when/if/*inasmuch as* we serve others—those who are hungry, thirsty, sick, naked, etc.—it is not just that we are doing things "for Him" (striving to be good disciples), but in some sweet, incredible way it is as if "*to* Him."

President Spencer W. Kimball said: "One can learn to be loving. If one patterns his life in the mold of love—if he consciously and determinedly directs his thoughts, controls his acts, and tries to feel and constantly express his love, he becomes a person of love, for 'As he thinketh in his heart, so is he' (Proverbs 23:7)."[24]

Don't you love experiences like when someone asks how you are and then waits to hear your answer? President Ezra Taft Benson wrote, "When we have the Spirit, we will love to serve, we will love the Lord, and we will love those whom we serve."[25]

There is a need for us to be filled with the Spirit—with oil for our lamps—and to cherish the gift of the Holy Ghost so that our lights may shine for others and we can help in the hastening of the work of bringing Heavenly Father's children back to Him.

In a group I was in, a Church leader told of visiting less-active members with another stake leader following a training meeting about working with Church members who were less-active. One woman they visited was a "porcupine." When she saw them on the doorstep she almost screamed at them, "I know why you're here!"

The leader responded with, "Why *are* we here?"

She said, "You're trying to get me to come back to church."

He said that had never entered his mind.

So she asked, "Well, then, why *are* you here?"

He responded with, "May we come in and tell you why we're here?"—and he did this with such love and gentleness that she let him in. (Maybe she was curious!)

They sat down in the living room, and with genuine love he said, "This evening the two of us knelt in prayer, asking Heavenly Father who needed us to visit. Your name came to mind. Can you think of any reason He'd want us to come and see you?"

She burst into tears and said, "Yes . . . because I'm *miserable!* And I've been miserable for *years!*" And she poured out her story and her heart to them. She was experiencing a spiritual drought and many doubts. What followed was a tender time of comfort and healing.

As they got ready to leave, he asked, "May we offer a prayer for you before we go?" She quickly said yes and told them she couldn't even remember the last time a prayer had been offered in her home. As the two brothers left, she was in tears, thanking them for their visit.

President Ezra Taft Benson said: "This latter-day work is spiritual. It takes spirituality to comprehend it, to love it, and to discern it. Therefore we should seek the Spirit in all we do. That is our challenge."[26]

Brothers Richard L. Bednar and Scott R. Peterson shared the following: "Trivializing spiritual activity is a major stumbling block to cultivating true spirituality. As long as we call activities spiritual when they are not, true spirituality is blocked and frustrated. . . . If we trivialize spiritual activities, we can easily take for granted what could be truly spiritual activities by executing them in a half-hearted way and still calling them spiritual, even though the Spirit is absent. Either way, we have sacrificed spiritual substance for its much more evident, yet empty, form."[27] The loss of spirituality is immediately noticeable and spiritual death is the most terrible of all deaths.

President Gordon B. Hinckley said: "It is not enough [for us, you and me, now, in our time] to simply be known as a member of this Church. A solemn obligation rests upon us . . . We must live as true followers of the Christ, with charity towards all . . . Be grateful, and above all, be faithful."[28]

And Elder Jeffrey R. Holland said, paraphrasing President J. Reuben Clark Jr., "Our faith must not be difficult to detect."[29] He also said: "Drawing upon my vast background of children's bedtime stories, I say you can pick your poultry. You can either be like Chicken Little and run about shouting 'The sky is falling; the sky is falling' or you can be like the Little Red Hen and forge ahead with the productive tasks of living, regardless of who does or doesn't help you or who does or doesn't believe just the way you believe."[30]

Doctrine and Covenants 11:12–14 says: "And now, verily, verily, I say unto thee, put your trust in that Spirit which leadeth to do good—yea, to do justly, to walk humbly, to judge righteously; and this is my Spirit. Verily, verily, I say unto you, I will impart unto you of my Spirit, which shall enlighten your mind, which shall fill your soul with joy; and then shall ye know, or by this shall you know, all things whatsoever you desire of me, which are pertaining unto things of righteousness, in faith believing in me that you shall receive."

I love the hymn "Let the Holy Spirit Guide":

Let the Holy Spirit guide;
Let him teach us what is true.
He will testify of Christ,
Light our minds with heaven's view.

Let the Holy Spirit guard;
Let his whisper govern choice.
He will lead us safely home
If we listen to his voice.

Let the Spirit heal our hearts
Thru his quiet, gentle pow'r.
May we purify our lives
To receive him hour by hour.[31]

May we do all we can do—in this season of our lives—to replenish and fortify our spiritual reserves—our spirituality.

I am convinced that as we do this the best we can, the theme of this conference will come true in our lives: "No good thing will he withhold from them that walk uprightly" (Psalm 84:11). And this promise will also be kept from the Doctrine and Covenants: "And at that day, when I shall come in my glory, shall the parable be fulfilled which I spake concerning the ten virgins. For they that are wise and have received the truth, and have taken the Holy Spirit for their guide, and have not been deceived—verily I say unto you, they shall not be hewn down and cast into the fire, but shall abide the day. And the earth shall be given unto them for an inheritance; and they shall multiply and wax strong, and their children shall grow up without sin unto salvation. For the Lord shall be in their midst, and his glory shall be upon them, and he will be their king and their lawgiver" (D&C 45:56–59).

NOTES

1. See Nephi Jensen, "What Does It Mean to be Spiritual?" *Improvement Era* 43:9 (September 1940): 538.
2. Bible Dictionary, s.v. "Gift of the Holy Ghost," 704.
3. Bruce R. McConkie, *The Millennial Messiah: The Second Coming of the Son of Man* (Salt Lake City: Deseret Book, 1982), 234.
4. Dallin H. Oaks, *Pure in Heart* (Salt Lake City: Deseret Book, 1988), 120.
5. Ezra Taft Benson, "The Great Commandment—Love the Lord," *Ensign*, May 1988, 4.
6. Dieter F. Uchtdorf, "Come, Join with Us," *Ensign*, November 2013, 23; see also F. F. Bosworth, *Christ the Healer*, 9th edition (Grand Rapids, MI: Fleming H. Revell, 2000), 22.
7. Spencer W. Kimball, *Faith Precedes the Miracle* (Salt Lake City: Deseret Book, 1972), 253–54; see also Matthew 25:1–13.
8. James E. Faust, *To Reach Even unto You* (Salt Lake City: Deseret Book, 1990), 16.
9. Oaks, "Spiritual Gifts," *Ensign*, September 1986, 72.
10. David O. McKay, *Pathways to Happiness* (Salt Lake City: Deseret Book, 1957), 377.
11. Wilford Woodruff, *The Discourses of Wilford Woodruff*, G. Homer Durham, ed. (Salt Lake City: Deseret Book, 1946), 125. See also *Journal of Discourses*, 26 vols. (Liverpool: Latter-day Saints' Book Depot, 1854–86), 22:208 (9 January 1881).
12. McKay, *David O. McKay* [manual], in Teachings of Presidents of the

Church series (Salt Lake City: The Church of Jesus Christ of Latter-day Saints, 2003), 31–32; see also Conference Report, April 1946, 113.

13. David B. Haight, "Solemn Assemblies," *Ensign*, November 1994, 14–15.
14. Marion G. Romney, in Conference Report, April 1954, 132–33.
15. Howard W. Hunter, *The Teachings of Howard W. Hunter*, Clyde J. Williams, ed. (Salt Lake City: Deseret Book, 1997), 212; emphasis added.
16. Benson, *God, Family, Country: Our Three Great Loyalties* (Salt Lake City: Deseret Book, 1974), 199.
17. Romney, "Gratitude and Thanksgiving," *Ensign*, November 1982, 50.
18. Benson, "The Book of Mormon and the Doctrine and Covenants," *Ensign*, May 1987, 85.
19. Benson, at the Atlanta Georgia Temple cornerstone laying, 1 June 1983; quoted in Dean L. Larsen, "The Importance of the Temple for Living Members," *Ensign*, April 1993, 12.
20. Gordon B. Hinckley, "Why These Temples?" *Ensign*, August 1974, 40.
21. Hinckley, Regional Representatives' Seminar, 6 April 1984; quoted in Dean L. Larsen, "The Importance of the Temple for Living Members," *Ensign*, April 1993, 12.
22. Boyd K. Packer, *The Holy Temple* (Salt Lake City: Bookcraft, 1980), 265.
23. Ibid., 182.
24. Kimball, *Teachings of Spencer W. Kimball* (Salt Lake City: Deseret Book, 1982), 245–46; formatting altered.
25. Benson, *Come unto Christ* (Salt Lake City: Deseret Book, 1983), 22.
26. Benson, *The Teachings of Ezra Taft Benson* (Salt Lake City: Deseret Book, 1988), 92.
27. Richard L. Bednar and Scott R. Peterson, *Spirituality and Self-Esteem: Developing the Inner Self* (Salt Lake City: Deseret Book, 1990), 127.
28. Hinckley, "The Dawning of a Brighter Day," *Ensign*, May 2004, 84.
29. Jeffrey R. Holland, "Terror, Triumph, and a Wedding Feast," Brigham Young University fireside address, 12 September 2004; available at http://speeches.byu.edu/?act=viewitem&id=1371; accessed 9 July 2014; see also *The Charted Course of the Church in Education*, rev. ed. (Salt Lake City: The Church of Jesus Christ of Latter-day Saints, 1994), 7; available at https://www.lds.org/bc/content/shared/content/english/pdf/language-materials/32709_eng.pdf?lang=eng; accessed 9 July 2014.
30. Ibid.
31. Penelope Moody Allen, "Let the Holy Spirit Guide," *Hymns of The Church of Jesus Christ of Latter-day Saints* (Salt Lake City: The Church of Jesus Christ of Latter-day Saints, 1985), no. 143.

"Fear Not, I Am with Thee": Christ's Atonement and Our Personal Growth

Bruce C. and Marie K. Hafen

Bruce: It is a privilege to be part of this wonderful gathering with you. As I think of the Relief Society general presidency's significant role in cosponsoring this Women's Conference, I'm reminded of what Elder LeGrand Richards reportedly said years ago when he was attending a Relief Society meeting with Belle Spafford, then the Relief Society general president. Just before Elder Richards spoke, Sister Spafford said, "Elder Richards, we sisters want you brethren to know that the Relief Society is 100 percent behind the Priesthood." Elder Richards went to the

---

Bruce C. Hafen was called to the First Quorum of the Seventy in 1996 and received emeritus status in 2010. An internationally recognized family law scholar, he has served as dean of the Brigham Young University Law School and as president of BYU–Idaho (formerly Ricks College). He is also well known for his best-selling trilogy on the Atonement. Elder Hafen most recently served as president of the St. George Utah Temple.

Marie K. Hafen was raised in Bountiful, Utah. She obtained both her bachelor's and master's degrees in English from Brigham Young University in Provo, Utah. She has served as a Relief Society president, a Laurel adviser, and as the matron of the St. George Utah Temple. She has written for the Relief Society general curriculum committee and has served on the Young Women general board and on the board of directors for the Deseret News. *She has taught religion, literature, and writing at both Brigham Young University–Idaho and Brigham Young University in Provo.*

Bruce and Marie are the parents of seven children and the grandparents of forty-four.

pulpit and said, "Sister Spafford, I'm glad to know that the Relief Society is 100 percent behind the Priesthood, because the Priesthood is 100 *years* behind the Relief Society!" That's still true, but we're working on it.

Introduction: Severe Mercy

Marie: At our dinner table the other night, a friend shared a story from what she calls her "spiritual first-aid kit." It's a story she remembers when life feels cold and harsh—when the exhaustion is deep, the snow is getting deeper, and "Rocky Ridge" is still ahead. It comes from the high plains of Wyoming in October of 1856. Our friend calls this story "Severe Mercy."[1]

Nine-year-old Agnes Caldwell had been wading through the wind-driven snow with the rest of the Willie handcart company for what must have felt like an eternity when relief wagons appeared on the trail ahead of them. Before the storm hit, Agnes had been taking each mile of the autumn trail in stride, even the one that had been strewn with rattlesnakes. For that mile, she and her friend Mary held hands and jumped again and again over the snakes until they were out of danger, mercifully unharmed.

But after days of dragging her nearly frozen feet through the deepening snow, she wasn't skipping any more. And she was literally starving. The death toll in her company was rising with every passing night. Yet, of the arrival of the relief party, all Agnes records in her understated history is, "It certainly was a relief." And then she describes her own rescue: "The infirm and the aged were allowed to ride, all able-bodied continued to walk. When the wagons started out, a number of us children decided to see how long we could keep up with the wagons, in hopes of being asked to ride. One by one they all fell out, until I was the last one remaining, so determined was I that I should get a ride. After what seemed the longest run I ever made before or since, the driver, [Brother] Kimball, called to me, "Say, sissy, would you like a ride?" I answered in my very best manner, "Yes, sir." At this he reached over, [took] my hand, [then clucked] to his horses [which made] me run, with legs that seemed to me could run no farther. On we went [for what] seemed miles. [I thought] he was the meanest man that ever lived or that I had ever heard of, and other things that would not be a credit . . . coming from one so young. Just at what seemed the breaking point, he stopped. Taking a blanket, he wrapped me up and lay me in the bottom of the wagon, warm and comfortable. Here I had time to change my mind, as I surely did, knowing full well [that] by doing this he saved me from freezing [to death]."[2]

Can you see why our friend calls this story "Severe Mercy"? "I thought he was the meanest man that ever lived." Sitting here in our climate-controlled comfort, can we put ourselves in Agnes's shoes? If I had been Agnes, I would have expected a *little* compassion from this "angel of mercy." Couldn't one look into my frost-bitten face or at my bony, rag-wrapped hand have entitled me to a crumb of kindness? But no. This man took Agnes by that little hand and instead of swinging her up into his lap in an act of mercy, he signaled his team to go faster, forcing her into a run, which increased her circulation. His severe mercy saved her life.

This story has much to teach us about the redeeming and strengthening powers of the Atonement of Jesus Christ. You can see the symbolism. The wilderness strewn with rattlesnakes; the brutal and unexpected blizzard that turns that trail to Zion into a refiner's fire; the young girl with her passion and determination to give the journey everything she's got; the wagon master who was loving enough to lend his strength yet wise enough to stretch her to her limits—and courageous enough to volunteer for the rescue in the first place. This man didn't *have* to leave the comfort of his home and this young girl didn't *have* to hang on to his hand when he pressed her to give more. Yes, he saved her life, but *so did she!* To be successful, the rescue effort had to be reciprocal. They both had to give it their all.

To phrase these next questions in today's vernacular, where is the enabling power of the Savior's Atonement in this story? What is the role of grace here?

You may have noticed, as we have, that in the last few years more and more Latter-day Saints are using Atonement-related words and phrases in talking about their spiritual experiences. This growing dialogue may be coming out of the muddy trenches of each of our lives and our sometimes desperate need to be assured of God's deliverance. Reaching deeper into the heart of the gospel is exactly what we should be doing when the storms are beating us down. But in our searching to explain our experiences, articulate our feelings, and teach our Sunday lessons, we may inadvertently draw one another away from the simple clarity of the restored gospel because, at least in part, we share so many of the same key words with other Christian churches. With the increased volume of our discourse, we are also sensing a little confusion.

One LDS woman, in trying to unravel the confusion for herself, made a list of stories from the Book of Mormon in which God's power delivered or strengthened someone, often miraculously. Going down the list she asked, "When is this the Atonement's enabling power, when is it priesthood power, or when is it simply an answer to a prayer?" She asked us, "Are there situations when we should be calling on one of these powers rather than another one?" The doctrine of the Atonement was feeling like a puzzle to her.

Our hope is that we can help clarify some key elements of the doctrine of the Lord's Atonement, including how we participate in that doctrine. In doing this, we hope you will feel reassured about Christ's desire to help us lift our burdens, and that you will feel more confident in your ability to stick with Him no matter what. We also hope that as we increase our understanding of what Christ has *done* for us, we might also increase our willingness to submit to whatever He may *ask* of us.

THE PURPOSE OF CHRIST'S ATONEMENT—OUR GROWTH AND DEVELOPMENT

Bruce: Our doctrinal discussion of the Savior's Atonement begins with the story of Adam and Eve. A friend once asked me, "If Jesus Christ is at the center of the gospel and the center of the temple, why doesn't the temple endowment teach the story of the life of Christ? What's all this about Adam and Eve?" As I have thought about his question, I have come to believe that the story of Christ's life is the story of *giving* His Atonement. The story of Adam and Eve is the story of *receiving* His Atonement—and their story is our story.

Lehi told his children that if Adam and Eve had remained in the Garden of Eden, they would have known only innocence, and their spirits could not have grown and developed. "And they would have had no children; wherefore they would have remained in a state of innocence, having no joy for they knew no misery." (Oh, I get it—no children, no misery!) But there's more: "Having no joy for they knew no misery, doing no good, for they knew no sin. Adam fell that men might be [mortal], and men are [mortal] that they might have joy" (2 Nephi 2:23–25).

So the Fall was not a disaster, as traditional Christianity teaches. It was a grand victory that opened the door to the school we call mortality for all of us. When we walk through that door, we will learn from daily experience—some of it harsh experience—the difference between evil and good, misery and joy. Yet this earth is not our home. We are away at school. Knowing just that much gives us a unique understanding of who we are, who God is, and why we are here—and why we need the Atonement of Jesus Christ.

Let us look then at the overall *purpose* of the Atonement, which relates directly to our own purpose in coming to earth. That purpose-driven perspective explains why the Lord would at times take us by the hand and stretch us into a run.

We see the purpose of the Savior's grace and His Atonement in an entirely different light from the way other Christian churches see it. To understand that difference, let's take a brief look at what happened during the Great Apostasy. Since about the fifth century A.D., traditional Christianity has taught—incorrectly—that because of the Fall, we are born with an evil nature. As one well-known Christian creed states, Adam and Eve "by their disobedience . . . lost their purity and happiness, and . . . in consequence of their fall all men have become sinners, totally depraved."[3] This idea says that man's inborn evil nature is the primary cause of human sins; people sin mostly because they can't help it. In this incorrect view, only Christ's grace can overcome man's depraved nature, and overcoming that depravity is the main purpose of grace. And only God decides to whom He will extend grace; being evil, man couldn't choose it for himself. This view inaccurately sees grace as a one-way infusion, not as the two-way interaction it really is—as we will see shortly.

So we Latter-day Saints have a challenge when we use terms like "grace" and "enabling power," because those terms, long used by other churches, sometimes proceed from incorrect doctrinal assumptions. That means the vocabulary of traditional Christianity won't always work for us, and it may confuse us. On the other hand, the Restoration corrected those doctrines with clarity and light about who we are and why we're here. That clear light resonates in the heart of every child who sings "I Am a Child of God,"[4] with echoes of divine parents, of having wandered from another sphere, of an inward yearning for home in the arms of a Father who has not only a body, but also a *heart*—a heart like ours.[5] We came to the earth not as depraved sinners but trailing clouds of glory, carrying the seeds of a potentially divine nature within us.

Modern-day scripture teaches us that we are born neither evil nor good by nature; rather, we are born "whole" (Moses 6:54) or "innocent" (D&C 29:39). Then, in a mortal environment that is subject to death and sinful influences, we will taste some sin and bitterness—not because we are innately bad, but because we can't learn to prize the sweet without actually tasting the bitter (D&C 29:39; see also Moses 6:54–55). And because the effects of that bitterness may separate us from our Heavenly Father, we need Christ's Atonement to overcome whatever separates us from Him—such as the physical separation caused by death and the spiritual separation caused by our sins. That's what the word means: "at-one-ment," the act of reuniting what has been separated.

In addition, we need the Atonement to help us grow to become like our Father, because we cannot be "with Him" forever in His celestial realm until we are "like Him." In this sense, our immature capacity separates us from Him—that's why He sent us away to school. So at birth we are completely innocent, literally babes in the woods. Then, as we grow up, like our first parents we wrestle with afflictions—sin, misery, children—and that wrestling, paradoxically, teaches us what joy means. In that way, our children also help us discover the "joy" part. The Savior's Atonement makes that process possible by protecting us while we learn from practice what love really is or why wickedness cannot produce happiness (see Alma 41:10). Because of the Atonement, we can learn from our experience without being condemned by it. So the Atonement is not just a doctrine about erasing black marks—it is the core doctrine that allows human development. Thus its purpose is to facilitate our growth, ultimately helping us to develop the Christlike capacities we need to live with God.

Marie: With that purpose in mind, the Lord's Atonement plays a key role in two categories of essential blessings—(A) unconditional and (B) conditional blessings. Unconditional blessings are given freely to everyone. The conditional ones require our *participation*. There are three kinds of conditional blessings: *forgiving, strengthening*, and *perfecting* blessings. We will discuss each of these in that order, even though these blessings may at times overlap and interact with each other in our lives.

THE UNCONDITIONAL BLESSINGS OF MERCY AND GRACE

First are the unconditional blessings. The mercy and grace of our Father and His Son bless all mankind endlessly, no matter what we do. Their mercy is in some sense the source of all our blessings, starting with the Creation and our very presence on earth. For example, we heard one LDS woman express the absolute wonder she felt when she realized, "I live in a world where the Master of the Universe—the most powerful being in existence—just happens to know me and love me and to care about my eternal happiness. What did I ever do to deserve this? Aside from choosing to come to earth, not one thing."

The gift of the universal resurrection is an unconditional miracle of the Atonement for every person. Because He is risen, all will rise, and eventually all will kneel to acknowledge Him. The Savior's Atonement also paid for Adam's original sin. Other Christian churches believe, incorrectly, that each person still needs grace to be cleansed from Adam's stain, which caused man's sinful nature. But as the second Article of Faith states, men will not be punished for Adam's transgression.

THE CONDITIONAL BLESSINGS OF CHRIST'S ATONEMENT—FORGIVING

Bruce: The Atonement offers us three *conditional* blessings. We can be (A) forgiven, (B) strengthened, and (C) perfected—on the condition that we participate in those processes.

The eternal law of justice requires payment for our sins. Yet the eternal law of mercy allows Christ's suffering to pay justice for our sins—if we repent. As we repent, then, the grace allowed by the law of mercy assures our forgiveness. As we sometimes stumble along, we have a perpetual need to repent and learn from our mistakes. This repenting and learning are matched by His perpetual willingness to forgive. Our repentance does not repay Christ—in that sense, we don't "earn" His grace. However, as a condition of extending grace to us—and to help us grow—He asks us to undertake a process of change or rehabilitation that begins with forsaking our sins. In this context, grace is a two-way street, interacting with our repentance. Thus will He help us change, if and as we humbly do all within our power—even when our sins are of the habitual or addictive kind, and we therefore need to draw on the continuous power of Christ's Atonement.[6]

In terms that apply both to forgiveness and to the other conditional blessings of strengthening and perfecting, Nephi said, "It is by grace that we are saved, after all we can do" (2 Nephi 25:23). Some people think this means the Lord won't help us until we have totally exhausted ourselves. But the larger doctrinal context makes clear that "after" in this verse means "along with"—His grace is with us before, during, and after we do all we can.

Conditional Blessings—Strengthening

When we take our repentance seriously, we can have the conversion experience that Alma called the "mighty change of heart" (Alma 5:12–26; see also Mosiah 5), which may be either sudden or gradual. Thus begins the Atonement's interactive strengthening process, as our obedience interacts with His grace. When this happened to King Benjamin's people, they desired good rather than evil, and they made covenants to become "the children of Christ." They took upon themselves His name, for He had "spiritually begotten" them—they were born again, then began to follow Him (see Mosiah 5).

Their experience demonstrates the covenant *relationship* Christ creates with His disciples through the covenants of baptism and the sacrament. As our lives show that we are sincerely *willing* to take upon us *His name*, always to *remember* Him, and to *keep his commandments*, He keeps his covenant to us—we will *always* have His Spirit to be with us. Through this intimate, two-way relationship, the Savior offers us the ongoing assurance of forgiveness, strength, and the increasing light of becoming like Him. He continually nourishes our spirits, like a flowing spring. Then, as we comprehend more of His light, He offers us more because we are able to receive more. This *relationship* is then the foundation and the source of the strengthening and perfecting blessings that follow baptism.

Marie: Thus begins the process of becoming a saint—sanctified—through the Atonement of Christ, as we yield "to the enticings of the Holy Spirit," and put off "the natural man" and become "as a child, submissive, meek, humble, patient, full of love, willing to submit to all things" which the Lord sees "fit to inflict upon [us]" (Mosiah 3:19). If, however, we yield to the adversary more than we do to the Spirit, we will become as Adam and Eve's children, who "loved Satan more than God" (Moses 5:13). Alma said that pursuing this carnal, sensual, and devilish path will ultimately "subject you to the spirit of the devil" who will "*seal you his*" (Alma 34:35; emphasis added). Chilling! In contrast, if we remain on the covenant path, we have the priceless promise from King Benjamin that Christ will eventually "*seal you his*" (Mosiah 5:15; emphasis added). We'd like to illustrate this strengthening process with two stories.

Allison was married in the temple and had several children. As they became teenagers some of them fell into deep trouble, which created turbulence in her marriage. For years their family had tried to do everything "right"—scriptures, prayer, Church, temple, family home evening. Yet she said, "What I had imagined and hoped for was not happening and I [felt] completely stuck. My frustrated mind cried out to Him, 'I was faithful and you left me anyway. Where [is] my support when all the fiery darts [are] being thrown at us?'"

Then, after four years of such dark times, a scripture opened to her as if it were a personal message from the Lord. "But remember, God is merciful; therefore, repent and thou art still chosen, and art again called to the work" (D&C 3:10). In response, Allison said, "Hope began to again peek through my doubts. That small particle of hope in me stretched heavenward. Was God really merciful? Could I repent, [let] go of my doubting, and again be worthy of his support? I was willing to try."

She worked as hard as she knew how to keep her spiritual commitments and to reach out to her family members in healing ways. The healing didn't happen overnight, but over years it came in small and simple ways. " Our burden," she said, " is being lifted—one scripture at a time, in a quiet prompting in the temple, as Primary children sing their testimonies, and through the kind words of friends who sometimes have no idea [about] the past heartache."

After seven years of exerting herself and continuing to interact with the Lord, Allison describes how her children began to return. "[My daughter] came into my room, sat on the bed, and for nearly two hours we talked, laughed, and cried. I had dreamed of moments like this. [From my son], I [now] receive my daily hug, which is expected and initiated by him. To see the light of Christ again reflected in him brings such marvelous, peaceful joy that it far outweighs the sorrow of his past choices." Allison said that she simply trusted Jesus. He carried her when she felt she could no longer move forward. She supplied her desire and her work, and He supplied His strength.

Bruce: Another friend we'll call Tyler had long been an active Church member, but he had been so abused during his early years that he couldn't believe the Savior's strengthening promises would apply to anyone as broken as he felt. As he began learning that those promises were anchored in the deep roots of the Atonement, he sensed that the promises were real, but he still thought they were for other people. He was afraid to reach for those blessings because he thought they would be tainted by his touch. Gradually he found that Christ would strengthen him to fuel the process of developing his spirit. Then came the key insight that, with the Savior's help, the pain he had suffered in his life could fill him with empathy and compassion that would help him be of greater service to the Lord and His other children in need. He has since become an inspiring teacher and counselor, helping others find what he found—that the Savior could help him grow his weaknesses into strengths.

The experiences of Allison and Tyler echo a pattern in many scriptural stories about how the Lord strengthens His people *in* their afflictions. He does this because of His covenant relationship with them. When the children of Israel were in Egypt, "God heard their groaning, and [He] remembered his covenant with Abraham, with Isaac, and with Jacob." And God said, "I have seen the affliction of *my* people. I know their sorrows" (Exodus 2:4–7). Then this to Moses after crossing the Red

Sea: "Ye have seen what I did to the Egyptians [now that's an understatement!]—and how I bare you on eagles' wings, and *brought you to myself*." To myself. At one. "Therefore, if ye will obey my voice and keep my covenant, ye shall be unto me an holy nation" (Exodus 19:4–6).

The same pattern and language appear in the Lord's interaction with Alma's people when Amulon held them captive. "I, the Lord God, do visit my people in their afflictions." Note that He says "my" people—not "the" people—because of His covenant relationship with them. "Lift up your heads and be of good comfort, for I know of the covenant which ye have made unto me" (Mosiah 24:13). He keeps His covenant to strengthen us as we try diligently to keep our promises to Him.

However, He may not always deliver us out of bondage—at least not immediately—even if we are faithful. But He will strengthen us until our burdens feel lighter, often using the burdens to bless and teach us. Perhaps we can't exactly say that He "atoned for" our burdens beyond death and sin, and it may not be logically precise to say that "the Atonement" delivered the people of Moses or Alma—or Allison or Tyler. But His Atonement is what qualifies Christ to enter into a personal, covenant relationship with His faithful followers, then Christ Himself strengthens them through that Atonement-based relationship. In His words, "Fear not, for I have *redeemed* thee, and thou art *mine*" (Isaiah 43:1; emphasis added). "I will strengthen thee; yea, I will help thee" (Isaiah 41:10).

The place of covenants in these stories shows that Christ extends His strengthening power on certain conditions. We needn't be perfect, but we must strive wholeheartedly, not halfheartedly. As Jacob put it, "Come [to Him] with full purpose of heart, and *cleave* unto God as he *cleaveth* unto you" (Jacob 6:5; emphasis added). This doctrine of conditional grace differs from the traditional Protestant idea that grace is entirely a free gift. But this pattern of two-way, interactive covenants is the Lord's way of encouraging us to do what only we can do—exert ourselves enough to participate meaningfully in the growth process. *Without our exertion, even God can't make us grow, no matter how much grace He extends.* Think of the nearly frozen Agnes Caldwell. That severe mercy was unbelievably hard for her—but it pulled her into action that only she could exert, and it saved her life.

Latter-day scriptures and hymns use the term "grace" in a rich variety of strengthening ways—nearly all of them conditioned on our taking some clear, energetic action. Some samples: "Teach ye diligently, and my grace shall attend you" (D&C 88:78). Alma's "priests were not to depend upon the people for their support; but for their labor they were to receive the grace of God" (Mosiah 18:26). To Moroni, "My grace is sufficient for all men that humble themselves before me; then will I make weak things become strong unto them" (Ether 12:27). "Though hard to you this journey may appear, / Grace shall be as your day."[7] That promise from "Come, Come, Ye Saints" is echoed in another favorite hymn, "As thy days may demand, so thy succor shall be."[8] In the midst of our journeys, He will succor and strengthen us as fully as our hardest days may require.

Marie: For some of us, "as thy days may demand" can mean unspeakable grief and pain from tragedies beyond our control. A man we know, for example, unaware that his child was behind his car, ran over and killed his own two-year-old in the family driveway. This was the most devastating experience of this faithful man's life. He blamed himself and felt unworthy before God and with his family. But his mistake was not his fault and it wasn't a sin. It was an accident. How does the Atonement help this man? Or is the question better stated, how does Christ help him, or any of us, in the deepest anguish of our lives?

A woman we met asked her version of the same question. She had been severely abused as a little girl. She felt betrayed, abandoned, and alone—tormented, psychologically and spiritually. "For years," she said, "I have felt unclean and shut out from God's presence. But I didn't sin; I was sinned against. Will the Atonement help me?" We can answer her sincere question with a resounding yes! Because of His Atonement, Christ *will* help her—and you, and us. Help from that source is His ultimate expression of compassion toward each of us whatever our circumstances may be.[9]

Alma tells us that Christ, apparently as part of His Atonement, took upon Himself the "pains" and "infirmities" of "His people" (Alma 7:11–12). That means, at the very least, that we do not suffer alone. And if we let Him, He will also lift the burden of our cross *with* us—His hands beneath ours, His shoulders helping us bear the brunt of the load.

But beyond that, did Alma mean that the Savior somehow "paid" justice for our infirmities the same way He paid for our sins? Or, more broadly, did Alma mean that Christ *unconditionally* took upon Himself all human misery, thus relieving mankind of all unfairness, injustice, and all other forms of suffering?

We don't believe so, because these interpretations would undermine both the Atonement's reach and its purpose. For one thing, He took upon Himself the infirmities of "His people," not "the people"—Alma is talking only about how Christ strengthens His covenant children. Yet even for them, He does not always eliminate the burden altogether, because doing so would not further the Atonement's purpose of helping His children grow and mature to become "purified even as He is pure" (Moroni 7:48).

To snatch us completely out of life's unfairness and injustices—out of our "effectual struggles," to use King Limhi's phrase (Mosiah 7:18)—would negate the very reason we came to earth, which is to master the traits of godliness even while under intense pressure. His grace allows us to be healed from and sanctified by that pressure without being crushed by it.

Christ earned the right to extend His grace by "suffering pains and afflictions and temptations of every kind." And He did so "that He may know according to the flesh how to succor his people" (Alma 7:11–12). *Succor* means to help, aid, or relieve in time of need or distress. So His succoring can bless us with support, healing, and strength.

However, we could miss what this understanding of succoring and grace *offers* us if we don't also grasp what it *asks* of us, and why. It's not that God will simply remove the hard things if we decode the hidden messages or if we just push the right button, such as when the computer screen says, "click here to enable." He asks us to give all we have to the refining process of grace—not to appease *Him*, but rather to engage *us*. There's Agnes again.

Being engaged in the crucible of refinement can, in our hardest times, make us feel like we are walking through hell. And perhaps we literally are! But if we stick with Christ, He will show us the way *through*. He can do this because He walked through hell himself without getting lost in it.

One of the survivors who had waded through the hellish handcart tragedy in Wyoming said, "We became acquainted with him in our extremities. . . . The price we paid to become acquainted with God was a privilege to pay."[10] When we also dig deeply enough to find Him and know Him in such places, fears can become faith and trust, anger melts into meekness, anguish becomes empathy. Line upon line, grace for grace, He causes—if *we* will—the affliction to be consecrated for our gain (see 2 Nephi 2:2).

How does He consecrate our afflictions for our gain? It has something to do with what Elder Neal A. Maxwell called Christ's "earned empathy,"[11] derived from submitting Himself to all of life's bitterness, descending "below all things" (D&C 88:6), so He could know from His own flesh-and-bones experience how to succor His people.

Perhaps His divine empathy was also partly a gift from His Father in answer to His prayer for His disciples. "Father, I pray . . . for . . . those . . . that . . . believe in me, that I may be in them as thou art in me, that we may be one" (3 Nephi 19:23).[12] It is as if He were saying, "Let me feel *with* them, Father, the way Thou dost feel *with* me. Let me feel their pain the way Thou, Father, dost feel mine."

By being *in* us, He can feel with us so completely, so perfectly, as to be "at one" with us in our afflictions. And so He whispers to strengthen us in our darkest nights of the Refiner's fire:

> *Fear not, I am with thee; oh, be not dismayed.*
> *For I am thy God and will still give thee aid.*
> *I'll strengthen thee, help thee, and cause thee to stand,*
> *Upheld by my righteous, omnipotent hand.*
>
> . . . .
>
> *When through fiery trials thy pathway shall lie,*
> *My grace, all sufficient, shall be thy supply.*
> *The flame will not hurt thee; I only design*
> *Thy dross to consume and thy gold to refine.*[13]

Conditional Blessings—Perfecting

Bruce: Now we are ready to consider how the Lord's *perfecting* blessings can endow us with divine qualities through a process of becoming holy, like Christ. After He has helped to cleanse us from our earthly stains and has strengthened us through our tribulations to the greatest degree possible, we can become "invested, over a lifetime, with holiness from God."[14]

Of this perfecting process, Moroni wrote, "*If* ye shall deny yourselves of all ungodliness, and love God with all your might, mind, and strength, *then* is his grace sufficient for you, that by his grace ye may be perfect in Christ" (Moroni 10:32). The "if-then" connection here says the Lord's perfecting grace is also conditional—*if* we forsake ungodliness and love Him, *then* He will endow us with holiness.

Here is an image that depicts this process. An early convert from Australia wrote that her past life was a "wilderness of weeds," but after she found the gospel, "flowers [began springing] up [everywhere]."[15] The Savior's Atonement helps us with both the weeds and with the flowers. Through the interactive miracles of repentance, forgiveness, and grace, Christ works with us to remove our sinful weeds and any other obstacles between ourselves and God. Then He can plant and help us nourish the seeds of divine qualities, like meekness, charity, and holiness. The Lord's grace does help these flowers grow. But even then, there may still be a few weeds in our flowers, and a few flowers in our weeds—it's an organic process.

Marie: As an example of His helping us to become holy, we can look at the gift of charity, the saintly capacity to love others as Christ does. Moroni explained, "Pray unto the Father with all the energy of heart, that ye may be filled with this love, which he hath *bestowed* upon *all who are true followers of his Son, Jesus Christ,* that when he shall appear we shall be like him" (Moroni 7:48; emphasis added). Is charity, then, a gift of grace? Yes, it is "bestowed"—it comes from outside us. But on what condition, since charity is also a conditional blessing? Those who receive charity are they who have become "true followers" of Jesus. The participation required of us at this higher level is more demanding.

Bruce: So in looking at "all we can do" to enjoy the perfecting blessings, the Lord asks us more about the spirit of the law, less about the letter of the law; more about our core internal attitudes, less about a mechanical list of do's and don'ts; more about consecration and sacrifice, less about our activity percentages. Scriptures that describe the perfecting attributes say they are given to those who are "submissive, meek, humble, patient, [and] full of love" (Mosiah 3:19); or who are "meek and lowly in heart" (Alma

37:34); or whose lives reflect a "peaceable walk with the children of men" (Moroni 7:4); or those who yield "their hearts unto God" (Helaman 3:35). Moroni asked that we "love God with all *your* might" (Moroni 10:32; emphasis added). We must love Him as fully as our limited personal capacity allows, but that doesn't mean we must reach some unreachable level of perfection by ourselves—for finally His grace is sufficient to perfect us in Him.

Marie: As we give everything we have to the Lord and He gives us everything He has, together we replace our noxious weeds with abundant flowers. There is a passage in Moroni 8 that describes the complete process we've discussed today better than any scripture we know—from forgiveness through spiritual strength to the perfections of charity and sanctification: "And the first fruits of repentance is baptism; and baptism cometh by faith unto the fulfilling the commandments; and the fulfilling the commandments bringeth remission of sins; and the remission of sins bringeth meekness and lowliness of heart; and because of meekness and lowliness of heart cometh the visitation of the Holy Ghost, which comforter filleth with hope and perfect love, which love [charity] endureth by diligence unto prayer, until the end shall come, when all the saints [the sanctified] shall dwell with God" (Moroni 8:25–26).

To illustrate how charity can come, we remember Elder Neal A. Maxwell. The quest of his life became his desire to be a true disciple of Jesus Christ. For years he thought about discipleship, he prayed about it, talked and wrote about it. In his later years, he began to see in the lives of others that adversity could be sanctifying. He saw three sources of suffering—our own mistakes, life's natural adversities, and, at times, afflictions the Lord might "inflict" on us to teach us. Of the latter category Elder Maxwell wrote, "The very act of choosing to be a disciple . . . can bring to us a certain special suffering. . . . [It is a] dimension that comes with deep discipleship. [Thus] all who will can come to know [what Paul called] 'the fellowship of his sufferings' (Philippians 3:10)."[16] He also wrote, "If we are serious about our discipleship, Jesus will eventually request each of us to do those very things which are the most difficult for us to do."[17]

After years of teaching others about these principles, at age seventy Elder Maxwell was stricken with leukemia in 1996. As he worked to absorb the shock of that news, he said to those who knew the link he saw between discipleship and suffering, "I should have seen it coming." This was what he came to call the "wintry doctrine"[18]—the idea that we can't internalize real consecration without our own "clinical experiences."[19]

During the following eight years until his death in 2004, Elder Maxwell's own empathy toward other people increased. He discovered for himself what he had tried to teach others: The Savior is able to succor us in our afflictions because he has drunk the cup of affliction himself. "Earned empathy," he called it. And those who knew him during his own season of the wintry doctrine saw a sanctifying process at work in his life, in his teaching, in his interaction with others, and in his visits to the homes of fellow sufferers. At one point, he sensed the Lord answering his question about why. "I have given you leukemia so that you might teach the people with more authenticity." No wonder Neal Maxwell would feel drawn to a phrase like "severe mercy."

Bruce: We believe he was receiving the gift of charity, as he discovered the connection between charity and affliction. Those who seek to be Christ's true followers may need to emulate His sacrificial experience, not only through physical pain but in other ways, at least enough to taste His empathy and His charity. For only then are we like Him enough to feel His love for others *the way He feels it*—to love "*as I have loved you*" (John 13:34; emphasis added). It may well be that charity and suffering are but two sides of the same coin. Little wonder, then, that Christ will not take away all of our suffering. After all, He said, "those who will not endure chastening *cannot* be sanctified" (D&C 101:5; emphasis added). May we not be surprised, and may we not shrink, when we discover, paradoxically, how dear a price we may need to pay to receive charity—which is, finally, a gift of grace.

I'd like now to offer a final thought before Marie concludes for both of us. I have the personal sense that those who receive the full gift of charity will feel Christ's love not only for others, they will also feel His love for *them* in a way that assures them beyond any question that—despite their remaining weaknesses—their sacrifices and their lives are finally and fully acceptable to Him. I foresee that day as the culminating moment of Christ's Atonement for us, when we shall be "like him, for we shall see him as he is," and we will be "purified even as he is pure" (Moroni 7:48). Perhaps that was Lehi's experience, when he felt himself "encircled about eternally in the arms of his [Redeemer's] love" (2 Nephi

1:15). The Lord has promised that those whose "hearts are honest and are broken, and their spirits contrite, and are willing to observe their covenants by sacrifice are *accepted* of me" (D&C 97:8–9; emphasis added). Acceptance—with Him, like Him.

We knew a very faithful older woman in Brisbane, Australia, who was present on a night in 1997 when President Gordon B. Hinckley talked to several thousand Australian Saints in a large stadium. As he concluded, he testified of the Lord's love for them, and he expressed his confidence in them in a way that somehow invited an especially calm spirit to descend. The next day, this sister said to us, "I have never believed that my life could really be acceptable to the Lord. But as President Hinckley spoke to our hearts, I felt for the first time that, despite all of my frailties, the Lord could *accept* me. I was astounded."

Our friend Donna grew up desiring to marry and raise a large family. But that blessing never came. Instead, she spent her adult years serving the people in her ward with unmeasured compassion and counseling disturbed children in a large school district. She had crippling arthritis and many long, blue days. Yet she always lifted and was lifted by her friends and family. Once, when teaching about Lehi's dream, she said with gentle humor, "I'd put myself in that picture on the strait and narrow path, still holding on to the iron rod, but collapsed from fatigue right on the path." In an inspired blessing given just before her death, Donna's home teacher said the Lord had accepted her. Donna cried. No word could have meant more to her.

These two women discovered that the Lord not only forgives us and eases our burdens, but ultimately He will also accept and perfect the honest in heart who observe every sacrifice with a contrite spirit—even when their lives fall short of flawless perfection. The Atonement of Jesus Christ makes this acceptance both real and possible—and He stretches forth His accepting hands unto us "all the day long" (Jacob 6:4). I testify that each of us can one day experience that ultimate acceptance, if we really want it—so long as we don't want anything else more.

Marie: The heart of Agnes Caldwell's rescue lies in the moment her hand met the hand of the wagon master in that lifesaving clasp. So it is between each of us and Christ. The full blessings of His Atonement cannot be unveiled in us until our hand reaches for, and hangs onto, His. In all of His power, He can't force us to take His hand, but He does invite and beckon us to come to Him.

And He is waiting to meet us in His holy house. The temple's saving, healing, and perfecting powers come from the Atonement of Christ, but we can receive them only if we get ourselves there—like Agnes running for the wagon.

For the last three years we have spent cherished time in the St. George Utah Temple looking into the faces of those who have taken hold of and are hanging on to the Lord's hand. His presence in their lives is evident in their faces. A mom with an infuriating teenage daughter at home told me how sacrificing to be in the temple more often, and living what she learned and felt there, was helping. "Not a lot of changes yet with my daughter," she said. "But I am becoming a different person, a better person."

In light of section 84, we can see that this young mother—and any sacrificing disciple like her—is absorbing the power of the higher priesthood and higher ordinances. Without these, the mysteries of godliness—or the power to become like Him—*cannot* be manifest in the flesh. If you want this power in your mortal body—inscribed in the "fleshy tables of [your] heart" (2 Corinthians 3:3)—put yourself in the temple. Wherever we may be, could we take the shoes off our hearts when we think and speak of Him and His Atonement, just as we do when we enter the temple?

As I was walking up to the temple one day, I came upon a grandmotherly woman—one of our temple workers—bending over, tending to the flowers near the front door. She looked up. Her aging face was alive with light, the face of a lifetime of temple worship and temple living. Her countenance enveloped me in the aura of the temple and filled me with the desire to have that same happy holiness in me. We will find Him in the temple. He is the template of the temple. He is making a temple of us.

"He marked the path and led the way, / And every point defines / To light and life and endless day, / Where God's full presence shines."[20]

NOTES

1. This phrase apparently originated with C. S. Lewis. See Sheldon Vanauken, *A Severe Mercy* (New York: Harper & Row, 1977), 20.

2. Susan Arrington Madsen, *I Walked to Zion: True Stories of Young Pioneers on the Mormon Trail* (Salt Lake City: Deseret Book, 1994), 57–59.
3. Salvation Army, Doctrine 5; available at http://www.salvationarmy.org.za/index.php/our-faith/doctrines-of-the-salvation-army; accessed 2 July 2014.
4. Naomi W. Randall, "I Am a Child of God," *Hymns of The Church of Jesus Christ of Latter-day Saints* (Salt Lake City: The Church of Jesus Christ of Latter-day Saints, 1985), no. 301.
5. We first heard this phrase from Terryl Givens.
6. See Craig Cardon, "The Savior Wants to Forgive," *Ensign*, May 2013, 15–18; see also Brad Wilcox, *The Continuous Atonement* (Salt Lake City: Deseret Book, 2011).
7. William Clayton, "Come, Come, Ye Saints," *Hymns*, no. 30.
8. Attributed to Robert Keen, "How Firm a Foundation," *Hymns*, no. 85.
9. For a fuller discussion about healing from abuse inflicted on us by others, see "Forgiveness and Christ Figures" in Bruce C. Hafen, *The Broken Heart: Applying the Atonement to Life's Experiences, Expanded Edition* (Salt Lake City: Deseret Book, 2008), 239–49.
10. Quoted in David O. McKay, "Pioneer Women," *Relief Society Magazine*, vol. 35, no. 1 (January 1948):8
11. See, for example, Neal A. Maxwell, "'From Whom All Blessings Flow,'" *Ensign*, May 1997, 11–12.
12. See also D&C 50:40–44: "I am in the Father and the Father in me; and inasmuch as ye have received me, ye are in me and I in you."
13. "How Firm a Foundation," *Hymns*, no. 85.
14. Elouise M. Bell, "Holiness," in *Encyclopedia of Mormonism* (New York: Macmillan, 1992), 648–49.
15. Martha Maria Humphreys, quoted in Marjorie Newton, *Southern Cross Saints: The Mormons in Australia* (Laie, HI: Institute for Polynesian Studies, Brigham Young University–Hawaii, 1991), 227.
16. Maxwell, *All These Things Shall Give Thee Experience* (Salt Lake City: Deseret Book, 1979), 32, 34, 36.
17. Maxwell, *A Time to Choose* (Salt Lake City: Deseret Book, 1972), 46.
18. Maxwell, "'I Will Arise and Go to My Father,'" *Ensign*, September 1993, 67.
19. Maxwell, "The Pathway of Discipleship," Brigham Young University fireside, 4 January 1998; available at http://speeches.byu.edu/?act=viewitem&id=619; accessed 2 July 2014.
20. Eliza R. Snow, "How Great the Wisdom and the Love," *Hymns*, no. 195.

Thin Places

Virginia H. Pearce

I will never forget my first experience in an impoverished country. It was a Church assignment and there were many things that were new to me. As we drove from the airport to our lodgings, we passed huge heaps of smoking garbage, glimpsing people who were scavenging in the refuse for things to sell. We saw families in tents by the side of the road and children begging from cars whenever traffic slowed. I watched, smelled, listened, trying to make sense of it all. But the memory that is etched in my heart more than any other from that visit was of an afternoon on a small island. We climbed out of the ferry and walked down a wide dusty road. Mangy dogs, pigs, and beautiful children followed us until we came to our destination. Over wooden planks and ducking our heads, we entered the home of a family. Two small rooms. The walls were louvered slats, through which the children from the village watched us curiously. Limited by language, we couldn't communicate verbally. The family sang Primary songs. We joined in. We prayed together, hugged, and parted. I didn't quite know what to say as we left the island. I felt I should express

---

Virginia Hinckley Pearce is the author of the bestselling book A Heart Like His: Making Space for God's Love in Your Life, *and has edited and coauthored several additional books, including* Glimpses into the Life and Heart of Marjorie Pay Hinckley. *She has served as a counselor in the Young Women general presidency and on the Primary general board of The Church of Jesus Christ of Latter-day Saints. She and her husband, the late James R. Pearce, have six children and twenty-seven grandchildren.*

horror and sadness over the distressing circumstances in which these people lived. But, I couldn't—in fact, I felt a bit envious. I didn't really understand then, but I think I do now.

Sister Rosemary Wixom, general Primary president, spoke at a CES fireside at Utah State University of very different circumstances, but in a way that gave words to the feelings I had on that long-ago day in the Philippines. Sister Wixom recounted one of *her* memories: "It was a beautiful fall day as we loaded up the family car with all of our belongings. You see, I was off to college with my twin sister, and our mother was going to drive us and drop us off in Logan [Utah]. . . . We were excited. We had every piece of clothing and every shoe we owned, plus food to stock our cupboards, packed into that car. We could barely see out the windows. As we drove into this valley, I had butterflies in my stomach. I could hardly wait for the adventure ahead.

"On campus one could feel the excitement in the air as students were unloading their cars and moving their belongings into their dorms and apartments. . . .

"When the car was empty, we stood on the sidewalk . . . , holding the last few items from the backseat. There we were, with jars of bottled peaches in our arms as we waved good-bye to our mother. Then, as she drove away, reality hit. We turned to each other, and with tears running down our cheeks, we said: 'What have we done? What were we thinking? How could something we once thought to be so adventurous now seem so frightening and intimidating?' Little did I know that in the days and years ahead on this campus, I would make decisions that would define the rest of my life. It was here that I discovered I had my own beliefs, and I was faced with defending my faith. I made lifelong friends. My prayers became more sincere. My testimony began to grow. I learned it was a personal choice to stand up for my standards and stretch myself academically and spiritually.

". . . No wonder this Cache Valley, this university, this campus is so beautiful to me. For it was here that I would begin to come to know myself, and in the process of coming to know myself, I would begin to come to know the Savior."[1]

Thinking back to that little home on a dusty island, it is no wonder that it seemed so beautiful to me. Within those flimsy walls that family had come to know God. And for those few minutes we spent with them, we all shared heavenly light.

It is individual and collective experiences between God and His children that unite us and turn ordinary places into sacred places.

That is exactly what happened to those who listened to Alma at the Waters of Mormon. Fleeing from King Noah, Alma hid during the day in a thicket of trees in the borders of the land. Many who believed his words came to be taught. Gathering in tents with their families "in a place which was called Mormon" (Mosiah 18:4), they listened eagerly as Alma taught the gospel of Jesus Christ. And then, going into the waters of Mormon, they covenanted with God to serve him and keep his commandments. Baptizing Helam, the first of many, Alma "cried, saying: O Lord, pour out thy Spirit upon thy servant, that he may do this work with holiness of heart" (Mosiah 18:12).

"And now it came to pass that all this was done in Mormon, yea, by the waters of Mormon, . . . the forest of Mormon, how beautiful are they to the eyes of them who there came to the knowledge of their Redeemer; yea, and how blessed are they, for they shall sing to his praise forever" (Mosiah 18:30).

The Waters of Mormon was a place made beautiful and sacred through holy experiences.

Elder Marlin K. Jensen taught: "There are places on this earth that have been made sacred by what happened there. According to the Old Testament, one of these places is Sinai, Horeb, or 'the mountain of God' (Exodus 3:1; see also Exodus 3:12; 34:2), where the Lord appeared to Moses in the burning bush. As Moses approached the bush, the Lord said to him, 'Draw not nigh hither: put off thy shoes from off thy feet, for the place whereon thou standest is holy ground (Exodus 3:5).'"[2]

The Garden of Gethsemane; the shores of Galilee; the Sacred Grove; the John Johnson home in Hyrum, Ohio; the upper floor of the Red Brick Store in Nauvoo— because of what happened between God and men and women in these places, they are holy.

There is a Celtic expression, "thin places." A thin place is where the veil that separates heaven and earth is nearly transparent. It is a place where we experience a deep sense of God's presence in our everyday world. A thin place is where, for a moment, the spiritual world and the natural world intersect.

> *"Thin places," the Celts call this space,*
> *Both seen and unseen,*
> *Where the door between this world*
> *And the next is cracked open for a moment*
> *And the light is not all on the other side.*
> *God shaped space. Holy.*[3]

Certainly temples are "thin places." Think about that. Above the entrance to each temple the words "Holiness to the Lord" are written. We call a temple the House of the Lord. Certainly, it is God-shaped space.

I have had the unearned privilege of walking through newly finished temples the evening before dedicatory services as our leaders inspected the workmanship of the building itself—the finishings and furnishings, the paintings, the grounds, crafted and installed as a form of worship. After many months, even years, of skilled work, it all comes together on the day of dedication—a space that is peaceful, clean, orderly, and beautiful. Looking at the workmanship and materials, President Hinckley would usually say, "Nothing is too good for the Lord."

Temples are refuges in a world full of noise, fear, and sleaze. We dress appropriately, speak quietly, and enter with hearts turned toward our Creator and Redeemer. We bring our perplexities, our sorrows, our yearnings, and our joy into those sacred buildings. We come as our true selves, unadorned by position or distinctive dress. We come knowing that God accepts us in our imperfections and knows how much we desire—in spite of our weakness—to be like Him. We receive comfort, revelation, and love. We solemnly and gratefully accept the ordinances—within which lie the power of godliness. After all, it is in temples that we are endowed with His greatest gift—His unfathomable power. Herein lies the sacredness of temples.

But let me remind you of another building—one so different in construction, appointments, and purpose. A small, rough-hewn, impregnable prison in Clay County, Missouri. We know it as Liberty Jail. Joseph Smith and five other leaders were incarcerated there during the winter of 1838 through 1839—the coldest winter on record in the state of Missouri.

It was a grim place, with only one small heavy door on the main floor opening to the outside world. The dungeon on the lower floor was barely six feet high—floor to ceiling—making it impossible for Joseph to stand straight. Bare rough stones formed the floor, covered with a bit of loose, dirty straw. I quote from Elder Jeffrey R. Holland, as he describes that winter:

"The food given to the prisoners was coarse and sometimes contaminated, so filthy that one of them said they "could not eat it until [they] were driven to it by hunger." On as many as four occasions poison was administered to them in their food, making them so violently ill that for days they alternated between vomiting and a kind of delirium, not really caring whether they lived or died.

"In the Prophet Joseph's letters, he spoke of the jail being a 'hell, surrounded with demons . . . where we are compelled to hear nothing but blasphemous oaths, and witness a scene of blasphemy, and drunkenness and hypocrisy, and debaucheries of every description.' 'We have . . . not blankets sufficient to keep us warm; and when we have a fire, we are obliged to have almost a constant smoke.' 'Our souls have been bowed down' and 'my nerve trembles from long confinement,' Joseph wrote. 'Pen, or tongue, or angels,' could not adequately describe 'the malice of hell' that he suffered there."[4]

With all of that, B. H. Roberts referred to Liberty Jail as a "prison-temple."[5] What could he have meant? Certainly, the purposes of a prison are the exact antithesis of the purposes of a temple—one is to incarcerate, hold captive, punish. The other is to set free, to give power, to glorify.

And yet, as I think of those Celtic "thin places," I say, oh yes! Liberty Jail was a place where Joseph's very suffering and despondency made him ready to receive God. Desperately, he begged for help. The answer came. "My son, peace be unto thy soul" (D&C 121:7). "God shall give unto you knowledge by his Holy Spirit, yea, by the unspeakable gift of the Holy Ghost. . . . Nothing shall be withheld. . . . All thrones and dominions, principalities and powers, shall be revealed and set forth upon all who have endured valiantly for the gospel of Jesus Christ" (D&C 121:26, 28–29). Joseph was told that "the doctrine of the priesthood shall distill upon thy soul as the dews from heaven. The Holy Ghost shall be thy constant companion, and thy scepter an unchanging scepter of righteousness and truth; and thy dominion shall be an everlasting dominion, and without compulsory means it shall flow unto thee forever and ever" (D&C 121:45–46). Liberty Jail had become sacred space, a thin place,

> *Where the door between this world*
> *And the next was cracked open for a moment*
> *And the light was not all on the other side.*[6]

Joseph left that prison temple forever changed with increased moral strength and a greater capacity to influence for good.

A mother hummingbird builds a new home. She must create a place of physical safety and warmth, where she can give birth to, care for and then from which she will launch her wee ones into the world.

Finding bits of fluff, soft plant matter, twigs, straw, leaves—she weaves, pokes, and tamps them into shape. Adding spider webs to give the nest strength and flexibility, she works patiently, diligently. Back and forth, hither and yon, each nest is its own individual creation, made up of unique materials but perfectly, perfectly serviceable. This little cup will securely hold her tiny eggs as she seals the opening with her own warmth—her life force. Is this pure instinct? I think so.

Like our busy little friend, we mothers and fathers prepare for our babies. We instinctively want a home that can physically lock out intruders. One where we can be warm when winter storms rage. One with a roof to shelter us from scorching sun.

But we, you and I, are more purposeful than a hummingbird. You see, we desire more than physical safety. We add to basic instinct a God-given desire for the spiritual safety of our loved ones. We want a place where we can teach them, watch them grow in confidence and skill. We want them to know how to build loving and satisfying relationships. We want them to be prepared to contribute to the world, to be strong in the face of evil and adversity, to make and keep sacred covenants and ultimately be prepared to go back to their eternal home. And we know that as we teach them, we will also learn and grow.

Yes, we want our homes to be "thin places" where we, and all those who enter can experience God.

We are taught that "only the home can compare with the temple in sacredness."[7]

What does that look like? Surely it doesn't mean a building with the finest appointments and workmanship. A place of complete order where people speak only in hushed tones, with light colored carpet and occasionally some soft organ music?

Wouldn't that be lovely! But in truth, our homes often resemble busy airports with people constantly coming and going. There seems to be an abundance of "stuff" that grows on every surface and spills onto floors. In these home-temples, we laugh and cry together, experience anger and frustration as well as deep and spoken love. In our homes we sustain hurt and pain, make mistakes, learn, repent, forgive, change. Home is a refuge, but it is also a laboratory, a classroom. But in all this confusion we sense something grand. Isn't growing toward Godhood holy work? No wonder our homes are second only to temples in their sacredness.

Sadly enough, we have all been in homes that are dark, depressing, and chaotic. I'm not talking about the chaos of clutter. I am talking about the chaos and darkness that come from spiritual darkness—places large and small where the Spirit of the Lord has not been invited.

Think about your home. Is it a place where every individual is safe to be himself—to cry, to be vulnerable and tired? Is it a place where there is an underlying atmosphere of love, making it easier to grow and learn and repent and contribute? Most of all, is it a place where you can be personally involved with God—where angels minister? Is it a thin place?

If these are your desires, you may want to consider dedicating your home or your apartment if you have not done so. It is a sweet thing to dedicate a home—to give voice to our commitment to do all we can create a space where the Spirit of the Lord can dwell. If you have not dedicated your home and would like to do so, you may find informative help in *Handbook 2*, section 20.11.[8]

You may live in a home where a spouse or children or other occupants don't share your desire that it be a sacred place. What does that mean for you? Think back again to Liberty Jail. Nothing and no one can prevent us, as individual women, from having experiences with God. We can pray at any time in any environment. We can feast on the scriptures. He can fill us with His love and power anywhere, anytime. Perhaps there may even be a particular place—a corner of a bedroom or a closet—where you go when you are filled with a desire to worship and supplicate your Father in Heaven—a space and place that is yours alone.

Teaching about the relationship between temples and homes, Elder John A. Widstoe wrote, "Spiritual power is generated within temple walls, and sent out to bless the world. Light from the house of the Lord illumines every home within the Church fitted for its reception by participation in temple privileges. Every home penetrated by the temple spirit enlightens, cheers, and comforts every member of the household. The peace we covet is found in such homes."[9] President Marion G. Romney said, "The power emanating from temples is far greater than we realize."[10]

So, if women are, by nature, a moral force for good in the world, think of that innate moral power when it is added upon through the temple endowment of power.

If we are faithful to the covenants we make with God in His holy house, we literally bring His priesthood power into our environments—most particularly our homes. Joseph Smith, speaking to women, said, "if you live up to your privilege, the angels cannot be restrain'd from being your associates."[11] Angels for associates? Why would any of us fail to claim that privilege?

A little over four years ago, I found myself returning home from the funeral of my husband. My children and friends who had gathered and been ever-present during the days since his death had left reluctantly—"Do you want one of us to stay? It wouldn't be a problem. . . . Just for the night?"

"No," I said. "I'm okay." And so they left.

The door closed and I turned around, thinking of my new life ahead. I would be alone in this space that I had always shared with others. It was indeed quiet. Very quiet. And a wall of loneliness almost flattened me. But surprisingly, and at the same time, it felt oh-so-good. Rather than just a lonely empty house, I had been blessed with space that was holy, where the door between this world and the next had cracked open many, many times. I thought, with gratitude, of the blessings of the covenants I had made—the companionship of the Holy Ghost and temple covenants that had given me access to God's priesthood power. Power that I now felt filling every corner.

During the next few weeks, I found it difficult to be away from my home for more than a few hours at a time. I'm sure some of that was due to the fatigue of grieving, but I believe that it was, in part, a new and deep recognition of the sacredness of home. Finding the notes I had written when my husband dedicated our home decades earlier, I was reminded that he had invited the Lord to watch over and protect and bless our home. And He had done so—and continues to do so.

Light is light. It doesn't come with the price of the neighborhood or the square footage of the house. And God's light doesn't stay in those thin places—it flows into our souls. We assimilate it and take it with us. Yes, the place and space is sacred, but more sacred are we—the vessels who carry his power.

A thirteen-year-old boy said to his mother: "I love you, Mom! When I'm with you it's like I'm inside a bubble—it's just so safe and happy." Getting out of the car on another morning, he said, "Here I go, leaving your bubble." His mother said, "Oh, no, my boy, you can take the bubble with you wherever you go!"

This is what we women do. We go to our Father in Heaven. Sometimes in sheer gratitude. Sometimes in discouragement or even desperation. We study His word. We do His will. We seek and accept the blessings of the temple where He endows us with His power and life-giving light. We are faithful to our covenants and we *expect* experiences with Him and His angels.

Hallowed by those experiences, our homes become "thin places" and we, ourselves, become a safe and happy home for others wherever we go.

NOTES

1. Rosemary M. Wixom, "Coming to Know," Church Educational System fireside for Young Adults, Utah State University, 1 May 2011; available at https://www.lds.org/broadcasts/article/print/ces-devotionals/2011/01/coming-to-know?lang=eng; accessed 7 July 2014.
2. Marlin K. Jensen, "Stand in the Sacred Grove," Church Educational System devotional for Young Adults, Sacramento, California, 6 May 2012; available at https://www.lds.org/broadcasts/article/print/ces-devotionals/2012/01/stand-in-the-sacred-grove?lang=eng&clang=eng; accessed 7 July 2014.
3. Sharlanda Sledge, unpublished poem, n.d.

4. Jeffrey R. Holland, "Lessons from Liberty Jail," *Ensign*, September 2009, 27–28.
5. See B. H. Roberts, *A Comprehensive History of the Church of Jesus Christ of Latter-day Saints*, 6 vols. (Salt Lake City: The Church of Jesus Christ of Latter-day Saints, 1930), 1:521 (chapter heading); see also 1:526.
6. Sharlanda Sledge, unpublished poem, n.d.
7. Bible Dictionary, s.v., "Temple," 780–81.
8. See *Handbook 2: Administering the Church* (Salt Lake City: The Church of Jesus Christ of Latter-day Saints, 2010), 176–77; available at https://www.lds.org/bc/content/shared/content/english/pdf/language-materials/08702_eng.pdf?lang=eng; accessed 8 July 2014.
9. John A. Widtsoe, "The House of the Lord," *Improvement Era* 39 (April 1936): 228.
10. Marion G. Romney, *Look to God and Live: Discourses of Marion G. Romney*, compiled by George J. Romney (Salt Lake City: Deseret Book, 1971), 236.
11. Relief Society Minute Book, 17 March 1842–16 March 1844, 35; available at http://josephsmithpapers.org/paperSummary/nauvoo-relief-society-minute-book?p=35; accessed 8 July 2014.

Social Media: New Ways to Invite Others to "Come and See"

Stephanie A. Nielson

Dear Stephanie . . .

Hey Stephanie, SHAME ON YOU! You sicken me to the fullest—you don't fool anyone. Keep using your *now* pathetic blog to splatter your religion and beliefs that offend others. They are outdated and annoying! GAG ME & get over yourself![1]

• • •

NieNie, just wanted you (and your entire family) to know that you are extremely selfish. Telling your children to follow a religion at such an early age is why we have closed-minded idiots who live in this world. Just because you blog about it doesn't mean you are gaining followers, just wanted you to know I am no longer following you.[2]

• • •

Stephanie A. Nielson was born and raised in Provo, Utah. In 2005, she began NieNieDialogues.com, *a blog about her life as a wife, mother, and Mormon, which quickly became popular. Stephanie and her husband, Christian, survived a near-fatal plane crash in 2008, in which both were severely burned. Stephanie continues to share her personal journey on her blog, that receives four million hits every month. She has been featured on* The Oprah Winfrey Show, The Today Show, *and in* People *magazine. She serves in the Church as a ward missionary and Primary teacher. She and her husband have five children.*

> Stephanie, you are becoming ugly on the inside. And according to your own testimony, that is what counts in God's eyes. Your prophet and teachings are out of touch in our world. You are following a religion that doesn't and won't accept everyone; how can you even show your face on any social media. You are inappropriate, and offensive. One more thing, I sincerely want to know how you sleep at night.[3]

• • •

> Stephanie Nielson, it is disgusting that you use your blog to advertise Mormonism or weirdos for lack of a better word. I will continue to pray for you. Good luck to a self-righteous narrow-minded family.[4]

Those were just a few samplings that I have received via e-mail. Then you have my Instagram account, which just a few weeks ago was hacked into, my name stolen, and inappropriate photos began to be posted under my name! I know of six accounts that are set up just to hate me and my family.

And you are probably wondering why I do this.

Some days I do too.

I do it because the gospel of Jesus Christ needs to be shared with all of my brothers and sisters. I don't have a name tag on my chest, but that doesn't mean I am off the hook. I still have a responsibility to share this message of hope and love. I *want* the responsibility to share this message of hope and love. I also think that sharing the gospel through social media is relatively easy and natural and the effects are far-reaching.

I love sharing simple messages about God's plan for me and my family with those who maybe don't understand what a gospel-centered home looks like. I love to share my love for motherhood with those who maybe think having children is crazy. Because of my situation, it's natural for me to express my gratitude for the things I can do every day. It's pretty amazing.

I won't lie—those true e-mails I read hurt. They make me sad; they make me feel horrible, worthless, and stupid. But then again, I am pretty much summing up how Satan wants me to feel on a daily basis. He is trying to stop anything good, and when I realize that, then I usually feel a little bit relieved because it means I'm doing my job.

There is only one person I let my children hear me call a loser, and that's the devil.

In Elder Neil L. Andersen's talk titled, "Beware of the Evil behind the Smiling Eyes," he comes right out and says it, sisters, and I will quote:

> The devil . . . "persuadeth men to do evil" (Moroni 7:17). "He [has] fallen from heaven, . . . [has] become miserable forever" (2 Nephi 2:18). He is a liar and a loser. (See D&C 93:25; see also Bible Dictionary, "Devil," 656.)[5]

He wants to stop this work. He will do anything to stop this work. I have seen it daily in my life. I see it on my Instagram comments, in e-mails and letters, and even through conversations. I don't just see it, but I feel it.

Have you noticed that Satan is always quick to ruin and use his negative power with anything wonderful and new? He wants to blemish and corrupt and to counteract anything that is beautiful, important, and good.

I began my blog in 2005 after a very powerful charge from Elder M. Russell Ballard. He encouraged us to share the message of the gospel through social media.[6] At that time, social media did not have such a large impact as today. That man is inspired, and I am grateful I listened, because heaven knows it wasn't like I didn't have anything else to do with my time. I had three small children and was living back east. I was also sick and pregnant with my fourth child, and to me, making dinner was a *huge* task, so for me to somehow start, produce, and find the time to continue a blog was a miracle.

I must have had an angel beside me doing some pretty heavy nudging. All of us know that members of The Church of Jesus Christ of Latter-day Saints are encouraged continually to share the gospel with others. I believe that the Church is always looking for the most effective ways to declare its message. Guess what—they think it's through social media.

Sisters, we have a great opportunity to be a powerful force for good in the Church and in the world! We must be bold in our declaration of

Jesus Christ, and we can do that by prayerfully using and utilizing this great power and tool.

I have often heard mothers and fathers share with me their desire to teach by example. I remember that, while I was growing up, my father would often drop me and my siblings off at school on his way to work. When it started to get down to the wire and if he was at the foot of his bed praying, then we would run into the kitchen and announce to the others, "He's still kneeling . . . hurry."

We knew we had three to five minutes longer, give or take, to put on shoes or pop a piece of toast in the toaster, or hustle to find that missing homework. As a mother I look back at that and value that example of the importance of prayer. Perhaps we could value the example of a mother who finds time in her busy schedule to sit down and read scriptures when she feels like she also needs to prepare the dinner or do the laundry.

Yes, those are wonderful things that your children should see you do but they should also see you sharing the gospel online. I don't mean you should ignore your children and glue your face to your phone or computer. Try collaborating with or learning from your children about social media. Chances are they know *way* more than you. Try sitting down with your children and together search for the perfect Mormon Message to share with your friends.

I had a conversation recently with a couple who have several children. This couple prided themselves that they were not in the trendy world of social media. The husband explained there was no way they would let their daughter get a phone until she was sixteen, and even then it wouldn't be a smartphone.

"I don't need to let social media in my life," he explained, "I don't need my children part of that ugly self-centered world. They will be normal kids, and know how to talk to people instead of using a phone to communicate." By this time, he was a little defensive.

I really admired his conviction and I know he is the co-leader with his wife and that they know what is best for their family and situation. I trust him and his wife and know that they together lead a very beautiful gospel-centered home and life. But that night as I continued to ponder on his remark, I contemplated why *I* use social media in my life. The reason again is simple: missionary work.

The more I listened to this couple talk to me that day about the reasons why social media didn't have a place in their home, the more I thought about how the gospel was reaching people all over the world, thanks to brave men and women and boys and girls who share their beliefs, standards, and testimony of Jesus Christ through blogs, Facebook, Instagram, and other social media.

You can be a missionary on social media just by being a good example of a member of The Church of Jesus Christ of Latter-day Saints. For example, telling your friends you went to church on Sunday lets them know you participate actively in the gospel. By your everyday actions, others can also know that Mormons strive to follow Christ. It's not always easy—there is always some pushback from people who hate and despise and try to stop the work of the Lord.

I am not very savvy with technology. In fact, last week my twelve-year-old daughter, Claire—who doesn't even have a phone—showed me how to block people on Instagram. But what I can do is testify of Christ. Honestly, if I can do it, you can do it!

As you participate in and utilize the tools of social media—especially for missionary work—remember that we are Latter-day Saints. We don't need to argue or fight with others regarding what we believe in. We don't have to constantly feel defensive or frustrated, although there are times I do. Let's try to remember where we stand on issues and as good faithful representatives of Jesus Christ. Our position is solid, and the Church is true. Remember that sharing the gospel through social media is simply like having a conversation, like friends who are having lunch together at a cozy table. Hopefully our minds and hearts will be led by and sensitive to the promptings of the Spirit.

But for heaven's sake, sisters, let's remember some important points before we post, such as, "Is what I am wearing appropriate for my age? Is it even modest?" "Does my caption fit the photo I am posting?" "What is my intent for posting this photo?" "Would my stake president or bishop 'like' this photo?" "Would I be embarrassed if my children saw this photo?" "Would someone not of my faith question my actions?" "Will this strengthen my own legacy?" Lastly, "Am I striving to have my online presence reflect my values and standards?"

Often Latter-day Saints ask me what advice I have for them if they were to start a blog or post on other social media outlets. I always ask them to honestly answer a few questions that I ask myself daily as I continue to use social media:

Why do you want to blog? Why do you want to put yourself out in the world? Maybe it's for family history's sake, maybe it's because you are really good at cooking, maybe it's because you have a talent that you want to share online or make connections, perhaps you can make a living—or some extra cash for your family—by blogging. Whatever it is, I hope you can answer my second question:

Can you talk and testify of Jesus Christ through your blog? If you can't, will you? Do you want to? This is the time to hasten the work, and I am serious about this. If what we do in *any* capacity in life doesn't help this cause, then I think we need to rethink our priorities.

If you have any kind of social media account, begin thinking of ways you can introduce the gospel. The Lord will help you think of ways to do this—I know He will—if you are prayerfully asking and searching. I know it is possible.

Take a photo of the sunset on Instagram and caption it something that makes you happy, or take a photo of your family and caption how grateful you are that have a family here on earth. Are you married? Take a photo of you and your husband together. Caption your photo with a small part of the Family Proclamation.[7]

Do you have children? Take a photo of them doing something together and caption or write about how thankful you are that the Lord created siblings to help each other along the path of life. Do you have a baby? Caption or quote a favorite children's song like the famous—and my favorite—"A Child's Prayer."[8] Do you have grandchildren? Write some really great advice you have learned along the way.

Are you single? Try taking a photo of you with friends or family members serving someone or your love for the prophet.

Do you take selfies a lot? Well, push in those duck lips and smile—let the caption read how thankful you are that you are happy, have a body, can work, and can choose to be happy.

Take pictures after church, before church, at the temple, the Conference Center, while visiting teaching, of the celebration after a baptism or baby blessing. My husband and I always document when we are out serving with the full-time missionaries. Honestly, the possibilities are endless if you are living the gospel already.

In fact, I am going to take a photo right now and post it. . . .

Let's talk a little about the dangers. Is social media in your life too much? Are you ignoring your children? Do you find yourself talking to a child and checking the comments on your Instagram post at the same time? I have done that. I always feel bad about it, and try to actively remember my priorities. Don't teach your children that you can multitask both them and your social media account, or they will do the same to you.

Children today are being educated by the media, including on the Internet. Messages portrayed on television, in movies, and in other media nowadays are very often in direct opposition to what we want our children to embrace.

It is our responsibility not only to teach them, but to be wise and strong in spirit, to continue to follow the prophet, keep the commandments, and do what is right. This will require a lot of time and effort on our part. In order to help others, particularly our children, we need the spiritual and moral courage ourselves to withstand the evil we see on every side.

Perhaps the Lord's encouragement to "open your mouths" (D&C 33:9) might today include "use your hands" to blog and text-message the gospel to all the world! I like to think so.

A recent article entitled "Why I Can't Stop Reading Mormon Housewife Blogs," by Emily Matchar, a self-described "young, feminist atheist who can't bake a cupcake" but is "addicted" to several Mormon housewife blogs (including my blog) examined this interesting phenomena:

"So why, exactly, are these blogs so fascinating to women like us—secular, childless women who may have never so much as baked a cupcake, let alone reupholstered our own ottomans with thrifted fabric and vintage grosgrain ribbon? . . . To use a word that makes me cringe, these blogs are weirdly 'uplifting.' To read Mormon lifestyle blogs is to peer into a strange and fascinating world where the most fraught issues of modern living—marriage and child rearing—appear completely unproblematic. This seems practically subversive to someone like me, weaned on an endless media parade of fretful stories about 'work-life balance' and soaring divorce rates and the perils of marrying too young/too old/too whatever."[9]

In response, MMB (MormonMommyBlogs.com) argued that although the article was right that these blogs provided something missing in other people's lives, this missing piece was spiritual:

"It's easy to learn about people through their blogs. You are getting to peek inside their homes, you are getting to see how other people are living. And not only that, but those Mormons that you've only heard weird myths about are out there talking, and you're finding that they are regular people. These are regular women, [whom] you admire. These are people just. like. you.

"Some of them stay at home, some of them work. But they do it all with a grace and greater understanding of their purpose. . . .

"When we write about our personal struggles, we do so in a respectful and uplifting way. Yes, we struggle with depression. Yes, we argue with our husbands. Yes, our children even drive us nuts. . . . But through all of that, the readers of Mormon mommy blogs feel the love. . . .

"Mormon Mommy Bloggers are a powerful force for good in this world, and they are spreading that goodness by sharing their lives through their blogs."[10]

When I began this presentation, I shared with you some mean e-mails, but I get wonderful ones too. My favorite e-mails are those from families who invite me to their baptisms. I am thankful and grateful that I am not afraid to open my mouth and share my beliefs and life with the world. The more I share the easier it is.

If you feel overwhelmed because you are in the middle of a very busy life, raising children, holding down a job, maybe doing both and other responsibilities that take up your time and you don't have time to serve more, to have the missionaries over for dinner, or to drive the sister missionaries to appointments, you can be just as effective in bringing the world the gospel by retweeting an inspired quote that the Mormon Newsroom just published. Simple. Or snap a photo of your sleeping baby and boldly proclaim that you are doing the most important work in the world as a mother. Simple as that.

Sometimes, I like to think I am a missionary serving in the World-wide Web Mission. It's kind of a hard language; the people are sometimes cruel; I get made fun of a lot; I don't fit in sometimes—actually more than most times. But I have seen a lot of good too. I've seen baptisms, and lives change for the better. I am preparing my children to serve in this mission as well. These are the ups and downs, the ins and outs, the dangers and the beauty of social media.

We must all defend our Savior and testify that He is the Christ. Through social media we can kindly remind that there is such a thing as right and wrong. Sisters, we must find the courage to speak out and defend the Church even when it's hard.

Hopefully I have given you some ideas and tools to be more bold, more excited (even if you are not, I promise you your kids are, so be excited for them), and more involved to share the gospel of Jesus Christ using something you utilize every day—social media.

May the Lord strengthen you with faith, courage, and perseverance so that as you actively use this tool for others to "come and see," you will have a powerful influence on those with whom you come in contact. Your words are powerful and incredible. Let your voice be heard in this great cause of the gospel of Jesus Christ.

A few months ago I received a letter in the mail from Elder Ballard. My eyes swelled with tears as he thanked me for sharing the gospel on social media. Before he ended the letter he wrote:

"I know that the criticism that comes through the Internet can be particularly harsh and cruel, and I am glad that you are able to continue on and focus in the good that has come into your lives. Satan knows that one of the best tools we have to share the gospel to a global audience is the Internet, which is why he works so hard to corrupt it instead. Keep helping spread the good word of God and you will continue to have missionary opportunities."[11]

Another e-mail I received recently says:

"Dear Stephanie,

"Tomorrow with my three sons, two daughters, and husband, we are getting baptized as members of The Church of Jesus Christ of Latter-day Saints. I first learned of the church because you mentioned God in an article that was published in a popular women's magazine. I was impressed and decided to look you up. I was so excited when I saw that you had a blog, and now I follow you on Instagram. I requested a Book of Mormon from your blog, and called the missionaries' number you added in the book. They came and began teaching me about who I was as a daughter of a God. Thank you for not being afraid to share what is right, good and true."[12]

I add my testimony to Elder Ballard's when he said:

"This is not a time for the spiritually faint of heart. We cannot afford to be superficially righteous. Our testimonies must run deep, with spiritual roots firmly embedded in the rock of revelation. And we must continue to move the work forward as a covenanted, consecrated people, with faith in every footstep."[13]

Sisters, don't be discouraged. Don't give up, work hard, and testify harder is my prayer for all of you.

NOTES

1. Personal correspondence in author's possession.
2. Personal correspondence in author's possession.
3. Personal correspondence in author's possession.
4. Personal correspondence in author's possession.
5. Neil L. Andersen, "Beware of the Evil Behind the Smiling Eyes," *Ensign*, May 2005, 46.
6. See M. Russell Ballard, "Sharing the Gospel Using the Internet," *Ensign*, July 2008, 58–63.
7. See "The Family: A Proclamation to the World," *Ensign*, November 2010, 129.
8. Janice Kapp Perry, "A Child's Prayer," *Children's Songbook* (Salt Lake City: The Church of Jesus Christ of Latter-day Saints, 1989), 12–13. Used by permission.
9. Emily Matchar, "Why I can't stop reading Mormon housewife blogs," Salon.com, 15 January 2011; available at http://www.salon.com/2011/01/15/feminist_obsessed_with_mormon_blogs/; accessed 14 July 2014.
10. See "MMB and ABC's Nightline: Why people REALLY read Mormon Mommy Blogs," MormonMommyBlogs.com, 6 March 2011; available at http://mormonmommyblogs.com/2011/03/mmb-and-abcs-nightline-why-people-really-read-mormon-mommy-blogs.html; accessed 14 July 2014.
11. Personal correspondence in author's possession.
12. Personal correspondence in author's possession.
13. Ballard, "The Truth of God Shall Go Forth," *Ensign*, November 2008, 84.

Perfect in One

Russell T. Osguthorpe

Most of us are probably familiar with Harry Anderson's painting of the Savior praying in the Garden of Gethsemane in which He is kneeling by the slanted trunk of a gnarled olive tree, clasping His hands, and looking heavenward. This was the scene of His final prayer before being betrayed by Judas, judged by Pilate, and crucified by the Romans. Consider your own thoughts or feelings as you contemplate the scene depicted in this painting. What words best describe your thoughts and feelings?

We live in a world that floods us with words every day. Texts, e-mails, headlines, captions—a continual avalanche of words. Sometimes the words help us understand something new. Other times the words make life more confusing. So I want to discuss with you a single three-letter word today—a word we all understand, a word we use every day. That's all—just a single, tiny little word. The word is *one*. That's it. And I am completely confident that this is a word we can all remember.

Russell T. Osguthorpe holds multiple degrees from Brigham Young University, including a PhD in instructional psychology. He is a former director of the Center for Teaching and Learning and a professor emeritus in the Department of Instructional Psychology and Technology at Brigham Young University. He was serving as a member of the Fifth Quorum of the Seventy when he was called as the general president of the Sunday School. He has also served as a stake president, president of the South Dakota Rapid City Mission, and as a member of the Mormon Tabernacle Choir. He and his wife, Lolly, are now serving as president and matron of the Bismarck North Dakota Temple.

But the brevity of this word belies its power. This word—only three letters—is scriptural. It's doctrinal. It embodies some of the most important truths of the Restoration. Consider the following phrases: *one heart, one mind, one spirit, one soul, one body, one faith, one baptism, one fold, one Shepherd, one God.*

As you review these phrases, notice the principles of the gospel that emerge when the word *one* modifies the noun that follows it. If I say the words *mind* or *heart* alone, you might think of many verses of scripture. But when I say, "of one heart and one mind," the idea of Zion likely comes to mind—an idea unique to the Restoration (see, for example, Moses 7:18).

The phrases *one fold* and *one Shepherd* may bring to mind the scene in the Book of Mormon when Christ appeared to the Nephites and told them that He had "other sheep" which were not of the fold of the Nephites, but that there would be one fold and one Shepherd (see 3 Nephi 15:17).

Even more compelling is the phrase *one God.* Historical Christianity has a dramatically different notion of what this means. As members of The Church of Jesus Christ of Latter-day Saints, we know that it refers to three separate beings united in purpose and mission (see D&C 130:22).

Now, before returning to the Savior in Gethsemane, let's consider the placement of the word *one* in the word *atonement.* When we encounter the word *atonement,* we may not think first of the word *one.* But it is central to the all-encompassing doctrine of the Atonement. Christ's sacrifice in the Garden and His death on the Cross were all aimed at helping us become "at one."

In this prayer of all prayers—the prayer that caused Him more pain and anguish than we can imagine—He asked His Father to help us become one. "That they (all of us) may be one; as thou, Father, art in me, and I in thee, that they also may be one in us" (John 17:21). Notice how the word *one* appears twice in this verse. It is the Savior's central thought and desire—that we, through His sacrifice—could become one with Him and His Father. Without the Restoration, His plea would be confusing because we know that we cannot become one *being,* as the Godhead is conceived by historical Christianity. Christ is saying, in essence, please help all of these Thy children—who are separate beings just as we are—to become *one* just as "thou, Father, art in me, and I in thee."

If we are to become one with God the Father and His Son, Jesus Christ, we might ask: so how do I do that? First, we need to become one with ourselves.[1] This is the first step to becoming one with God.

I like the Apostle Paul's description of the challenge of becoming one with ourselves: "For the good that I would—I do not; but the evil which I would not—that I do" (Romans 7:19). This is a verse we may need to read twice to get the full impact. Paul is expressing in this verse the frustration we all have at doing things we know we should not do and not doing things we know we should do. It's the war that goes on inside us periodically—the desire to do right, when the impulse is to do wrong. Paul's lament is not unlike that of Nephi when he said, "O wretched man that I am!" (2 Nephi 4:17). Nephi was frustrated that he felt that he could not control his desires.

Several years ago, while I was serving as a stake president, a couple came to me for help with their relationship. They had been married for about five years and had decided that they simply could not endure each other any longer. No serious transgression had been committed. They just did not love each other anymore. As they sat with me in my home, they verbally picked at each other, chronicling every complaint that came to mind.

They shared some frustrations with each other that they had never shared before. I was surprised that they did not seem to know each other very well even though they had been married for years. Their words were laced with negative emotion and harshness. It was not a pleasant scene—either for them or for me. The husband and wife I was counseling were obviously not at one with each other. Neither were they at one with themselves. And they certainly were not at one with God. So, if it's not too unpleasant for you, hold this image in your mind for a few minutes, while we return to the Savior's prayer in the Garden.

The Savior knew that becoming one would be our main challenge in mortality, and so this was His central plea. "And the glory which thou gavest me I have given them; that they may be one even as we are one" (John 17:22).

"I in them, and thou in me, that they may be made perfect (or complete) in one . . ." So this word *one* keeps appearing in His prayer—again and again. Then He gives us the key to becoming one. That key is to feel God's love. When we're at war with ourselves or with each other—as this couple was—we preclude ourselves from feeling His love. So Christ prayed, "and that the world may know that thou has sent me, and hast loved them, as thou has loved me." Consider the depth of this plea. The Savior was praying that we would know that the Father has loved us just as He has loved His only Begotten Son. This same divine love comes to all of us, every one of us.

As President Thomas S. Monson has taught: "Heavenly Father loves you—each of you. That love never changes."[2] We might change. We might distance ourselves from Him. But His love is always there ready for us to receive. When we are at odds with ourselves or with each other we cannot feel God's love for us. But when we become one with ourselves and with each other, then God's love for us is so evident we cannot deny it.

Now back to that couple who came to me for counsel. At the close of the session, I did not know what to say. I had just listened to so much harshness that I could not see how we could end our visit on a positive note. Then, out of desperation, I said, "You know, we don't have harsh words in this home. We just don't. So I personally need to hear or see something positive before you leave me this evening. Could you just give each other a hug or something?"

They stood, looked at each other, and gradually placed their arms around one another. They began to cry. Then they apologized for how they had spoken to each other. They asked for forgiveness. We all felt better. I saw this as a small miracle. Their harshness toward each other had departed. Their anger had disappeared. And love entered the room.

Several weeks later, the husband approached me after a church meeting and said, "Hey, president, I just wanted you to know that we're doing okay. We've decided not to get divorced. Things are so much better."

I've reflected often on that visit. When the couple came to me, they were definitely not keeping the covenants they had made with God and with each other. At baptism they had committed to take the Savior's name upon them. They had also covenanted with each other in the temple. They had somehow forgotten those promises. But at the close of our visit, the power of those covenants came rushing back. This is why we are a covenant people. Without covenants, we cannot become one with each other and with God. This is why the ordinances are so essential.

My wife and I will soon be going to Bismarck, North Dakota, to preside over the temple there. The temple is a place where those who come to worship make covenants with God. Each of these covenants is a promise to do something. But it's a promise also to do it out of love.

The Lord knew from before the world was that making and keeping eternal covenants was the only pathway to becoming one. A covenant is a two-way promise. We promise to do what God would have us do, and He promises us blessings. Each time we make and keep a covenant, we become one with the Savior and our Heavenly Father. We are in essence answering Christ's prayer in Gethsemane: "That they may be one in us."

After we make a covenant, we renew it every Sunday in this ordinance of ordinances—the sacrament. It is during these sacred moments each Sabbath day that we symbolically take Christ within us. When Jesus said, "I in them," He knew that this ordinance would help us know what he meant. We symbolically take within us *His* flesh and *His* blood—all so that we can become *one* with Him.

I urge you to reread chapters 11 through 26 of 3 Nephi. In these chapters, we learn of Christ's visit to the Nephites following His Resurrection. He first teaches them. Then He prays—much as He prayed in Gethsemane prior to His Crucifixion—that we might be one with each other and with Him and His Father. Directly after that prayer, Christ institutes the sacrament, showing how essential this ordinance is to the whole process of becoming one. Then He launches the gathering—missionary work—and finally establishes the Church.

These chapters show us how we can all become an answer to Christ's prayer in Gethsemane. The people progressed from covenant to covenant, ordinance to ordinance. Then, finally, at the end of the chapters, the people became one with each other, so that Zion could be established.

Someone might ask, "So how do I become one with someone else if that someone else is not interested in becoming one with me?" The process that leads to becoming one with each other is not a do-it-yourself project. Both need to make covenants and keep them, just as the couple who came to my home for help. Sometimes a person chooses to take a different path, and the process of oneness ceases. We cannot control another person's choices. That is why becoming one with each other is such an amazing process. It is all based upon agency. And if our spouse or friend decides to take a different path, then our task is to forgive and move forward.

Forgiveness takes away anger, resentment, and revenge. It brings us close to God, so we can become one with Him. And it makes it possible for us to become one with others who likewise want to become one.

The love that leads to forgiveness draws us closer to God. The more we become one with God and with each other, the more our actions will be motivated by love. And the more our actions are motivated by love, the more we become one with God and with each other.

When we feel at one with ourselves, at one with God, and at one with others, we are partaking of both the strengthening and redeeming powers of the Atonement simultaneously. As we forgive ourselves and others, we are partaking of the redeeming power, but at the very moment we forgive or feel an increase of love toward another, we are strengthened also. When Christ prayed that we might be "made" perfect in one, He understood that His act of atonement was the power that would make us perfect in one.

I once listened to a teacher of a youth Sunday School class in Oaxaca, Mexico, recount how she began her lesson on missionary work with a question:

"You are all acquainted with Sister Alonso. You know that she has not yet joined the Church. She is my neighbor. What do you think I could do to help her come closer to the Church?"

The teacher then explained how the class members had suggested that she invite Sister Alonso to sacrament meeting.

"Good," she said. "I will do that. Any other ideas?"

Then one young man said, "Sister Alonso is poor. It's hard for her to feed her family, and she doesn't have a husband. We should take food to her."

Then a young woman said, "Let's all bring food to class and then take it to her next Sunday. It's fast Sunday next week. We can bring the food we would have eaten and take it to her." So that is what they did. As the teacher told this story, tears began to course down her cheeks. She was moved by the thoughtfulness and generosity of these thirteen- and fourteen-year-old youth.

Even though no one would have used the term, her class had become a council. In the process of counseling together they all agreed on a plan of action to help Sister Alonso. They were becoming one. The teacher did not know before the class what the outcome would be. She made space for the Spirit, and the Spirit worked in the hearts of the young people. The teacher told how the class took the food to Sister Alonso the next week and how grateful she was for the goodness of these young people.

They acted out of love, and so they became one with each other and with God. They were keeping their baptismal covenant to take the name of the Savior upon them. No contention. No one trying to be better than another. No one seeking praise. Just thoughtful service to someone in need—all of it leading to a deeper feeling of oneness.

What blessings come as we become one? All the blessings of the gospel. Yes, all of them. This is precisely why the Savior prayed in Gethsemane—that we might experience all of the blessings that had been prepared for us before the world was. He knew that those blessings all hinged on our becoming one.

Perhaps one of the most overarching and immediate blessings that comes from our trying to be one with God and with each other is the peace of knowing that we are pursuing the path God wants us to follow. The couple I counseled felt peace as they embraced each other. The class members in Mexico felt peace twice—first as they suggested giving food to their neighbor, and then a second time as they actually carried out their plan.

So that's it. That's my message. And it's all contained in a single three-letter word: *one*.

I know that the more we become one with each other and with God, the happier we will be in this life and throughout eternity. I bear witness that as we reflect on the Savior's prayer in the Garden—even for a moment—we will be drawn closer to Him and to each other. His plea shows how much we are loved by Him and by our Heavenly Father. I testify of His love. I feel it every day. I know His love never changes. I know that we can all be made perfect in one.

Notes

1. See D. Todd Christofferson, "That They May Be One in Us," *Ensign*, November 2002, 71–73.
2. Thomas S. Monson, "We Never Walk Alone," *Ensign*, November 2013, 123.

Living the Commandments Brings Happiness and Joy

Mary G. Cook

Dear sisters, I feel such love for the sisters in the gospel. I realize that you love the Lord, you love His gospel, and you want to be involved in the kingdom. I, like you, know we are daughters of our Heavenly Father. His marvelous plan of happiness is to receive the ordinances and covenants here in mortality that will make it possible for us to return to His presence.

I don't know when it was that I knew the restored gospel was true. For me it was a gradual thing. I do know that as I grew up in the Church, attended Primary and all the other meetings, read my scriptures, prayed to Heavenly Father, and sang the songs of the gospel I knew it was true in my heart and I never doubted.

Shortly after I was baptized, my parents filed for divorce. Part of it involved disputes over Church commitment and conduct incompatible with the gospel. My mother, sister, brother, and I went to live with our grandmother—our mother's mother. She was a widow, and I can't

---

Sister Mary G. Cook met her husband, Elder Quentin L. Cook, while they attended school in Logan, Utah. She earned a bachelor's degree from Utah State University, where she was valedictorian of her college and Scholar of the Year. She did graduate work at Stanford University. She has served the Church in numerous callings including as the Young Women president of the San Francisco California Stake and early morning seminary teacher. A talented musician, she has enjoyed teaching music and leading youth choruses in the Church, schools, and community.

She and her husband are the parents of three children and eleven grandchildren.

imagine how she dealt with three lively children for two years. I attended my third and fourth grades during this time. When I think back over those years, I remember feeling a little insecure about my family situation. One day, I was walking home from mid-week Primary, and I remember it was springtime, the flowers were in bloom, and I had to walk through a neighbor's yard into her backyard and into my grandmother's backyard in order to get home. The hollyhocks were almost as tall as I was, and the bees were humming throughout the garden.

I suddenly felt the most overwhelming feeling of love. It just enveloped me. I felt that the Lord knew me, and that I was important to Him. It was the first time I recognized the power of the Holy Ghost in my life.

I realized that we make our own happiness, no matter what trials, tribulations, or sorrows we face in this life. We choose, based on our faith in the Lord, Jesus Christ, to be of good cheer. The Savior has said, as recorded in Doctrine and Covenants 78:18: "Be of good cheer, for I will lead you along. The kingdom is yours and the blessings thereof are yours, and the riches of eternity are yours."

This situation in my family as well as this experience taught me three basic things:

- First, the blessing of having the Holy Ghost as a constant companion and the comfort provided when we are especially in need.
- Second, living the commandments brings happiness and joy.
- Third, I knew I wanted to have a happy family life.

My parents actually resolved most of their differences after two years of separation, and we reunited as a family. Things weren't always great, but years later when I was a wife and mother myself, my parents were sealed in the temple, and I was able to be sealed to them.

With the gospel knowledge we have, we should be the happiest people in the world. We can't let the sorrows and tribulations of mortality deflect us from the promise of a better, glorious, and magnificent eternal life. President Thomas S. Monson has quoted Charles Swindoll from *Lessons for Living* on the subject of attitude:

"Attitude, to me, is more important than . . . the past . . . than money, than circumstances, than failures, than successes, than what other people think or say or do. It is more important than appearance, giftedness, or skill."[1]

President Monson added, "We can choose to be happy and positive, regardless of what comes our way."[2]

Alma, speaking to his son Corianton, explains that men will be judged according to their works—"raised to endless happiness to inherit the kingdom of God, or to endless misery to inherit the kingdom of the devil" (Alma 41:4).

Having a happy heart—desiring to be happy—turns many a trying day into a tolerable one. Being able to laugh at a mistake or a disappointment keeps you going, not giving in or succumbing to feelings of depression or loneliness. More than once I have told myself, "This, too, shall pass." And it does. A wise person once said, "Today is a gift. That is why they call it the present." We need to cherish the gift of each new day and be happy therein.

In the gospel we sing about happiness. I learned this in Primary: "When we're helping, we're happy, / And we sing as we go . . ."[3] I also learned: "If you're happy and you know it, clap your hands"[4]—I clapped as loud as I could. In the hymn "Let Us All Press On," we sing, "If we do what's right we have no need to fear, / For the Lord, our helper, will ever be near; / In the days of trial his Saints he will cheer, / And prosper the cause of truth."[5]

My dear sisters, come what may, we can be of good cheer. As Victor Hugo said,

> *Be like the bird that, halting in her flight*
> *Awhile on boughs too light,*
> *Feels them give way, yet sings,*
> *Knowing that she hath wings."*[6]

The Savior, our sun and shield, has given us wings to fly and the covenant pathway to soar.

As we suffer the sorrows and joys of mortality, let us keep our eyes focused on the prize. Be of good cheer, for we know the outcome, we know the truth; we know the Savior and His infinite Atonement made in our behalf. We know the Father's plan of happiness. As the Prophet Joseph Smith said: "Happiness is the object and design of our existence."[7]

NOTES

1. Charles Swindoll, quoted in Thomas S. Monson, *Teachings of Thomas S. Monson*, Lynne Cannegieter, comp. (Salt Lake City: Deseret Book, 2011), 24.
2. Monson, *Teachings of Thomas S. Monson*, 25.
3. Wallace F. Bennett, "When We're Helping," *Children's Songbook* (Salt Lake City: The Church of Jesus Christ of Latter-day Saints, 1989), 198.
4. Anonymous, "If You're Happy," *Children's Songbook*, 266.
5. Evan Stephens, "Let Us All Press On," *Hymns of The Church of Jesus Christ of Latter-day Saints* (Salt Lake City: The Church of Jesus Christ of Latter-day Saints, 1985), no. 243.
6. Quoted, for instance, in *The Christian Advocate*, vol. 86 (June 15, 1911): 800.
7. Joseph Smith, *History of The Church of Jesus Christ of Latter-day Saints*, 7 vols., edited by B. H. Roberts (Salt Lake City: The Church of Jesus Christ of Latter-day Saints, 1932–51), 5:134.

The Rewards of Righteousness

Elder Quentin L. Cook

My precious wife, Mary is the love of my life, my best friend, and we have collaborated as equal and complementary partners in this marvelous venture we call life for over fifty years.

I have been blessed with exceptional women in my life, beginning with an incredible mother. My appreciation for all the women who have been such an influence on me is beyond my ability to adequately communicate. They have sought excellence in every aspect of their lives.

Elder Jeffrey R. Holland interviewed our children to write an article for the *Ensign* magazine when I was appointed to the Quorum of the

---

Elder Quentin L. Cook was sustained as a member of the Quorum of the Twelve Apostles of The Church of Jesus Christ of Latter-day Saints on October 6, 2007. Called as a General Authority in April 1996, he served in the Second Quorum, the First Quorum, and the Presidency of the Seventy.

At the time of his call as a General Authority, he was vice-chairman of Sutter Health System. He had previously served as president and CEO of a California healthcare system. Prior to that, he was a business lawyer and managing partner of a San Francisco Bay Area law firm.

He is a native of Logan, Utah, and received a bachelor's degree in political science from Utah State University and a Doctor of Jurisprudence from Stanford University.

He has served the Church as a bishop, president of the San Francisco California Stake, Regional Representative, and Area Authority. As a young man, he served in the British Mission. He and his wife, Mary, are the parents of three children and eleven grandchildren.

Twelve. Our only daughter, Kathryn, said some very nice things about me and concluded, "I adore everything about him. But my mother is a saint."[1] I concur with that assessment of Mary. Kathryn, our daughter, also fits that description. Both of them accomplish amazing things and never feel like they have done enough. I asked my daughter to comment on parts of this talk. Her helpful e-mail was sent at 2:30 A.M. She is probably like many of you and never gets enough sleep.

I chuckled the other day as I read the heading of a blog post of a faithful member working on family history. That entry was posted at 2:20 A.M. and was titled: "I am sorry, Elijah, but I really need to get some sleep."

I feel a great responsibility in speaking to you wonderful women. You have my love and admiration for who you are and what you accomplish in this difficult world.

Dear sisters, please do not underestimate the power and impact of your capable, loving, and sensitive influence on those with whom you associate. You bless many as they pass through the vicissitudes of life.

It seems to be part of your special nature to feel that, no matter how hard you work and what you do, it is never enough. Sometimes, despite the fact that everyone else feels you have been spectacular, you may feel inadequate and ineffective. Yet the excellent work you do, the kindness you show, and the love you exhibit are blessings beyond measure to those who have the privilege of associating with you. And it is enough!

Our theme for this Women's Conference includes the scriptural promise, "No good thing will he withhold from them that walk uprightly" (Psalm 84:11). My purpose today is to identify some of the rewards of righteousness and point out ways in which we can be and are now blessed in these turbulent times.

Before doing so, I will mention some difficult circumstances that we face today. *The world is literally in commotion.* Many of the challenges are in the spiritual realm. They are societal issues we as individuals cannot necessarily resolve but nevertheless concern us. After I have briefly discussed these troubling issues, I will highlight practical rewards we *can* as individuals achieve, even at a time when righteousness across the world is in decline.

The very idea of "rewards of righteousness" is a concept that is under siege in today's world. Convincing people to choose righteousness is an age-old challenge. "The natural man is an enemy to God" (Mosiah 3:19). There has always been "opposition in all things" (2 Nephi 2:11).

The difference today is that the "great-and-spacious-building" skeptics are louder, more contentious, and less tolerant than at any time during my life. They evidence their diminished faith when, on many issues, they are more concerned with being on the wrong side of history than on the wrong side of God. There was a time when the vast majority of people understood they would be judged by God's commandments, not by the prevailing views or dominant philosophies of the day. Some are more concerned about being mocked than they are with being judged by God.

It isn't that the battle between good and evil is new. But today a much higher percentage of people are willing to mistakenly conclude that there is not a moral, righteous standard to which all people should adhere.

A few examples might help you understand the progression of changes that give rise to my concern. First, David Brooks, writing in the *New York Times*, has chronicled the decline in the use of moral words. Researchers can use a Google database of 5.2 million books published between A.D. 1500 and 2008. They can type in a search word and find out how frequently the word was used in different epochs of time. One example Brooks cites is "a long decline of usage in terms like 'faith,' 'wisdom,' . . . 'evil,' and 'prudence,' and a sharp rise in . . . social science terms like 'subjectivity.'"[2] Brooks notes that the frequency of words like "thankfulness," "appreciation," "modesty," "humbleness," "kindness," and "helpfulness" has dropped approximately 50 percent.[3]

A second example: At one time, Christian themes undergirded or figured into most fiction. One prominent writer points out that fiction has now lost its faith, stating that "Christian belief figures into literary fiction in our place and time: as something between a dead language and a hangover."[4]

A third example: A host of writers and researchers have established the decline in institutions such as marriage and religion and the increase in out-of-wedlock births, poverty, and other factors that adversely impact society.[5]

Notwithstanding all that I have mentioned, the Church has never had more faithful members. Members of The Church of Jesus Christ of Latter-day Saints, together with others who have similar moral values, represent an island of faith in a sea of doubt and disbelief. We know as the Prophet Alma declared, "wickedness never was happiness" (Alma 41:10). The Father's plan for His children is a "plan of happiness" (see Alma 42:8, 16).

My desire is to chronicle some ideas that may help you individually and your families to better understand and achieve the rewards of righteousness.

First Is the Reward of Spirituality

A question many have raised is: How do I put material concerns in the proper perspective as I attempt to achieve spiritual progress? We are so much a part of this world. The material aspects of day-to-day living are a specific challenge. Society tends to look at everything through the lens of worldly rewards. With modern communications, we are bombarded with advertising for products that were not even dreamed of in prior generations, and images of glamorous people who appear to be living comfortable, frustration-free lives.

In the preface to the Doctrine and Covenants, this very problem is highlighted to warn us of dangers and give us guidance to prepare and protect ourselves now and in the future. Section 1 of the Doctrine and Covenants provides significant insight on this subject:

"They seek not the Lord to establish his righteousness, but every man walketh in his own way, and after the image of his own god, whose image is in the likeness of the world, and whose substance is that of an idol" (D&C 1:16).

President Spencer W. Kimball taught that idols can include credentials, degrees, property, homes, furnishings, and many other material objects. He pointed out that when we elevate these otherwise worthy objectives in a way that diminishes our worship of the Lord and weakens our efforts to establish His righteousness and perform the work of salvation among Heavenly Father's children, we have created idols. The creation of idols has always been a serious concern.[6]

Sometimes the lens of the world causes us to focus on issues not quite as dramatic as aspiring to great wealth, but nonetheless takes us away from deep spiritual commitment.

Many years ago I was made aware of an interesting display that had several unique scenes. The different scenes were underneath a large banner that read: "If Christ came tonight, to whom would He come?" If I remember the depictions correctly, they contained the following situations:

- One was of an elderly woman in bed being attended by a nurse. She appeared to be very ill.
- A second was of a young mother with a newborn baby. Joy radiated from her face.
- A third scene displayed a family with crying children. It was clear that there was not enough to eat.
- A fourth scene showed an obviously wealthy family.
- A fifth scene was a sweet, but humble family with many children joyously singing together.

As I thought about the five displays and the banner, "If Christ came tonight, to whom would He come?" several thoughts went through my mind. First, we know that when the Savior comes the second time, we will not know the day nor the hour. We also know that as Christians, we care for the poor and needy and the widow and the orphan. Nevertheless, the banner would have been more accurate if it had read, "If Christ came tonight, who would be prepared to greet Him?"

My second thought was that the scenes told us everything about the physical condition of the people, but nothing about their spiritual condition. We could infer from the various scenes that some were old and sick and some were healthy and newly born. Some were rich and some poor. But these facts don't tell us what is most important, which is the condition of their spirits.

The baseline, or starting point, for reviewing our life and commitment to the gospel of Jesus Christ is baptism. The spiritual nature and requirements for baptism are set forth in the Doctrine and Covenants 20:37. It reads in part: "All those who humble themselves before God, and desire to be baptized, and come forth with broken hearts and contrite spirits, and witness before the church that they have truly repented of all their sins, and are willing to take upon them the name of Jesus Christ . . . shall be received by baptism into his church."

For many of us, except for new converts and the very young, our baptisms were many years ago. The great prophet Alma speaks eloquently to us when he states: "And now behold, I say unto you, my brethren, if ye have experienced a change of heart, and if ye have felt to sing the song of redeeming love, I would ask, can ye feel so now?" (Alma 5:26).

Alma continues with a profound message that is completely relevant to our day. He essentially asks the Saints, if they were called to die, would they be prepared to meet God? Alma then emphasizes four qualities in order to be blameless before God:

First, are we "sufficiently humble?" (Alma 5:27). In a sense, this is a return to the requirement for baptism—humbling ourselves and having broken hearts and contrite spirits.

Second, are we "stripped of pride?" (Alma 5:28). In speaking of pride, Alma warns against trampling the Holy One under our feet and being puffed up in pride—setting our hearts upon the vain things of the world and upon riches—supposing we are better than one another, and persecuting those who are humble.

Third, are we "stripped of envy?" (Alma 5:29). For those who have great blessings, but do not feel gratitude because they can only focus on what others have, envy can be most pernicious. "Lifestyle envy" has increased as fame and fortune have replaced faith and family as a core aspiration for much of society.[7]

Fourth, do we mock (or persecute) a brother or sister? (Alma 5:30). In today's world we would probably call this bullying.

Could anything be more relevant to the issues that exist in our own day than this message about pride, envy, and persecutions? The great debate across much of the world is about temporal day-to-day economic issues. Yet there is very little discussion about returning to Christlike principles focused on preparation to meet God and the condition of our spirits. We need to focus our lives and increase emphasis on spiritual matters.

SECOND IS THE REWARD OF RIGHTEOUS FAMILIES

The question often asked is: Should we be raising our families in areas where there are few members of the Church and we are surrounded by much evil, contention, and opposition to righteousness? It should be noted that today no community is immune from evil, contention, and unrighteous temptations.

My wife and I had these concerns as we were beginning to raise our children in the San Francisco, California, area in the late 1960s. The Latter-day Saint population was relatively small. But while the vast majority of people were wonderful, the Bay Area had become a magnet for drug usage and all manner of promiscuous and sinful conduct. The Haight-Ashbury area in San Francisco was one of the first places where a drug culture became significant. Civil unrest and demonstrations became prevalent in the schools and universities. The change in society was significant enough that a concerned stake president asked the leadership of the Church if he should encourage Church members to remain in the area. Elder Harold B. Lee, then a senior member of the Quorum of the Twelve, was assigned to address the issue. He explained that the Lord had not inspired the construction of a temple in our area only to have the members leave. His counsel to us was simple but profound:

- First, create Zion in our hearts and homes.
- Second, be a light to those among whom we live.
- Third, focus on the ordinances and principles taught in the temple.

We cherished Elder Lee's counsel and tried to follow it in our family.

In building Zion in our hearts and homes, we need to emphasize religious observance in the home by having daily family prayer and scripture study, and holding weekly family home evening. In this context, we can teach and train our children. We do this with love and kindness, avoiding undue criticism of both our children and our spouses. Errors children make should not be treated as sins, but as mistakes to be corrected. Only sins require repentance (see D&C 1:25, 27).

Regardless of where we live and even if we do everything right, some children may make unwise choices that lead to forbidden paths.

Accordingly, it is important to help our young people determine in advance what they will say or do when improper or immoral conduct is proposed. Our children attended schools where there were only two or three Latter-day Saint children. At the beginning of each school year and before school activities, we discussed in family home evening appropriate responses if they found themselves in compromising situations. We asked them what they would say to friends who might tell them, "Don't be silly, everyone does it"; "Your parents won't know"; or "Just once won't matter."

We talked about our accountability to the Lord. We reviewed one of my favorite stories of the boy who was going to steal some merchandise and looked around to make sure no one was watching and then his friend said, "You forgot to look up."

We pointed out that we follow Christ's example when we dress modestly, use clean and appropriate language, and avoid pornography, which, by the way now needs to be taught to Primary-age children so that they can have pure lives. We talked about Joseph of Egypt who found it necessary to flee when confronted with inappropriate attention from Potiphar's wife.

Each of our children had at least one experience where this preparation was essential, but most of the time their friends protected them because they knew their standards and beliefs.

Our daughter pointed out that after she was away at school, when she talked with her mother on the phone, Mary would tell her some things she loved about the Savior. Mary constantly used His example or character to help with the problem Kathryn had called to discuss.

I personally believe we can raise righteous children in almost any part of the world if they have a firm foundation of Jesus Christ and His gospel. As Nephi described teaching his family, "We talk of Christ, we rejoice in Christ, we preach of Christ, we prophesy of Christ, and we write according to our prophecies, that our children may know to what source they may look for a remission of their sins" (2 Nephi 25:26). If we do this, when our children make unwise choices, they will know that all is not lost, and they can find their way home.

I am thrilled with the new youth curriculum and the reports on what it is accomplishing in the lives of our young people. As they purify their lives, the Spirit will guide them. I want to assure you that you and your family will be blessed as you strive to strengthen each member of your family through faith in the Lord Jesus Christ.

If we follow Elder Lee's counsel to be a light to those among whom we live, we cannot be in camouflage as to who we are. Our conduct should reflect our values and beliefs. Where appropriate, we should participate in the public square.

When Elder Lee was teaching us, there were only a handful of temples. Today there are temples spread across the world. This weekend [4 May 2014] the 143rd operating temple will be dedicated in south Florida.[8] Living worthy of a temple recommend, receiving temple ordinances, and living true to our covenants gives us the focus and vision to stay on the covenant pathway. When our youth live worthy to perform baptisms for the dead, their lives will be in order.

My counsel is that we need to focus our energy on strengthening our families by talking, rejoicing, preaching, and prophesying of Christ that we may enjoy the reward of righteous families so we can be eternal families.

For those who are single at this time but living righteous lives, our doctrine is reassuring. *Handbook 2*, Section 1.3.3 declares, "Faithful members whose circumstances do not allow them to receive the blessings of eternal marriage and parenthood in this life will receive all promised blessings in the eternities, provided they keep the covenants they have made with God."[9]

THIRD IS THE REWARD OF HAPPINESS

The question raised here is: How do I provide enough advantages for my children to be happy and successful in life? Lucifer has created a counterfeit or illusion of happiness that is inconsistent with righteousness and will mislead us if we are not vigilant.

Many of the problems across the world are occurring because the secular world has been pursuing an incorrect definition of happiness. We know from the Book of Mormon that this problem has existed throughout all generations. We also know the blessings that come from living the commandments. In King Benjamin's marvelous address, he states: "I would desire that ye should consider on the blessed and happy state of those that keep the commandments of God. For behold, they are blessed in all things, both temporal and spiritual; and if they hold out faithful to the end they are received into heaven, that thereby they may dwell with God in a state of never-ending happiness. O remember, remember that these things are true; for the Lord God hath spoken it" (Mosiah 2:41).

Over many years I have followed a research project that commenced in the 1940s. Initially there were 268 men in a premier university who were periodically studied over their entire lives. Later, additional groups were included as women became part of the study. This study covered approximately seventy years. The doctors had regular recurring interviews with these men and women. The goal of the original study was to find out as much as possible about success and happiness.

The study showed that college entrance scores and grade averages did not predict either success or happiness in later life.

One area where there was a high correlation was childhood family happiness. The successful happy adult usually reported that their mother, in particular, verbally expressed love and affection and did not use severe discipline. Both parents were demonstratively affectionate with each other and available and accessible to their children with whom they had warm and emotionally expressive relationships. The parents created a stable family environment and were believed to have respected the autonomy of their children.

A concluding book on the study, published in 2012, reports: "Many measures of success throughout life are predicted less reliably by early financial and social advantage than by a loved and loving childhood." A "warm childhood" correlates with achievement more than intelligence, social class, or athleticism.[10] The study also found that "what goes right in childhood predicts the future far better than what goes wrong."[11]

The study as a whole indicates that even when there are significant challenges and some things go very wrong, most children are very resilient and the trust that is built by loving relationships with parents, especially the mother, can result in lasting, lifetime happiness. What was interesting to me, but not surprising, was that the study was completely in line with what the scriptures and the Church have taught about the family. The emphasis the Church has made on family home evening, family prayer, expressions of love, family togetherness, and family traditions are the very kind of activities that the study indicated would produce happy, successful adults.

While Nephi begins the Book of Mormon expressing gratitude for goodly parents, the real lesson to be learned is that we each determine what kind of parent we will be so that our posterity can happily report they were born of goodly parents.

Dear sisters, the most important thing you can do is to make sure your children and those you nurture know that you love them. Love is the key ingredient to happiness.

FOURTH IS THE REWARD OF PROSPERING IN THE LAND

The question here is: Our family is not achieving significant material success, is that because we are *not* righteous enough? Let me assure you that prospering in the land is not defined by the size of your bank account. It has a much fuller meaning than that. The scriptures are clear that living the commandments allows us to prosper in the land. The prophet Alma, speaking to his son Helaman, teaches, "inasmuch as ye shall keep the commandments of God ye shall prosper in the land; and ye ought to know also, that inasmuch as ye will not keep the commandments of God ye shall be cut off from his presence" (Alma 36:30). Accordingly, having the Spirit in our lives is the primary ingredient in prospering in the land. We also have certain specific promises (see Ephesians 6:1–3; the "first commandment with promise"). Doctrine and Covenants 89 promises that in living the Word of Wisdom we will have health blessings and great treasures of knowledge.

Isolating one element of the Word of Wisdom, avoiding alcohol, is instructional. The longitudinal study I mentioned earlier found that alcohol abuse touches one American family in three, is involved in a quarter of all admissions to general hospitals, and plays a major role in death, divorce, bad health, and diminished accomplishment.

Another long-term study of active Church members in California found that women live on average 5.6 years and men 9.8 years longer than comparable US females and males. The study noted that these "total death rates . . . are among the lowest ever reported" for those followed for twenty-five years. The physicians indicated at least one reason was adherence to the Word of Wisdom. Truly living the Word of Wisdom allows us to prosper in the land.[12]

In a conversation I had with President Gordon B. Hinckley on a flight to a temple dedication, he joyfully reported that the Church had the funds to increase the number of temples because the Latter-day Saints had prospered in the land. As faithful tithe payers, they had provided the resources to build temples where sacred ordinances could be performed. Prospering and being wealthy are not necessarily synonymous. A much better gospel definition of prospering in the land is having sufficient for our needs while having the abundant blessing of the Spirit in our lives. When we provide for our families and love and serve the Savior, we will enjoy the reward of having the Spirit and prospering in the land.

The Final Reward I Will Mention Is Peace

The ultimate promised reward of righteousness is set forth clearly in Doctrine and Covenants 59:23, "But learn that he [or she] who doeth the works of righteousness shall receive his [or her] reward, even peace in this world, and eternal life in the world to come."

Thirty-five years ago, President Spencer W. Kimball taught that major growth would occur in the Church because many good women will be drawn to the Church in large numbers. He declared, "This will happen to the degree that the women of the Church reflect righteousness and articulateness in their lives and . . . are seen as distinct and different—in happy ways—from the women of the world."[13] This has truly happened and will continue to do so in the future.

As we have been taught so beautifully in this Women's Conference these last two days, the Lord God is indeed a sun and shield and will give grace and glory. No good thing will be withheld from them that walk uprightly. I have mentioned a few of the rewards of righteousness—the reward of spirituality, the reward of righteous families, the reward of happiness, the reward of prospering in the land, and the reward of peace.

My prayer and blessing is that you may reap these rewards as you faithfully follow our Lord and Savior Jesus Christ. I testify of the reality of the Atonement and the divinity of the Savior.

NOTES

1. Jeffrey R. Holland, "Elder Quentin L. Cook: A Willing Heart and Mind," *Ensign*, April 2008, 21.
2. David Brooks, "What Our Words Tell Us," *New York Times*, 21 May 2013, A21; available at http://www.nytimes.com/2013/05/21/opinion/brooks-what-our-words-tell-us.html?_r=0; accessed 7 July 2014.
3. See ibid.
4. Paul Elie, "Has Fiction Lost Its Faith?" *New York Times Book Review*, 23 December 2012, 1; available at http://www.nytimes.com/2012/12/23/books/review/has-fiction-lost-its-faith.html?pagewanted=all; accessed 7 July 2014.
5. See, for example, Charles Murray, *Coming Apart* (New York: Crown Forum, 2012).
6. See Spencer W. Kimball, "The False Gods We Worship," *Ensign*, June 1976, 3–6.
7. "The Instagram Effect," *Deseret News*, 15 April 2014, C7.
8. See "Fort Lauderdale Florida Temple Open House and Dedication," available at https://www.lds.org/church/events/fort-lauderdale-florida-temple-open-house-and-dedication?lang=eng; accessed 7 July 2014.
9. *Handbook 2: Administering the Church* (Salt Lake City: The Church of Jesus Christ of Latter-day Saints, 2010), 4. President Boyd K. Packer reaffirmed this in his April 2014 general conference talk.
10. George E. Vaillant, *Triumphs of Experience: The Men of the Harvard Grant Study* (Cambridge, MA: The Belknap Press of Harvard University Press, 2012), 109.
11. Ibid., 108.
12. James E. Enstrom and Lester Breslow, "Lifestyle and reduced mortality among active California Mormons, 1980–2004," *Preventive Medicine* 42 (2008): 135.
13. Kimball, "The Role of Righteous Women," *Ensign*, November 1979, 104.

Index